Praises
for *Ownership Spirit*

Ownership Spirit is the key to having a highly productive, self-motivated work-force. Every organization *wants* more of it. Every organization *needs* more of it. This is the book to make that happen. We can cultivate ownership in ourselves and those we work with. All of us will benefit. Read this book!! Embrace the *Ownership Spirit* in your own life, and spread the word.

—Jim Cathcart
Author, *Relationship Selling* and *The Acorn Principle*

Dennis Deaton's book spoke directly to my heart. At a time when many are retreating in fear and hopelessness, this book will propel all who choose to listen to pick up the key of ownership and blaze new paths into the future.

—Molly Davis
Author, *Letters to Our Daughters*

If you want to become a world class performer, read this book. Dennis Deaton drills down to the core of what makes the great ones great.

—Steve Siebold
Author, *177 Mental Toughness Secrets of the World Class*

Dennis Deaton teaches powerful principles that have the capacity to change humanity. This book inspires the reader to claim full accountability for their lives and ultimately create whatever destiny they choose—in any and every situation. The writing is clear, the stories are captivating, and the truth is liberating.

—Heather Madder
Author, *Walking on the Ceiling*

From my experience in working with leaders in every field, great leaders are those who know how to hold themselves accountable and build accountability in their team as well. Dennis Deaton helps us understand those choices and their implications and gives us tools and inspiration to take more ownership of all aspects of our lives.

—Kevin Eikenberry
Author, *Remarkable Leadership—*
Unleashing Your Leadership Potential One Skill at a Time

In a world that is so full of people who unwittingly play the role of a victim, Dennis Deaton is a beacon of hope in the battle between pessimism and optimism. I will recommend this book to all of my clients.

—Paul Martinelli
President, Bob Proctor Life Success Consulting

At the core, great organizations are the products of tough-minded, accountable people—people who are capable of sustaining constructive thinking during periods of challenge and change and who refuse to think and act like victims. *Ownership Spirit* is a mindset operations manual designed to bring these traits to life in your business and your personal life.

—Steve Bodhaine
Group President Yankelovich

Ownership Spirit is about forgetting the luck factor and taking control. Dennis Deaton cuts to the heart of the difference between successful people or organizations, and those who never quite catch "the Spirit of personal accountability." Great job, Dennis!

—Leslie Householder
Author, *The Jackrabbit Factor* and *Hidden Treasures*

I must confess, I was unexpectedly pleased. As with so many business management books, I anticipated just another "feel good" regurgitation. This one is different—it has practical substance with the most meaningful content—and moreover, it gets directly to the heart of the principal reasons for sub-par performance and how to change for the better.

—Joe Biehl
Managing Partner, IDM Consulting

In just one sitting, the book literally helped me change my outlook. It taught me practical tools for applying timeless truths. The truly great thing about Dennis Deaton's book is that it helps you to take a closer look at yourself—to find ways to become even more of an owner and even less of a victim. The choice is ours.

—Mark Christensen
President, Learning Point, Inc.

In my own business and my life and for the nearly 50,000 entrepreneurs and business owners my company has worked with, "ownership thinking" is an absolutely necessary quality for success. In his book, *Ownership Spirit*, Dennis Deaton teaches clearly, with wit and insight, how to strengthen your ownership qualities. I highly recommend this book.

—Ethan Willis
CEO, Prosper Corp. and Author, *One Minute Entrepreneur*

All too often, we attribute success to luck, favoritism, market forces, and the like. *Ownership Spirit* gives each of us the blueprint to take more responsibility, accountability, and ownership for our own thinking and actions to create more successes in our life.

—Dr. Tony Alessandra
Author, *The Platinum Rule* and *Charisma*

Having been in business for nearly 40 years, I have been on both sides of the Owner/Victim fence. Dr. Deaton conveys a powerful lesson in positioning one's mind and thoughts to overcome challenges in your business and personal life.

—Lawrence Hummel
Director Managed Care, Amerisource Bergen

Great book! I have always believed that achievers have an ownership spirit— Dennis Deaton's words speak volumes to how people who embrace ownership can continue to cultivate this spirit and grow exponentially to get through difficult times both professionally and personally.

—Jodonna Lucas
Director of Team Sales, Adidas America

Dennis Deaton brought the *Ownership Spirit* to our company, and his presentation and content were amazing. He has the ability to reach deep inside and make you alter your thinking and alter the thinking of your employees. This uncanny ability leads people down a better path that makes them want to be more invested and productive.

—Russ Beckner
Vice President, Charles Schwab

The principles taught in *Ownership Spirit* are timeless and timely. In this day of economic down turn, you can't afford not to know and practice Dr. Deaton's principles of ownership.

—R. Fred Houston
President and CEO, Columbia Ultimate

Ownership Spirit

Other Books by Dennis R Deaton

The Book on Mind Management
Money: An Owner's Manual
The Ownership Spirit® Handbook

Audio Seminars by Dennis R Deaton

The Ownership Spirit®
Visioneering
Money: An Owner's Manual
Power Up! Sustaining Peak Performance
Creating Connections

For information about Own It! our online teen empowerment and accountability course:
    www.GrandKeyEd.com

For additional accessory products:
    www.Quma.net

For seminar, keynote and workshop information:
    800-622-6463

For quantity discounts for *The Ownership Spirit®* book:
    800-622-6463

Ownership Spirit

The One Grand Key
That Changes Everything Else

Dennis R Deaton

Quma Learning Systems, Inc.
Mesa, Arizona

Publisher's Cataloging-in-Publication Data
Provided by Cassidy Cataloguing Services

Deaton, Dennis R

Ownership spirit : the one grand key that changes everything else / by Dennis R Deaton. — Mesa, Ariz. : Quma Learning Systems, c2009.

p. ; cm.

ISBN: 978-1-881840-22-0

1. Leadership. 2. Success in business. 3. Self-actualization (Psychology) 4. Success—Psychological aspects. 5. Work—Psychological aspects. 6. Character. I. Title.

HD57.7 .D43 2009
658.4/092—dc22   0910

Editors: Cecily Markland, April Price, Torri Black
Proofreaders: Susan Deaton, Chelcie Dunlap, Jeff Garney, Tori Spencer
Cover design: Rachel Stewart
Interior design and layout provided by Jorlan Publishing, www.JorlanPublishing.com

Printed in the United States

For reprint permission, seminar information, or purchasing, including quantity discounts, contact:

Quma Learning Systems, Inc.
480.545.8311
www.Quma.net

Published by Quma Learning Systems, Inc.

To Susan,

for all the love and beauty
you have brought
into my life—
most notably the nine diamonds
who now shine in their own settings
with their complements and attendant jewels

Contents

Special Thanks

To the team of minds, way back when, that first conceived of *The Ownership Spirit®* seminar: Reece Bawden, Steve Chandler, Steve Hardison, Ray Madaghiele.

To Steve Chandler who, in particular, gave life to the message through his wit and intellect.

To April Price for sound and sensible content editing, advice, and coaching.

To Cecily Markland for diving into the nitty-gritty of detail editing and wordsmithing.

To Torri Black for the pinpoint grammatical editing.

To the team of advisors, proofreaders, and kindly critics who refined the articulation of the message in manuscript form: Susan Deaton, Chelcie Dunlap, Jeff Garney, Tori Spencer, Rachel Stewart.

To Rachel Stewart for the artistry and technical work in designing an electrifying cover.

To each of the growing body of certified instructors—dedicated exponents of *The Ownership Spirit*—who work to make some of the finest companies in the world even stronger.

To the courageous individuals who graciously consented to have their personal stories bring life and substance to the extraordinary power of Ownership in all of our lives.

The Ownership Spirit

Introduction

Why should you read this book? You may have several reasons.

- You might be a business leader looking for a way to improve execution and foster greater accountability in your culture.

- You might be a team leader needing to focus and energize your team in times of change, challenge, or adversity.

- You might be looking for something on a personal plane— insight on how to conquer a habit, cultivate character, or enhance your leadership skills.

- You might be struggling to strengthen your relationship with a friend, co-worker, or loved one.

- You might be facing a perplexing personal dilemma or a seemingly insurmountable challenge.

- You might be seeking to add power to your goals or find ways to take more control over your career or your future in general.

- Or, you might want to enjoy more peace, happiness, and satisfaction.

If so, you have selected the right book. This book is about a key. Not just any key. Not just one of many keys on a ring of useful keys. This is the book about the most fundamental and indispensable key of them all—the key to willfully alter outcomes and improve results. With this one grand key you gain the power to change everything else in or about your life.

Is there really *a key* that makes the telling difference between individuals and teams who consistently achieve extraordinary results and those who don't?

Is there *really* one grand key that enables people to triumph over daunting challenges to attain their goals, no matter what?

Is there *really* one crucial dynamic that can unlock the door to success in virtually any circumstance, for anyone, anytime?

Yes! The One Grand Key is *Ownership—the Ownership Spirit!*

In this book, I offer you proven ways to wield that key more skillfully and effectively. Your skill in applying the key of Ownership ultimately determines how far you will go in your career and in life; how effectively you will utilize your knowledge, skills, talents, experience, training, and education; and how much of your potential you actually develop and realize.

Why am I so confident in making such bold statements? I have spent the last three decades studying, teaching, consulting, coaching, and working with people in all walks of life and in all sizes of business, involving tens of thousands of people—and I have never once seen *The Ownership Spirit* come up short. It is a universal principle that always works.

By skillfully applying the Grand Key of Ownership, you will open door after door for yourself and others and accomplish what you most desire to achieve in your life and work.

The Ownership Spirit is the **One Grand Key that Changes Everything Else.** Now, let's explore *Ownership Spirit*—what it is, the science behind it, and how to apply it.

Section 1

Premises:
Choice and Consequence

*"The consummate truth of life is that
we alter our destiny by altering our thoughts."*

—Dennis R Deaton

The power to choose is universal; we all possess it. The choice is continual and perpetual. There is hardly a moment in our lives when it does not apply. Consciously or unconsciously, countless times each day, you and I stand at the crucial crossroads of choice. At those split-second intersections, we make one fundamental decision in particular: we choose whether to respond as an Owner or react as a Victim.

The importance of these Owner/Victim choices can't be overstated. Though most of them may seem inconsequential, they are the make-or-break moments in life. Each option, Owner or Victim, has its consequence, and each consequence leads to a result.

Every time we choose Owner over Victim, we access the power to take charge of the circumstance, its consequences and results, for there we decide whether we will act or be acted upon.

5

I have spent most of my life studying the Owner/Victim choice and the stunning contrast in consequences that flow out of those decisions. I invite you to explore this subject with me and embark upon a journey of deeper self-discovery—the fruit of which will astound you. As you will discover, the harvest you can reap by amplifying your *Ownership Spirit*—employing The One Grand Key—is worth every ounce of effort you sow.

Chapter 1

The Owner/Victim Choice

Rich Hamill was talking amiably with his friends when their vehicle hit black ice, spun out of control, and slammed into a bridge abutment. The crash not only cancelled Rich's ski plans for the day, it cancelled most of his life's expectations as well. In those few calamitous seconds, the spinal cord in his athletic, 18-year-old, six-foot-one-inch, 210-pound body was severely damaged, and he lay paralyzed from the neck down.

After a successful operation, Rich eventually regained some control of his arms and some hand movement but no fine-motor dexterity. The extensive loss of so many of his faculties triggered an understandable grieving process. Rich went through the full cycle. Initially, there was shock and disbelief. Then anger. The other stages followed.

Amid his struggles to come to grips with this new reality, Rich hit upon an insight that reversed his initial downward momentum and became the upward driving force in his life. That one insight transformed his life. He discovered the power in his power to choose.

By consistently choosing Ownership, Rich Hamill and people like him cultivate what I call *Ownership Spirit*. Ownership Spirit is the One Grand Key that gives us the power to change everything else. Everything. Our emotional states, physical states, intellectual and creative states, and everything that flows from those states. Our subsequent expressions, gestures, actions, behaviors, and communications, and, hence, everything that flows from them. Our consequences, outcomes and results. Everything. Everything we do and everything we are is the sum total of the choices we make at the Owner/Victim intersection.

Owner and Victim: Patterns, Not Personalities

Owner and Victim are not identities. They are not personalities or labels for types of people. They are not intended to denote classifications or categories, or to be terms for rating or ranking ourselves or other people. Such taxonomic tactics actually impede our growth and progress. Owner and Victim are simply descriptions of two fundamental patterns of thought and ways of viewing the world. Owner and Victim represent contrasting mental approaches that lead to markedly different behaviors, results, and destinations. Victim thinking is powerless and begets more powerlessness. Owner thinking is powerful and leads to more power.

When we think like Victims, we take the bumps and jolts of life as personal affronts. Disappointing events don't just happen, they seem to happen *to* us, and in Victim mode our tendency is to then find a scapegoat—someone close by to blame. Victim thinking even resorts to blaming God or life, as though life had a purposeful agenda to make certain individuals as miserable as possible. "That's life for you. Never pays to get your hopes up. Life will just come along and knock you down." Unlike Owners, who are occasionally down and disappointed, Victims operate from a fundamental premise of patent pessimism. To them, life is just one long sinister plot, a cruel and calculated series of baleful setbacks.

Because they perceive they can't control *everything*, people in Victim mode overreact and assert they can't control *anything*. Hence, they cast aside *all* responsibility and deny any accountability for their outcomes with a woeful, "What's the use?" lament. That hopeless, helpless, hapless, "life sucks" mentality leads to other drawbacks. In that state of mind, circumstances, events, and other people seem to "make" us do, be, and say things we don't want to do, be, or say. Feeling coerced, Victims justify their actions with phrasing such as, "I had to ...," "They made me ...," and "It'll be your fault if I ...."

In Victim thinking, we don't spend much time *working on* challenges and problems, let alone goals. We're too preoccupied being shocked, dismayed, and resentful. In Victim mode, we are easily offended. We carry lifelong grudges and almost wear them as war medals on the battlefield of perpetual injustice.

In Victim thinking we recognize few, if any, opportunities to improve things or make a difference. Nothing, from our moods and attitudes to our actions and behavior, ever seems to be dependent on our own choices but rather on fiendish outside forces beyond our control. That mentality saps energy, clogs creative arteries, and corrodes our will to deal with and live life, and that leads to "heart" failure of the worst kind.

When we think in Owner terms, we live independent of circumstance. The ups and downs of the day don't define who we are, our mood, demeanor, or commitment. When something goes awry, Owners can be disappointed and frustrated, but they don't find someone to blame or resent, as Victims often do. Owners tend to focus their thinking on what to do—what options they have and what courses of action to pursue. When Owners suffer losses, they grieve. They also heal. They look for what they can learn or appreciate, and they go on. They do not hang on to their grief or prolong their suffering. When people treat them rudely, Owners seldom take offense. They could, of course, but they see that as a waste of time and energy. They don't carry a lot of grudges, nurture perceived slights and wounds, or keep score of who owes them what or who deserves what and why.

Owners understand that life is not easy, and they don't expect it to be. They are not looking for obstacles or hoping things will get hard, but at the same time, they are seldom surprised by trouble. In the face of adversity, they don't fret nor flee; they stand their ground and do their best to figure out ways of meeting, shouldering, or overcoming. In the face of success, they don't gloat. They stay focused on the principles that triggered their progress, applying what they have learned with a tone of gratitude for the breakthrough.

When we think like Owners, we recognize we may not control the winds in life, but we do regulate our own sails. When the gales blow against us, we can learn to tack into the headwind. When, as Owners, we reach our intended ports, the headwinds and crosswinds of adversity leave behind an unexpected windfall. The joy and satisfaction we feel upon arrival is much greater than from the tailwind-aided pleasure cruises. The joy of victory is always proportionate to the degree of opposition.

Building Ownership Muscle

Soon after the accident, Rich Hamill faced a pivotal Owner/Victim choice as he entered rehab. He could choose to take the Victim route—to pout, seethe, and go through half-hearted motions, resenting his trainer. On the other hand, he could choose to take the Owner route, to accept the reality of his condition, make the most of what he had left, and be grateful for his trainer's help.

Rich began his rehab program as a "Level 1"—meaning he couldn't do anything, not even roll over. When patients progress to Level 4, they graduate rehab. The doctor estimated it would take Rich about six months to progress from Level 1 to Level 4.

Having been a football player with a stubborn streak, Rich had learned to push himself hard against his limits. He told his doctor, "Explain to me on paper what I have to do to get out of here. In two and a half months I am leaving here and not coming back."

"Mr. Hamill, that will never happen."

Despite his doctor's skepticism, Rich worked ferociously, and true to his word, he completed rehab two and a half months later.

Moving Forward

Rich said, "Rehab wasn't that hard. It was clear what I had to do, but from then on, everything was up to me. I had to step back and ask, 'What am I going to do with my life? I'm no longer an athlete, and nothing comes easily any more.'"

Sorting through his options, he realized his best ones involved going to college, but there were a few problems with that. For one, he'd never been much of a student. His whole life had been focused on sports and the outdoors. "Can I develop the mental skills to handle the rigors of college?" he wondered. Second, he could not write or use a keyboard. He would have to develop some degree of refined motor skills so he could write in some fashion. Again, he wondered, "How am I going to take notes and tests?" Furthermore, he had very little physical strength: no triceps, almost no biceps, no ability to move his body in and out of vehicles or his chair. On top of that, he had virtually no endurance whatsoever. That was verified when he went to a track to see how far he could "run" in his wheelchair. One lap was it. After a quarter mile, Rich was physically exhausted and fighting for air.

Had Rich chosen Victim mentality, he could have easily justified not going to college—no scholastic discipline, couldn't write, couldn't move in and out of his wheelchair, no stamina. However, operating from Owner mentality, he viewed those obstacles as his "to do" list. They simply became things to work on and overcome.

Rich began by enrolling himself in a demanding exercise regimen. "I was never more determined about anything in my life. I was going to get my strength back so I could be as independent as possible," he said. Within four months, he was doing six-mile "runs" in his wheelchair and had developed significant upper body strength to go along with his increased stamina. He now could transfer in and out of his chair without aid or assistance.

Simultaneously, Rich worked on improving the motor skills in his arms so he could write and take notes. Unable to grasp a pen with his paralyzed fingers, he obtained a pen-holding device that slips over his palm, making handwriting feasible. Acquiring the device was easy. After that came the discipline—hours of tedious practice. Eventually the hours of effort paid off, and Rich fine-tuned his hand and arm movements to the point that he could produce legible writing.

Feeling at least physically prepared, he entered college. Ownership skills in one facet of our lives are portable and reusable in every other facet. The aptitudes and attitudes—the mental skills—he developed to *prepare for* college were precisely the strengths he needed to *succeed in* college. Rich graduated with a degree in business administration and decided to move from Michigan to Arizona where "at least my fingers wouldn't freeze to the spokes of my chair."

New Challenges

When Rich moved to Arizona, he had no job and no prospects, not even a promising lead. Drawing on his Ownership Spirit, he battled through one obstacle after another. Just finding an apartment was no small challenge. Finding hotels with roll-in showers is no big deal, but finding an apartment with that feature is harder than one might think. Overcoming one hurdle at a time, Rich secured a suitable apartment and a good job.

Rich loved his job, but it wasn't long before he was back on the streets looking for another one. The company he worked for was new and undercapitalized. A few months after he started, Rich and several other employees were laid off, and Rich remained unemployed for five months. His savings depleted, his straits were dire. He was out of money and living on credit, but he never panicked. Whenever the question, "What am I going to do?" entered his mind, he was ready for it. He harnessed the mindset, "One way or another, I'll figure it out."

Rich had three or four interviews a day but with no success. During this time, he encountered obstacles he had never met before. It was the first time he'd experienced any discrimination. Back home, getting a job was no big deal. Everyone in town knew Rich and his family. In Arizona, he was a nobody—a partially disabled nobody. "Dealing with the discrimination was harder than breaking my neck," he said.

Ownership Spirit always finds a way. The skills that had prepared Rich for college and propelled his way to graduation still applied. He had learned how to persevere. Nearly five months after being laid off, Rich finally landed a job with a respected insurance company with great opportunity for advancement. His first position, working in the mailroom, wasn't exactly his dream job, and it didn't pay what he needed, but he appreciated what he had and made the most of it. A year later, Rich heard about an opportunity in the claims department, and he applied. Many of the interview questions dealt with skills in handling adversity. He sailed through those questions and the rest of the interview. His life's experience spoke volumes. Rich got the position and flourished. Rich has become a very skilled and respected claims representative with a bright future.

One of Rich's Favorite Mottos

If you were to drop by Rich's office, you'd see a placard that helps him maintain his Ownership Spirit: **The only person who can tell you that you can't is yourself, and you don't have to listen.**

The first time I read it, I chuckled. Later, I realized how profound a statement it is. I said, "Yes, that's it! It's right on target." We all have inner voices telling us to doubt ourselves, urging us to think, "I can't,"

"It's just too hard," and "It's not fair." Those internal mutineers tell us to whine and give up, but we don't have to listen. We can close our ears to those Victim solicitations and focus on more worthwhile themes.

Minute by minute, we are presented with a continuous succession of Owner/Victim choices. These moments of choice happen so frequently, so rapidly, and so subtly, that we hardly sense we are even making a choice. In a flash, we opt for one or the other, largely oblivious to the ramifications of these choices and their cumulative consequences.

For example, a self-defeating thought flits through our mind, or someone puts a negative spin on something happening at work. At that split second, we have the choice as to whether we will buy in to the negativity or reject it. The Victim option calls out to us with seductive appeal because it usually requires less effort. Yet, when we reject the "poor me, poor us" Victim monologues and choose the higher planes, we feel better about ourselves, gain ascendancy over circumstance, and enable ourselves to "figure it out."

The Choice is the Differentiator

We all get our 24 hours in a day, our seven days in a week. Why are some of us making so much more out of life? Why does one person in an organization rise to the top while another flounders? What is it that makes the difference between the life of a Rich Hamill and the life of another paraplegic who turns to bitterness and spends hours stewing in self-pity?

Attitude? Beliefs? Perspectives? Character?

All of those answers are accurate—to a degree. Each of these elements plays a role in shaping our behaviors and molding our outcomes. Yet, none in and of itself can be considered a *determinant* since each of them is *determined* by something else. Attitudes, beliefs, perspectives, and traits of character are determined by something deeper and notably even more fundamental.

That determinant is thought.

Ultimately, we determine what we will believe or reject through our thoughts—through our mental choices that determine what kind of a person we are and on what plane of life we will live. Attitudes, traits, behaviors, actions, and reactions are all *creations* of thought—*our* thoughts. Rich Hamill gets constructive results because he chooses constructive thoughts. He *thinks* like an *Owner* not a Victim.

They Are Us

The patterns of Owner and Victim are familiar and common to us all. Nobody holds exclusively to one posture or the other. Nobody is a perfect Owner and nobody is a complete Victim. Each of us is a composite of both. We slip in and out of these patterns frequently, often lapsing into Victim thinking so seamlessly we don't even notice.

Like Rich, we go sailing along quite nicely, minding our own business, when, in the blink of an eye, something happens that disrupts our pleasant journey. Someone cuts us off in traffic. Almost instantaneously, we feel irritated and resentful toward that person, not noticing that the source of our irritation is our own Victim-toned interpretation of the other driver's motives—that his maneuver was a deliberate act of disrespect directed at us personally. Meanwhile, the driver in the other car is feeling irritated with us because *his* Victim-toned interpretation of what just happened depicts us as intentionally flouting the laws of common courtesy because we were too arrogant to let him pass in front of us.

Consider the many ways and times it happens in the workplace. Picture, for example, a group of people sitting around a conference table, each of them thinking he or she is the very epitome of optimistic Ownership, each oblivious to how easy it is to unknowingly slip into Victim mode. The team leader presents a plan requiring Mark to make some procedural changes to accommodate the work flow performed by Mary. Is Mark immediately elated and excited? Not likely. His first response is more likely to be reluctance, driven by Victim thoughts, such as, "Why do I always have to be the one to accommodate Mary? If she would just step up and do her job, we wouldn't even have to get bogged down in all these meetings." Mark may never come right out and state his thoughts, but his Victim-toned attitude is communicated nonetheless.

What's Mary thinking? She's Victimized by Mark's vibes of reluctance. "All we're asking is for Mark to make one simple change.

What's the big deal? Mark always talks about teamwork but when it comes down to it, he's very inflexible and hard to work with."

Meanwhile, sensing the chilly reception to the proposed plan, the team leader has a Victim monologue going, too. "Why does everything have to be such a struggle? We've got bigger changes than this ahead of us. Are my people ever going to get it?"

Ironically, if you were to ask any of the people in the meeting, if they were an Owner or a Victim, they would immediately contend that Victim thinking is as foreign to them as a yak-drawn sleigh.

Again, not one of us *is* an Owner or a Victim. We all exhibit characteristics of Owners and Victims based on our thoughts at any given moment.

My colleague, Steve Chandler, provides this profound insight:

> That you have a fixed personality is a myth. It is self-limiting and it denies your power of continuous creation. In your ongoing creation of who you are, nothing has a greater impact on that process than the choices you make between optimism and pessimism. There are no optimistic or pessimistic "personalities," there are only single, individual choices of optimistic or pessimistic thoughts.

Once we accept that none of us has a fixed personality—meaning nobody is a type, nobody has permanently encoded traits and characteristics, and each of us is a work in progress gaining greater competency through upgrading our mental software—then we are ready to break through all kinds of barriers.

The Value of Ownership Spirit

Opportunities to unleash the power of the Owner/Victim choice abound. We hear a rumor about lay-offs in our department at work, we get called at an inconvenient time to jury duty, or we hear from a teacher that our child has been misbehaving in school. None of these events is catastrophic, and yet each event presents us with the chance to build Ownership muscle—the strength and composure to think clearly and respond calmly despite the conflict and clamor around us. Moreover, we are preparing ourselves with the muscle we may need at some point when we, too, face a life-jolting challenge.

The events differ in magnitude, but the fundamental choice is always the same: We can choose to respond as an Owner or react like a Victim—and the decisions we make at the Owner/Victim intersection determine our routes and our destinations. Those decisions spell the difference between a pleasant conversation with our spouse or an argument that lasts for days, between sharing a laugh with a co-worker or feeling deeply offended by a sarcastic remark, between happiness and unhappiness.

Chapter 2

Our Essence:
The Thinker of Thoughts

People who exhibit consistent Ownership traits recognize and leverage one crucial distinction. They are able to see the difference between their choices and themselves as the chooser.

As human beings, we each *have* a body, but we are not our bodies. We *have* emotions, but we are not our emotions. We *have* feelings, but we are not our feelings. At the core, who we are is *the thinker of thoughts* inside our bodies, and what that thinker of thoughts chooses to think has everything to say about the quality of life we experience.

As the thinker of thoughts, we can step outside of our thinking, examine it, sort through options, and make judgments. We can take Ownership of the thinking process itself and everything that flows out of it. We can assess where each line of thinking will take us and consider whether or not we want those consequences. In moments of assessment, we are free to choose any of a vast array of options. The choice is ours alone. Hence, we alone are responsible for the outcomes. There is no place to hide. We are the sole selectors of our emotions, feelings, actions, and the corresponding biochemical impacts upon our bodies. Owning that truth is the key to changing everything else.

The degree of Ownership we wish to assume is solely up to us, as is also the extent of the corresponding benefits we enjoy. At this moment, your thinker of thoughts is assessing how eagerly and deeply you will respond to the message, concepts, methods, and tools this book has to offer. Because of that truth, as the common disclaimer states, "Individual results may vary." Still, Ownership, along with all of its inestimable benefits, flows from only one uniquely self-managed source—the innermost workings deep inside each of us—the thinker of thoughts.

The Thinker of Thoughts Runs the Brain

The underlying premise of my message is this:

> *The consummate truth of life is that*
> *we alter our destiny by altering our thoughts.*
> *The mind is our most crucial faculty, our crowning asset,*
> *our ultimate arena of battle.*

I invite you to take the word "destiny" out of this statement and replace it with a practical alternative, such as "our future," "our results," "our relationships," or "our attitudes." Explore several options. Now, I suggest another valid alternative: "We alter the very biochemistry of our bodies, at any given moment, by altering our thoughts."

Neurotransmitters

We can alter our destiny by altering our thoughts. We can *affect,* and even *effect,* the biochemistry of our bodies by taking Ownership of our thought processes and controlling our states of mind.

Medical research provides insights as to *how* those changes happen. We now know that a thought—something that we can choose deliberately and intentionally any time we want—is immediately translated into molecular equivalents (neurotransmitters) in our bodies. Neurotransmitters are chemical messengers that "speak" to the cells, tissues, and organ systems of the body, telling them what to do and at what rate to do it. *A specific thought generates a specific neurotransmitter (or transmitter set) which, in turn, has a specific impact on the body.*

Thoughts really are *causes* that are producing direct *effects.* Thoughts can elevate or depress activity in the immune system. For example, conjuring and harboring sentiments of anger, fear, or frustration creates chemistry that weakens our immune system and makes us more susceptible to illness.

Thoughts *Design and Redesign* the Brain

The connection between thoughts and neurotransmitters is only the proverbial tip of the iceberg. Our more prevalent thoughts even make *anatomical* changes in the brain itself. Note what respected scientist, Dr. Jeffrey M. Schwartz, has to say:

> Contrary to the notion that the brain has fully matured by the age of eight or twelve, with the truly crucial wiring complete as early as three, it turns out that the brain is an ongoing construction site. The hardware of the brain is far from fixed at birth. Instead, it is dynamic and malleable.
>
> Neuroplasticity refers to the ability of neurons to forge new connections, to blaze new paths through the cortex, even to assume new roles. In short, neuroplasticity means rewiring of the brain.

Our brains are not permanently set in their ways but can be altered and reconfigured. What governs this reconfiguration? The thoughts we think.

A single, fleeting thought is hosted by a spontaneously formed circuit of brain cells, called neurons, and leaves barely a trace of its course. However, as we repeat a given thought, the interconnections in that circuit become more durable with each repetition. Neurons that fire together, wire together. Patterns in our thoughts become patterns in our brains. Our brains wire and re-wire themselves in response to our most-used thought patterns.

Even the neuronal circuits in our brains are a product of our thoughts. Our brains continually and dutifully reconfigure themselves in order to get better at the exact functions we request of them. Dr. Schwartz continues:

> Conscious thoughts and volitions can, and do, play a powerful causal role in the world, including influencing the activity in the brain. Willed mental activity can clearly and systematically alter brain function. The exertion of willful effort generates *physical force* that has the power to change how the brain works and even its physical structure. The result is directed neuroplasticity.

Science reaffirms what we have intuitively known for decades— our thoughts literally make us or break us. This power the thinker of thoughts wields—the ability to actually transform itself and make itself better (or worse)—is both sobering and utterly energizing.

Think of the opportunities we forfeit when we ignore these perspectives and allow our thoughts to take the course of least resistance. In contrast, think of the possibilities we gain when we respect, discipline, and elevate our thoughts! That is what I am trying to convey through my use of the term "Ownership." I'm talking about *mental accountability*. Taking responsibility for what we allow ourselves to think is to take charge of the rate and degree of our development and the magnitude and richness of our outcomes. Through the prudent exercise of this prerogative, we wield the power to alter our destiny (and everything else) by altering our thoughts.

Learning to take more Ownership, to be more selective about the subjects we allow our minds to dwell on, amounts to a proficiency with life-changing, soul-enhancing impact. What can be more encouraging and exciting than to know we can think our way to greater proficiencies in thinking itself? With those new and improved neuronal assets, we can then leverage even higher planes of thought, which enable higher neuronal circuits and higher planes of thought beyond that.

Taking Advantage of Neuroplasticity

We constantly face opportunities to build better brainware, although we generally don't see our Owner/Victim choices from that standpoint. Each decision produces its own stream of immediate outcomes. By those same choices, we are also designing and redesigning our neuronal networks, thus producing changes in the brain with long-range effects. That insight underscores the importance of making consistent Owner choices.

Since neurons that fire together, wire together, each time we think a certain thought, we engage that particular neuronal circuit. The neurons involved reinforce their connection to one another and even recruit more neurons into the circuitry, solidifying a network of interconnections. Conversely, when we cease or drastically diminish the usage of any given circuit, the opposite sequence of events occurs. The interconnectivity of those neurons diminishes. In effect, we can unlearn behaviors and mental tendencies by de-selecting them through the choosing of a different thought with some consistency.

The neglect of a given thought pattern weakens the prominence of that circuit and lowers its rank on the search list of our personal mental Internet browser (like search engine de-optimization). The more we refrain from firing any particular circuit, the weaker it becomes and the further it drops on the search list. As we stop calling on certain circuits, we unwire those circuits.

The Gap

The way you can take best advantage of this powerful insight is to pay more attention to your decision points. When you do, you will detect the split-second pause or gap between the time an event occurs and your *almost* instantaneous reaction to it. That small gap is a big deal.

For example, suppose you receive an email from your boss informing you of an abrupt change in your schedule. If the email isn't worded to your liking, you may experience a sudden surge of resentment. Decision point. If you choose, at that instant, to take the path of least resistance and go with the resentment, then the veins in your neck start bulging, the arteries constrict, your heart pounds wildly, and your blood pressure goes sky high. You now have a full-blown case of Victim mentality because, in the moment of decision, you chose to be upset, and your body obediently followed suit. All the while, you excuse yourself from responsibility, telling yourself your boss is at fault for being such a power freak. The truth remains, however, at the decision point you could have taken Ownership and opted for a different response, and the stream of ensuing events within your body would have been correspondingly different.

Between stimulus (email) and response (what happens in your body) we experience a **mental interpretative gap.** In that gap, we make choices, and in those moments of choice, the juice of life is squeezed.

To Panic or Not to Panic

I have a friend who owns a Harley-Davidson motorcycle. He loves to ride it at high speed, without a helmet, along Arizona's Superstition Freeway. (Aside from that, he's a very intelligent human being.) Frequently, he carves time out of his busy schedule to climb on his Harley and hurtle over black asphalt at shocking rates of speed. Saguaro cacti and palo verde trees buzz by on the periphery, and molecules of nitrogen and oxygen whip through his hair. In his mind—in his interpretative gap—all of that sensory data is configured as "joyride." He's having a ball. He throws his head back, laughing and cackling. If he has any pent-up frustrations, he blasts those out into the stratosphere. After this 30-minute experience, the pharmacy inside his body will perfectly reflect his chosen state of mind. His body will be secreting copious amounts of very beneficial substances, including Interleuken-2, an immuno-accelerant that enables the immune system to perform all of its functions. His body's ability to recognize improperly dividing cells that could foster cancer is improved. Its ability to recognize outside antigens that could produce infection is enhanced. He has literally "inoculated" himself with greater health and strength.

In my friend's case, the interpretation he makes pays off with an array of notable benefits—more energy and improved immune function, which, in turn, lead to better health and more vitality for life, facilitating more happiness and prosperity.

In contrast, when I accompany him on these *joyrides,* my choices in the gap are much different. As I'm hurtling over the asphalt, I have the same molecules of nitrogen and oxygen whipping through my *helmet;* however, my medically-oriented mind chooses to focus on the threats, hazards, and dangers of this jaunt. I harbor an abiding concern for my physical well-being, having flashes of panic, even moments when I wish I had invested in a box of Depends (if you get my drift). After my 30-minute experience, the pharmacy inside my body reflects my fear and apprehension. Instead of Interleukin-2, my body pumps out stress hormones, including cortisol, a fine immuno-*suppressant.*

So, what makes the difference? It's not the motorcycle, asphalt, or molecules of nitrogen in the atmosphere. It's the mental *creation,* the configuration of thoughts. One person's joy is another person's panic, and both are mental constructs formed in the interpretative gap.

Minding the Gap

Without awareness, the gap between stimulus and response narrows to the point that it seems to vanish altogether. When that happens, our responses become fairly mechanical and predictable—just a series of conditioned responses to the routine flow of repeated stimuli, and we become unwitting Victims of our habits. When we are mindful of the gap, however, and pause for a split-second consideration, we widen the gap and that begets options. We then see a spectrum of choices, and usually opt for something better.

Being aware of our ability to choose and making consistent Owner choices constitutes the essence of mental discipline. Enhancing our mental discipline is not as difficult and foreboding as we may assume. Here again, we come to an Owner/Victim decision point. We could see the word *discipline* as disappointing bad news and decide to continue our quest for the quick, easy "secret" to success and happiness. Conversely, we can look at discipline as an exciting, soul-stretching invitation and gladly pay the price for something that is ultimately priceless—the realization of our true potential.

Retraining ourselves to see the value and possibilities that arise out of adverse circumstances is one reward that comes from looking at discipline this way. It might not be our natural tendency at first, but "natural tendencies" are not permanent or unchangeable. By taking Ownership, we can reconfigure weak circuits and turn them into strengths.

Opening Up Options

When we encounter a setback or loss, we can learn to resist our almost reflexive Victim thoughts like, "Oh, no; here we go again," or, "Why does stuff like this *always* happen to me?" We can learn to open up the mental interpretative gap and enumerate options. It can be as simple as saying to yourself, "Whoa, slow down and look at the options."

When my knee-jerk reaction takes over and I sense myself turning to the "why me" laments, I use a circuit breaker. Specifically, I say to myself, "Stop. What are your options here, Dennis?" The "stop" breaks the negative monologue. The follow-up question, "What are your options?" then triggers a constructive line of questioning—questions such as, "Mentally and emotionally, where am I right now? Is this *really* the end of the world? To what extent is my irritation (or any other emotion present at the time) due to my choice in how I am spinning this thing? How could I see this as good news or actually advantageous? Can I think my way to something better than what will turn out if I just moan about it?"

Whenever we direct our thoughts to such introspection, we "mind the gap," and with that Ownership, there is no limit to the applications and benefits we can accrue. From physical consequences to our creative output, from our interactions with other people to our deepest emotional states, Owning our thoughts puts us on the road to attaining richer destinations.

Not Just Positive Thinking, Analytical Thinking

The value of this quintessential insight goes far beyond our physical health. This supernal principle also offers immense possibilities for our emotional health, financial health, spiritual health, and every other health.

Ownership Spirit embodies a powerful mental approach to life that leverages higher self-awareness, enabling us to *use* our *presence of mind* as a tool to gauge and govern our *states of mind* and the corresponding effects that flow out of them. When we practice that degree of Ownership and continue to hone and perfect our skills through daily effort, we reap bountiful harvests of deeper happiness and accelerated personal growth, the end of which has no upper bounds.

By now, you can sense that positive thinking is not enough. Important as that is, we have to go deeper. We need to sharpen our skills in *analytical* thinking—more expressly, *self*-analysis of the thinking itself. We need to use our presence of mind to analyze our presence of mind. Each of us can benefit by doing a little more of that. We just have to pique our awareness a bit and give more consideration to doing that.

Over the years, I have taught thousands of engineers, scientists, and other talented professionals with highly cultivated abilities to analyze outside systems to impressive degrees of depth. However, when asked if they ever apply their finely tuned analytical skills to their own mental circuits, most of them openly admit that the idea had never even occurred to them.

Universal Crunch Questions

The crunch question is this: *How often* and *how well* do you use your amazing prerogative of intentional self-analysis? When was the last time you considered the possibility that you might have developed some mental habits that produce far more cortisol than Interleukin-2? When was the last time you examined your dominant thoughts about your career; approach to a crabby co-worker; or relationship with your child, spouse, or significant other? When was the last time you so effectively diagnosed your own mental tendencies that you discovered a self-written virus in your own mindware and achieved a breakthrough?

When was the last time you candidly evaluated your thoughts when you felt angry or depressed and realized that your emotional state at that moment had less to do with the circumstances than with your interpretation of those circumstances—that the situation was not causing your anger but that *you* were causing the anger? When was the last time you really thought about thinking about your thinking?

Chapter 3

The Othello Principle

Those of us who stayed awake during the Shakespeare portion of our English classes came to appreciate the Bard's uncanny ability to focus attention on the contradictory aspects of human behavior and the foibles that seem to show up and apply to one generation after the next. That is certainly the case with the tragedy, *Othello*. Embedded in a tragic plot of jealousy and rage lies a pearl of insight I call *"The Othello Principle."*

At the start of the play, Othello, a general in the Venetian military, enjoys a close relationship with the beautiful Desdemona, and his love for her is completely reciprocated. Othello and Desdemona are loyal and true to one another.

Into this ideal scene enters the evil Iago. He gains Othello's trust and friendship, but he's not a friend. Intensely jealous of Othello and masquerading as an ally, Iago insinuates that Desdemona is anything but faithful—that she is, in fact, carrying on a torrid love affair with one of Othello's military colleagues. In actuality, infidelity is the furthest thing from Desdemona's mind. She continues to conduct a virtuous life, fully loyal to Othello. Yet, in that behavior, Othello thinks he sees all the *evidence* he needs to justify the conclusion that Iago is steering him correctly and that Desdemona *is* unfaithful. Letting his fears and suspicions run unchecked in his mind, Othello works himself into such a jealous rage that he takes Desdemona's life with his own hands.

The tragedy doesn't end there. Too late, Othello figures out that Iago has been "unfaithful," not Desdemona. This horrifying realization is too much for him to bear. Fueled by even greater rage, Othello seeks out Iago and stabs him, and he then takes his own life.

Despite the gruesome elements of the plot, Shakespeare deftly leads us to consider a universal principle of human behavior—one that applies to each of us every waking minute. *The Othello Principle* states: **The eye sees what the mind looks for.**

Extensive Application

The Othello Principle influences all of our responses and behaviors. That influence is so pervasive it even extends to how we interpret and make sense of our experiences. Two people sitting next to each other in the same movie have two different experiences, depending on how each individual chooses to interpret the movie. In the same way, two people will reach markedly different conclusions while listening to the same speech or participating in the same meeting.

In virtually every context, we tend to see what we look for. Our results are strongly shaped by our underlying points of view and expectations. If we're *looking for* betrayal, we tend to see evidence of betrayal. If we're looking for loyalty, we tend to see evidence of loyalty.

Our ability to leverage this principle even depends on how we choose to look at the principle. From an Owner's point of view, *The Othello Principle* opens up unlimited vistas of self-determined and self-propelled possibilities. Knowing we may be limiting our outcomes by how we look at a situation, we can undertake careful re-consideration of our underlying assumptions and improve our results by improving our approach.

Individual Results May Vary

When I conduct seminars, I sometimes encounter people who are anything but thrilled about being in the class. Their Victim mindset is easy to recognize. They enter the room with cold, steely stares. They know they will hate the session before we've even said hello. Their body language and facial expressions tell it all. I can almost hear them muttering to themselves, "Oh, boy, here we go—nice little, fluffy, soft-skills seminar. Four hours of wasted time. Look at the name of this one. Hah! *The Ownership Spirit.* Isn't that sweet?"

If they maintain that Victim mindset, it wouldn't matter who might be teaching the seminar—Mother Teresa or Albert Einstein—they wouldn't find any value. In the end, they would walk away concluding (just as they predicted) that it was a big waste of time, and they would be right. For them, it would have been an utter waste of time. Prophecy made; prophecy fulfilled.

Consider the alternative. Sitting next to one of the people in Victim mode might be a couple of colleagues with receptive mindsets. They are not neutral about the opportunity to sharpen their skills. They might even go so far as to make a specific commitment to find great ideas that will improve their skills. From start to finish, their experience in the seminar will be entirely different. They will walk away with dramatically different results—a guidebook filled with ideas to ponder, digest, and apply.

Same seminar? Well, not really. Each person creates his or her own experience, based on how he or she decides to apply *The Othello Principle.*

We Create Our Own World

More than most of us realize, we each create our own culture—the "world" we dwell in—whether at work or at home. Recently, I was talking to two brothers who hold drastically different views of their childhood home life. One characterized his childhood as happy, and the other brother called it a nightmare. One was complimentary of the way he was raised, and the other, severely critical. Guess how life in general plays out for each of these men.

I invite you to take a deep, honest, pragmatic look at the results you are getting these days. How do you feel about going to work and coming home? How do you look at the people with whom you work and live? Do you tend to see the good and the commendable, or do you find yourself continually upset and dissatisfied with other people's efforts? A "prophecy check" or a reset of your operating system may be in order.

If we look for family members or co-workers who aren't pulling their share of the load, we tend to collect evidence of their lazy, slacking ways, and we become even more critical. If we are looking for hypocrisy and duplicity in upper-level management, we soon find ourselves awash in a culture of suspicion and negativity. In every memo or meeting, it won't take us long to spot the deception and manipulation. From there, our "evidence gathering" accelerates, and conversations with colleagues at work start going something like this:

> Did you see what they said in this memo? "We're all in this together." Hah! Did you see the bonuses they gave themselves last year?! If we took one-tenth of those bonuses, we could get six more engineers in this department, and we could really handle these demands. I can't believe they can peddle this stuff with a straight face. Who do they think they're kidding?

Once we get the Victim thing going, we like to *share* our evidence:

> In the 33 years you've been here, have you ever seen it worse? You know what they did in XYZ department? People couldn't even log on to their computers. Supervisors were standing by their desks saying, "Please empty your desks; we're escorting you to the parking lot." After 20 years, that's how they treat them.

Our colleague may join the crab session and try to top that story:

> You think that was a big deal? You should see what they did in ABC department; they lined some of them up against the wall, and they shot 'em.

The undermining starts fueling its own momentum, and the swapping of gossip and horror stories accelerates. In some companies, there seems to be an unwritten policy that if you haven't heard a negative rumor by 11 a.m., you're supposed to start one. Without realizing it, the Victim mentality pollutes the atmosphere, and all that "secondhand smoke" spawns a cancerous, cynical culture that becomes even more resistant to change.

Most of the time, the people actually responsible for the negativity infecting the team—the Victim thinkers with the megaphones in their hands—are generally the last ones to take responsibility for it. Everything wrong is management's fault, and they grumble out loud, "When will *they* ever wake up and smell the coffee?" (Anyone got a mirror?)

Unless reversed, this line of thinking will impede the rate of change and responsiveness, impacting everything from customer service to delivery time. When the Victim thinking becomes endemic and calcified, while upper-level management may set the direction, the 600-pound gorilla of cynicism (seeing what it's looking for) will ultimately determine the speed.

Applies to Relationships

What applies to the workplace applies equally to the home front. Wherever we go, we create our own environments and the quality of our relationships—everything is shaped or changed by how we choose to apply *The Othello Principle.*

Although we frequently see *The Othello Principle* applied in a negative way, it need not be so. The principle works just as consistently in the positive direction, exerting the power to build. When we look for the strengths and positive traits in our colleagues and family, we create and promote an environment of appreciation that leads to trust and cooperation.

My wife and I are good friends with a couple who enjoy a strong, loving marriage. It wasn't always that way. A few years into their marriage, they were both very unhappy and highly critical of each other. One sharp word led to another, and the wounds of criticism escalated. One day, the husband was advised, "Stop wondering if the marriage will work. Stop debating whether you've married the 'right person.' Make a firm, final decision that divorce is not an option. Focus on keeping your vow to love and honor your partner by looking for the good; offer more praise and appreciation."

The husband chose to follow that advice and to shift his point of view. He concentrated on looking for, and commending her for, her positive qualities. Rather than assuming the worst in her motives and intentions, he assumed the best. It didn't take long for the change in his viewpoint to exert its positive effects. His shift opened space in their relationship for her to make a shift too. Step by step, they closed the gap that separated them, and they have become a united team.

Applies to Cultures

In like manner, Victim cultures can be reversed and turned into positive, supportive environments. That shift must first begin with personal ownership, which most people are more than ready to adopt once they are awakened to it. When they start to own and analyze their own thinking, that awareness enables them to recognize and set aside petty grievances and counterproductive attitudes and find better approaches.

I have seen teams strengthen and accelerate their implementation of the Ownership principles by defining an "Ownership Code of Conduct." They simply made some agreements among themselves as to how they will respond to change, obstacles, and adversity when it occurs. One particular group also drew up a list of introspective questions they agreed to ask themselves when anyone on the team noticed a drift toward Victim thinking. Here are five questions I selected from their list:

+ Am I/Are we thinking in terms of "we" or "they" right now?

+ What constructive solutions or suggestions can I/we offer or implement?

+ What else can I/we do to meet our goals and execute our strategies?

+ How does my/our daily performance promote better teamwork and cooperation?

+ Am I/Are we demonstrating leadership in how we respond to change and challenge?

Questions like these leverage the power embedded in *The Othello Principle,* converting weak, nonproductive, change-resistant points of view into open, creative, change-driving mindsets.

If you can turn around one person, you can turn around two, three, or a team. Such turnarounds emerge from simple roots—higher awareness, personal responsibility, and commitment to more constructive outcomes. At first, it may take more effort, but the investment soon pays off. Before long, a creative solution-oriented culture supplants a problem-oriented focus, resulting in a more spirited climate and culture.

Two Brief Examples

The Emerging Markets Group of a large telecom company were drastically behind goal when *they* caught hold of the Ownership Spirit. By examining their mindset, the group leader and her direct reports recognized the "fatalist" Victim thinking in the group's emails and conversations.

Such phrases as "The market is soft," and "The economy is sluggish" are not necessarily Owner or Victim statements—it is what comes after those statements that tells the tale. Owners say, "So, what are we going to do about it? Who do we have to be, and what do we have to do, to reach our goals?"

The Emerging Markets Group had fallen into the subtle trap of concluding, "There's not much we can do," By mid-August, they had achieved under 40 percent of their goal for the year. With the awareness gained from our training, this group shifted their mental gears into a concerted Ownership posture relative to their annual goal. Within weeks, they experienced a dramatic, measurable shift in attitude and energy. The group leader remarked:

> We learned that nobody else was going to solve the problem for us. The cavalry wasn't coming. As a team, we agreed to get out of the Victim role and take Ownership of our numbers. With 60 percent of our work still in front of us and only four months left in the year, we finished the year by surpassing our annual goal (103 percent).

A second example of the impact of Ownership Spirit comes from the Cellular Infrastructure division of a well-known electronics company. The division was under fire. Product quality had sagged, customer complaints were rising, and they were getting drubbed by their competitors. Rumors were flying that management was seriously considering either shutting the division down or selling it off.

The initial reaction of some people in the group was to start polishing up their resumes. Those who were even more pessimistic became almost paralyzed by the prospects of the impending doom—assuring continued poor results for the group.

The division leader wasn't ready to concede so easily. He invested in a group-wide educational effort in Ownership thinking, asking his people to *focus* and *own* what the group *could* control. Essentially, he said, "We can't control whether the company will spin us off or not. We *can* do everything in our power to make drastic improvements in our quality and shorten our delivery time. Even if that doesn't convince the board, we will be a stronger, more attractive organization to whomever *does* buy us, and we are more likely to all land on our feet going that route. So let's stop waiting for the axe to fall and focus all our energy on eliminating defects."

Not everyone immediately jumped on the bandwagon, but most team members could see the sense in the leader's point and took Ownership. As the downward momentum slowed and a turnaround became ever more evident, most of the doubters joined in or moved on. And a few breakthrough ideas emerged from the team that accelerated improvements in both quality and production. In the end, there was no spin-off. The division not only over-achieved on their defect reduction goal, they generated huge chunks of profit for the company; and the doom-and-gloom rumors vanished.

The Othello Principle plays a powerful causal role in our personal and professional outcomes. For many people, it exerts its effects subconsciously. That need not be the case. We can increase our analysis of our points of view and make strategic upgrades that proffer stunningly improved results.

Chapter 4

Old Dogs and Leopards

Opinions vary among thought leaders about whether human beings are capable of changing their outlooks, attitudes, and behaviors. Some staunchly hold that people are only marginally reinventable, and once the die is cast the person is forever stuck in that mode. They claim people who learn helplessness in their youth will always be helpless adults.

Understanding *The Othello Principle*, we quickly see the weakness in that pessimistic point of view. Skeptical leaders fulfill their own prophecies. Their low expectations have a self-fulfilling impact on the performance of their people (the "Golem effect").

This bleak, once-the-die-is-cast position puts the organization on a hiring treadmill. The leopards-can't-change-their-spots doctrine virtually forces us to think in terms of hiring only "good people" or "the right people." When we happen to hire some closet Victim thinkers clever enough to outwit our hiring system, and later we find them contaminating our ranks, we expend all sorts of resources trying to adroitly and legally "get them off the bus."

We then throw a lot of energy and resources into developing a Victim-proof hiring system. We believe the contamination can be stopped by getting even more rigorous with our hiring protocols so we can unmask the weak links before we hire them.

Yes, we are wise to improve our screening and hiring processes, but we can't escape the fact that we are always hiring human beings. Since nobody's perfect, and there are no flawless Owners (or total

Victims) on this planet, we are inescapably in the business of educating human minds and assisting those thinkers of thoughts to think more responsibly.

The good news is that the thinker can be successfully educated. Leopards may not be able to change their spots, but *human beings* can definitively change the way they think. Victims can become Owners.

Change Happens

No one is hopelessly stuck in any given behavior, style, or attitude. Even when we settle into a certain posture for some time, we can change our programming any time we elevate our consciousness. We can do it for a few moments, such as when we decide to snap to attention when the boss walks by. We can also do it on more enduring levels.

Once, during an *Ownership Spirit* seminar I was teaching at a microelectronics manufacturing company, one leader shared an email he had received from an hourly worker. The young man started his email by mentioning he had been repeatedly exposed to the company slogans, one being "We make a difference." It meant little to him until one day, on his lunch break, he and a co-worker, both wearing shirts that bore the company logo, were at a fast food restaurant. An older man approached them, introduced himself, and asked if they really worked for that company. They answered, "Yes, we do." The man then poured out his most heartfelt gratitude for one of the devices made by that company and what it had done for him.

This man had experienced severe pain for more than 20 years. Sometimes the pain was so severe it would cause him to black out, endangering himself and those around him. No medications or treatments had ever helped—until this device was implanted in his body. The device had revolutionized his life, allowing him to work and hold a job again. It restored his ability to drive his car, function with his family, and live pain free. Tears of gratitude filled his eyes, and his voice choked with emotion as he expressed how happy he was to have a normal life again.

Within a few minutes, in one conversation, this young worker made a lasting shift in his attitude toward his work.

He wrote:

Even though I know I did not help in building that device, this conversation made me feel as if I do make a difference. For the first time I understood what *We make a difference* really means. When I come to work, I no longer look at the parts as if they are just parts. I see them as people, and I give each one of them not one, not two, but three looks to make sure that they are the greatest quality they can possibly be.

Why didn't this young man recognize his nonchalant attitude toward quality and make this shift earlier? Let's consider that question.

Generally, most of us are oblivious to the control we have over our attitudes and approaches. We simply follow the course of least resistance. We think we're thinking, but we're just recycling our old comfy ways—re-running behaviors we have solidified long ago by hours of repetition. In the case of the young man, it's possible that, being paid by the hour, he started viewing his work as a matter of so many ticks on the clock, overlooking the big picture. His role would then seem routine, empty, and meaningless. Before long, he would be completely bored, and all the company slogans would seem like vapid rah-rah.

Where does apathy and boredom originate? In our minds. If we aren't aware that we are dancing to the melody of our own orchestras, most of our greatest symphonies will never be composed. It is not because we are incapable. We are simply unaware of our capability.

Daily we hear people underestimating themselves and reinforcing some inane self-depiction. They may say, "I'm just not a detail person," as if they've been programmed a certain way and are absolutely powerless to be any other way. Sometimes they'll even point to *evidence*: "I'm just not a morning person, and I can prove it. That's why they don't let me teach preschool. I would have killed one of those kids that time of morning."

When we listen to ourselves, we discover how often we *sentence* ourselves to a pattern of behavior as though we are simply pre-programmed circuits. It sounds something like this: "Dennis, tell us a little about yourself. Who are you?"

"Well, I'm a real people person. I'm good at math and bad at oil painting. I have a short temper (which I got from my dad's side of the family). My father was a hot head, and my grandfather had a pretty short fuse, too. In fact, if you go back to the old country, you'd find that our whole family is that way—we're Italian, you know. My cousin is part Lebanese, and he's the same way. Both of us get that hot temper from our ancestors."

Are people really just the end-products of their nature and their nurture? I say no. While genetics and external environment do exert considerable influence, the final say comes from the thinker of thoughts—what we say and repeat in our minds, our *inner* environment.

A Significant Battery of Research

You don't have to take my word for this. Consider this summation from a body of work by a leading authority in human behavior, Dr. Martin E. P. Seligman. I quote from one of his books, *The Optimistic Child*:

> Why should we bother to learn to think optimistically? Isn't pessimism just a posture with no real effects? Unfortunately not. I've studied pessimism for the last 20 years and in more than 1,000 studies involving half a million children and adults, pessimistic people do worse than optimistic people in three ways. First, they get depressed much more often. Second, they achieve less on the job, at school, and on the playing field—much less than their talents would suggest. Third, their physical health is worse than that of optimists. So holding a pessimistic theory of the world may be a mark of sophistication, but it is a costly one.

Notice the first sentence! "Why should we bother *to learn* to think optimistically?" That's key phrasing! He didn't say, "Why is it important to be born optimistic?"

Heredity is overrated when it comes to its control over our individual behavior. The idea that most of our shortcomings and bad traits can be blamed on our genes is a seductive doctrine, but that notion leaves us powerless. Personally, I think we have a lot more to go on than just the fruitless wish that we had chosen our ancestors more carefully.

Seligman adds impressive support to my premise—no one is born or permanently programmed into a certain, unalterable pattern of thinking or behaving. His findings, based on a huge study population, contend that attitudes and attitudinal changes are a matter of pure will and decision—choice. People can decide to approach life optimistically (like an Owner would) or to approach it pessimistically (like a Victim).

Seligman also connects the attitudes of optimism and pessimism to physical consequences. His conclusions link closely with the work of Dr. David D. Burns, an expert on the subject of depression.

Depression can certainly facilitate negative thinking by producing a biochemical funk that makes it difficult to maintain positive states of mind. So, yes, states of body can definitely affect states of mind.

However, Dr. Burns takes the position that most cases of depression are not "endogenous," defined as depression stemming from malfunction of the body. Rather, most cases are what he diagnoses as "reactive depression," stemming from "malfunctions" in thinking. Admittedly, in especially prolonged periods of depression, it is difficult to tell whether the thinking threw the chemistry out of whack or the chemistry threw the thinking off course. However, in his book, *Feeling Good,* Burns ultimately concludes that the primary source of depression is *prolonged immersion in distorted thinking.*

The Mark that Leaves a Mark

Now, let's consider Dr. Seligman's reference to pessimism as a "mark of sophistication." He's pointing to the prevalent and inaccurate inference that intellectual sophistication and cynicism go hand in hand. In other words, if you are truly brilliant and astute, you could never fall for the shallow, insubstantial attribute of optimism. Positive attitude is for unsophisticated, naive airheads, Pollyannas, and mental canaries.

It wasn't always that way in American society. One quality of the "greatest generation," celebrated in the best selling book by Tom Brokaw, was its pervasive "can-do" attitude. Members of that generation didn't dwell on what was missing or what couldn't be done. Instead they thought: "We may not have the know-how right now, but we'll figure it out and make it happen anyway."

Movies of that era reflected the can-do approach to life. Mickey Rooney and Judy Garland made handsome livings portraying the can-do whiz kids who could find some way of making a bad situation better. If an orphanage was in sad shape and about to be torn down, Mickey and Judy didn't say, "Why doesn't the government stop this?" or "Why doesn't upper-level management do something?" Instead, they asked, "What can we do to help?" Before long, they'd hatch a plan. Judy would say, "I know what we can do. We'll put together a program, we'll sell tickets, and we'll raise enough money to save the orphanage. It'll be wonderful! We can do it."

Perhaps the plots in those movies were a bit oversimplified, but the can-do attitude got thrown out with the bath water when Hollywood began promoting the virtues of the anti-hero—like James Dean and Marlon Brando—rebels who were so brainless their rebellion didn't even have a cause; they were just down on everything. Those who played the anti-heroes found it to be an easy way to fame and riches because they didn't even have to memorize any lines. They just mumbled their way through the movie with furrowed brows presiding over dour, pained looks on their faces. That was the hallmark of true sophistication! People watching a Brando movie back then would say, "Man, isn't he cool?! You can't even understand what he says." We were so impressed, the leather jackets practically flew off the racks, and Hollywood and society have never been the same since.

Promoting Pragmatism

Nobody is advocating a Pollyannic naiveté here. Rather, I am asking us to take a pragmatic approach by asking ourselves, "What mental processes produce the best results?" Apart from Seligman's impressive body of research, the annals of human history testify that those who have made the biggest contributions have applied faith, hope, and concentrated hard work, driven by the belief that they could make a difference.

For example, tempered by the hardships of the Great Depression, the "greatest generation" forged a mindset of self-reliance. The pessimistic, cynical, "nobody will ever fix this mess" attitude was more foreign to them than the faraway continents where they fought to preserve their freedoms.

The thought processes that produced the values and virtues of that generation remain the formula for greatness. We derive greater happiness and fulfillment, along with markedly better results, when we assiduously resist the temptation of settling for the easy, but dead-end, road of pointing fingers, blaming, and shifting responsibility.

Again, attitudes and behaviors can be transformed by transforming the thoughts that originate them. None of us is dealing with locked-in habits that keep us bound down to any specific pattern or tendency. Note two conclusions that emerge from Dr. Seligman's research: (1) *optimism makes you more effective than pessimism,* and (2) *optimism can be learned.*

If optimism can be learned, then so can every other virtue and attribute. If we don't believe that, we might as well shut down all the churches, schools, and universities. People *can* shift their points of view. People can change and make dramatic alterations in their beliefs and behaviors.

As one representative example, I cite Bjorn Borg, the great tennis legend of the 1970s and '80s. During his brilliant career, Borg won 90 percent of his Grand Slam matches, en route to winning 11 Grand Slam tournaments. His six French Open titles are an all-time record, and he remains the only player to have won both Wimbledon and the French Open in three consecutive years. Considered one of the greatest men's tennis players of all time, Bjorn Borg was so well known for his stoic, composed, cool-as-a-cucumber demeanor that he was frequently referred to as "Iceborg." Unlike other tennis stars of his day— Jimmy Connors, Ilie Nastase, and John McEnroe, all of whom were known for their sophomoric, on-court tantrums—Borg never lost his cool concentration, even in moments of intense competition. His self-control and laser-like focus were keys to his prowess and success.

From what source did Borg get his classic composure? Was he born with these traits, the fortunate beneficiary of some superb self-discipline genes? Was he just the predestined product of a reserved, dignified Scandinavian culture? Decidedly not. In fact, at one time Bjorn Borg was as volatile and petulant as his temperamental opponents. In an article on Borg published in *Time* magazine, author B. J. Phillips wrote:

> Is Borg too good to be true? Maybe, but once he was too bad to believe. At eleven, young Bjorn cursed like a navvy, hurled his racquet, hectored officials and bellyached over every close call. "I was crazy, a madman on the court. It was awful. Then the club I belonged to suspended me for five months, and my mother took my racquet and locked it in the closet. For five months, she locked up my racquet. After that I never opened my mouth again on the tennis court. Since the day I came back from that suspension, no matter what happened, I behaved on the court."

Borg was not born "Iceborg," he created "Iceborg." He became what he became through conscious choice and conscious effort.

Our attitudes and states of mind are not products of our nature or our nurture. We can choose to revisit our attitudes, analyze them, and reconfigure them. We can do it again and again and again. Ownership can be learned, and it can be taught. That, in itself, is one of the most important Ownership concepts to "Own."

Section 2

Practices:
Ownership Thinking

"I've learned that you can tell a lot about a person by
the way he or she handles these three things:
a rainy day,
lost luggage, and
tangled Christmas tree lights."

—Maya Angelou

Our concept of *Ownership* evokes images of the lives and accomplishments of extraordinary people of the past and the present. We think of impressive examples of remarkable problem-solving, fortitude, sacrifice, and perseverance that cause us to evaluate ourselves. As we do, most of us can point to times when we displayed a fair degree of Ownership and to other times when we did not.

Knowing that we have substantial room for improvement leads us to another Owner/Victim choice. If we shift into Victim, we may think, "Why wasn't *I* lucky enough to be born with these traits?"

Or, "I wish *my* parents had taught me all of this when I was young." Victim thinking takes the position that character is a gift or genetic birthright—you are either born with it, or you are not. If you weren't born with the resolute determination of a Lincoln or the patience of a Gandhi, there isn't much hope.

If we take the Ownership posture, we might ask, "What can I do (practices) to become a stronger person? How can I show more tough-mindedness when things don't go my way? What mental skills can I learn to be more resolute and resilient when I meet a setback?" The more we gravitate toward Ownership, the more we see that we all have been given the gift of potential; however, fulfilling that potential is up to us, and nothing of value comes without a price.

Chapter 5

Blind Spots

If ineffective thinking patterns are not beneficial—and in most cases are downright detrimental, even lethal—then why are they so prevalent? Why would anyone choose self-impeding patterns of thought?

There could be many reasons. Maybe we have had some bad experiences that have traumatized our outlook on life. Perhaps we were raised in a negative environment, or we formed a circle of friends that dwelt on the gloomy side of life. It could be a subconscious attempt to avoid effort and responsibility. It's certainly easier to carp and criticize than to come up with solutions. Safer too. Sitting back and whining involves no risk. Nobody can take potshots at your actions if there aren't any. It could even be a misguided plea for attention. (Victims seldom suffer in silence).

All of these reasons have some validity, but my years of study, pondering, teaching, and coaching—along with my own thinking about my thoughts—have led me to conclude that *we choose unproductive thoughts because we don't **realize** we are choosing them.*

There's not a pessimist on the planet who thinks he or she is being a pessimist. They think they're being *realistic.* "Somebody needs to be a realist around here," they affirm, as they pride themselves on being the only pragmatic thinker on the team. Without an appreciation for *The Othello Principle,* however, they don't realize *everyone* is being realistic and pragmatic, and some people's realities work better than others.

"Sure Bill's happy and positive all the time," whines one Victim salesperson. "Look at all the units he sells every month. I'd be happy, too, if I sold that many units." This person fails to recognize what is cause and what is effect. He actually has them reversed. It seems preposterous to him that Bill sells more cars *because* he opts for a positive, people-attracting mindset; he doesn't realize Bill could actually be intentionally using *The Othello Principle* to his advantage. He cultivates that posture because it yields better results. The Victim's pessimistic approach is so ingrained in his thinking he doesn't even see optimism as a legitimate option. To him, people with an upbeat approach are just a bunch of insincere phonies.

Pessimistic points of view tend to limit the thinkers' options without the thinkers even realizing it. They take a brief look at the possibilities, and they don't see many; so they bail out of the creative process early on. They toss their hands in the air, and declare, "Nothing can be done." Meanwhile, someone else on the team may just as sincerely believe multiple promising options could exist. They stay in the creative process until they come up with one or two viable options and end up with a successful outcome. The end results in both cases, though diametrically opposite of each other, are produced by two completely sincere, completely *realistic* thinkers.

Taking Charge of Reality

The reality we need to strive for is that realism is a creation. We have all heard that "perception is reality," but few of us leverage that idea to our benefit. Rather than analyzing our perceptions and looking for areas where we may be limiting ourselves, we don't *realize* we're thinking unproductively. Nobody consciously goes about sabotaging their own progress and prosperity. Nobody gets up in the morning and says, "You know, I think I'll get out there and dodge a lot of responsibility today." In the final analysis, what impedes us most is not our bad habits but our inability to recognize the mental processes that author and perpetuate those habits.

Emmet Fox observed:

Thought is the real causative force in life and there is no other. You cannot have one kind of mind and another kind of environment. You cannot change your environment while leaving your mind unchanged. This is the real key to life. If you change your mind, your conditions must change, too. Your body must change, your activities must change, your home must change, the color tone of your whole life must change. This may be called the great cosmic law. The practical difficulty in applying it arises from the fact that our thoughts are so close to us that it is difficult, without a little practice, to stand back and look at them objectively.

Nothing offers us greater possibilities for enhancing the quality of our lives at home or at work than cultivating the skill of stepping outside of our thoughts, assessing their value, and making changes. When it comes to advancing our careers, improving individual and team results, or fulfilling our loftiest dreams and ambitions, applying that one skill will literally work wonders.

The Pointed Point

We're *all* creatures of the habits we've formed over the course of our lives. Many of those habits are solid and beneficial. Yet, even the most accomplished of us have written lines of code into our personal software that are not nearly as strong as they could be.

All of us have blind spots—ineffective mental habits that do not serve us. Most of the time, we are completely unaware of their existence or how often we resort to them. To support that point, I would like to present a paper written by a college student who was invited to a pilot class on *The Ownership Spirit*. Students were not told in advance anything about the content. They had no idea they were going to study thought processes and hone mind management skills. Most of them thought they were coming to some sort of elective English class.

At the very beginning of the class, the instructor asked the students to take 20 minutes and write a one-page paper about some aspect of their background. Most of them assumed, of course, that they would be graded on grammar, punctuation, content, and writing style; however the actual rationale for the exercise had nothing to do with English skills. The purpose was to have the students capture a sample of their thoughts, without it being affected by the knowledge that those thoughts would be analyzed for Owner and Victim patterns. Our goal was to create a discovery experience about blind spots. For most of them, the exercise worked like a charm. When they learned more about Owner and Victim language patterns and then went back to their papers, they were surprised to discover how often they had lapsed into Victim thinking. That realization opened their minds to what we had to teach about thinking tools because they could see the actual need for them.

With that in mind, consider this essay submitted by one of the students:

Student Essay: My Father

Most of my life, I have grown up without a father figure. I have always had a niche to be filled by a father figure. My mother did a good job raising me, but I feel as though my father has robbed me of something special, something all my friends had that I wanted.

I have never met my father, and I am not sure if I ever want to. I need to move on with my life. I feel as though I need closure. Growing up I have developed some harsh feelings toward my biological father. He made life tough on my sister and me. My mother came to America with just her possessions, her daughter, me, and my father. He left my mom after one year of living in the States. My father never helped out my mom in her time of need. He never paid child support. My mother had to work a full-time job, from morning to night. Not having a father really made me appreciate my mother.

I want to get back at my father somehow. I feel as if I need to, just because of the way he affected my life. It was messed up, and I don't think he had the right to do such a thing. Everyone I grew up with had both a father and a mother. I didn't have a father to teach me how to be a man, little things and big things. Like mowing the lawn or special things like girls. The future scares me because I hope that in the future I can be a great father to my family.

Now I have a stepfather and I can't accept him as a father figure. I love him like a father, but in the back of my mind, I know he isn't my pops. He came into my life too late for me to accept him as a father. He is the next best thing though. He has taught me some stuff that only a father can. I can't meet my father in the future because he doesn't want to see me. I feel solace knowing that most kids in my generation grew up without a full family. I just wish that I at least knew my father.

Seminar Discussion

Dennis: What is the prevailing tone of this essay—an optimistic, Owner tone or a pessimistic, Victim tone?

Answer (in an overwhelming chorus): *Pessimistic Victim tone.*

Dennis: Would you agree with me that the essay is virtually saturated in Victim-toned thinking?

Answer: *Yes.*

Dennis: Do you think the student realizes how Victim-toned his point of view actually is?

Answer: *No.*

Dennis: Clearly, he's blind to his own Victim statements. Do you think these thoughts came into his mind for the very first time when he was asked to write this paper?

Answer: *No. Definitely not.*

Dennis: This isn't the first time he's run this story. He's been replaying this series of thoughts hundreds of times, over and over, until it's now an automatic reflex. Do you think the student is unique?

Answer: *No.*

Dennis: No, we all are susceptible to blind spots. Some of our habits are so habitual, they have become transparent. We don't even notice how often we run them. Now, identify a specific Victim-toned statement you find in the paper.

Answer: *"My father has robbed me of something special."*

Dennis: Excellent. The word *robbed* is full of accusation and insinuation, isn't it?
　　　　Another one?

Answer: *"He made life tough on my sister and me."*

Dennis: Note that we are *not* disagreeing with his statement. He *has* had a tough life. Nevertheless, he is portraying himself as a Victim. *A Victim statement does not need to be untrue!* It *is* true that his father's decisions have had an adverse impact on his life, but his Victim thinking is compounding the challenges. His Victim viewpoint is making his life much rougher than it needs to be.

Another one?

Answer: *"I want to get back at my father somehow."*

Dennis: Why is the feeling that he has the need, even the right, to retaliate and inflict some retribution on his father indicative of Victim thinking?

Answer: *Because for someone to play the Victim, there has to be a counter-part—there has to be a Victimizer.*

Dennis: Yes! That's a very important point. For me to play the Victim, I have to portray someone else as the villain. Of course, that leads to another dangerous trap. I then feel justified in revenge and retaliation. Notice in your own thinking that whenever you are painting someone as an evil, malicious fiend whose sole motive is to make your life miserable, you have a bit of Victim thinking going on. Again, this is not to say that the other person is innocent of any devious acts or unkind words. He may be doing some underhanded things, but you are seeing yourself as a Victim, which gives the other person power over you.

Can someone give us another example of a Victim-toned statement in the essay?

Answer: *"I didn't have a father to teach me how to be a man."*

Dennis: Notice that he is painting himself as being the *lone sufferer* on the planet. Everyone else has these perfect, storybook families, with loving parents teaching, nurturing, and guiding them every step of the way. *He's* the *only* one who has to go it alone. Whenever you portray yourself as the lone sufferer, thinking that all your neighbors and co-workers have it easy compared to you and you're the only one who has to deal with such heavy burdens, that's a signal you are mired in a Victim puddle. One more Victim statement please.

Answer: *"He came into my life too late for me to accept him as a father."*

Dennis: That's an interesting one. He begins his paper by saying he has "always had a niche to be filled by a father figure." Then, along comes someone who makes a valiant attempt to fill that role, and the young man rejects his stepfather because apparently there was a deadline. (The stepfather arrived too late.)

Many of our Victim statements may be far more incongruous than his. When they rattle around in our own heads, they seem to make perfect, logical sense. It's only when we put them down on paper, and then examine them, that we realize how contradictory and ridiculous they actually are. We author our mental habits, but if we let them roll along and gain momentum, in a certain sense, they start to run us.

Switching for a moment to the Owner side, what is the student's highest positive aspiration?

Answer: *To be a good father.*

Dennis: Right. He aspires to be a great father, but he has huge doubts about it. Is there anything in his background that is preventing him from being a terrific father?

Answer: *No.*

Dennis: So what is holding him back?

Answer: *Himself. He's holding himself back.*

Dennis: Is *everything* about himself holding him back?

Answer: *What's holding him back are his thoughts.*

Dennis: But is it *all* of his thoughts? What's holding him back is this story line—these 29 sentences. He has been over this story dozens of times, possibly every day. What's holding him back is that very mental construct—that sequence of sentences. Unless he sees that and dismantles these very sentences, converting them into something more constructive, he'll continue to suffer the negative consequences, everything from depressed immune function to impaired relationships.

This final point made in this discussion is vital. If this young man were to attend a motivational rally and the speaker said, "You've got to think more positively," would the speaker be right? Yes. Would it help the student? Not that much, because the suggestion to think positively is too general in this case. If the young man went to a therapist and the therapist said, "You've got to unload some baggage," would the therapist be right? Yes. Would it help the student? Not until the therapist was able to guide the student to understand exactly what baggage needed to be unloaded.

If the student could recognize what is holding him back and redesign it, he would enjoy many new dimensions to his life—one of those being a better relationship with his stepfather, which would likely enrich his relationship with his mother as well. He would also gain confidence in his ability to be a good father. He would see his experience has put him in an excellent position to be a great father—that he is actually advantaged! He has a vivid, emotion-laden vision of what the father-child relationship could have been like. He knows exactly how meaningful and important it is to the child. He can picture the kinds of chats and teaching moments he wishes he had experienced. All of that could be the template he could follow to be a very caring, alert, and available father.

Sometimes, out of our deprivations and hardships come some of our clearest perspectives and greatest strengths. I think I am the beneficiary of something like what I'm describing here. My father's father died when he was 11 years old, during the depths of the great American Depression. Dad didn't seem to be neurotic or obsessed about it, but more than once he told me, "Dennis, I know what it's like to grow up without a father. In any way I can be there for you, I'm going to do my best to do it." I cannot recall many school events or ballgames I participated in where my dad did not move heaven and earth to be there.

Will our student's disadvantaged childhood hamper his progress for the rest of his life, or will it prepare him to be an intensely devoted father? It depends on how he chooses to look at it—as a Victim or as an Owner.

The Rest of the Story

So, what happened to the student? Was he able to recognize his Victim monologue and alter it? Are there any tools to help him (or us) detect unproductive habits and redesign faulty circuits in our thinking? The answer is "Yes," and the good news is the student, Joe, is only one of many success stories. In fact, I am using Joe's essay as a prototype in this book, not with his permission, but rather with his insistence.

When the 20-minute writing time ended, the instructor told the students they would not be handing their papers in for a grade. The compositions were for their eyes only. She then introduced the class to concepts of *The Ownership Spirit*, including *The Othello Principle*, and then taught the students three tools and gave them the assignment to apply the tools to their own essay and be ready to report on their experience.

The teacher had known the young man before he attended her class. She said, "The change that came over this young man in two days was phenomenal. It was like the weight of the world had been lifted from his shoulders."

In the chapters ahead, we will delve into the tools that can produce this phenomenal change.

Chapter 6

Re-encoding Circuits

Life-changing shifts in attitude can and do happen along the path of our progression. Indeed, they occur often when we earnestly seek to improve ourselves through honest analysis of our thought processes.

What made Joe's experience so meaningful to him was not that it came as some fortuitous fluke or bizarre stroke of luck. His excitement stemmed from the realization that his "epiphany" had happened because he had taken the steps to make it happen.

Such breakthroughs have happened for me, and they can happen for you—and for any of us—when we learn to apply three tools: The Suspecting Tool, The Detecting Tool, and The Rescripting Tool.

Rescripting Tool. When we identify a habitual Victim statement or unproductive flow of thoughts, we can use The Rescripting Tool to create a strong replacement for the ineffective mental habit.

Detecting Tool. Sometimes, we are not *sure* whether a given thought or flow of thoughts is problematic or not. Hence, we use the Detecting Tool to detect and verify the Victim-toned components in a given point of view.

Suspecting Tool. Before we use either of those tools to do any analysis and redesigning, we use the Suspecting Tool to uncover the need or compelling reason to employ the other tools.

A New Tool Set

Every thought has an impact and creates a spectrum of effects. Thoughts have the potential to change everything from our physical states, to our emotional states, to our creative intellectual activity, to our behaviors. Awareness that the origin of those consequences lies in our thoughts enables us to exert control over those effects. The converse is also true. We can use the effects (the products of our thoughts)—those very emotions, behaviors, actions, and physical consequences—to evaluate the quality and relative value of the thoughts that produce them.

Hence, if we notice an unwanted or counterproductive emotion flaring up inside us, this indicates we just selected and entertained a counterproductive thought. Rather than thinking that a neighbor's comment (something outside) "made us mad," we can take responsibility for our emotions as we think, "Now, what did I just say to myself (something inside) about what my neighbor said that generated this resentment?"

As the proverb states, "By their fruits, ye shall know them." We can use the *consequences* of our thoughts to assess the *quality* of our thoughts. This insight forms the basis of a useful method for self-analysis and evaluation of our own thought patterns. In fact, we can formalize it into a tool—The Suspecting Tool.

The Suspecting Tool

"Bitter water comes from a bitter spring," paraphrases a Native American adage that applies to the cause-and-effect relationship between thoughts and outcomes. Logically, an ineffective or undesirable consequence would point us back to an ineffective or undesirable thought. By heightening our awareness of these indicators, we can improve our ability to discover and expose counterproductive thoughts.

The Suspecting Tool consists of a list of *indicators* or *consequences*—signs or symptoms, if you will—of unproductive thinking patterns or mental habits.

Indicators of Unproductive Thinking Patterns

1. Results

If we notice a repeated pattern of disappointing results in some facet of our life, we've likely found an indicator of underlying self-sabotaging thoughts. We've heard the phrase, "The numbers don't lie." Neither do results. Naturally, we think we're predominantly sensible, clear-thinking individuals. Yet, if we continue to see disappointing results in our work life, our personal life, or both, these disappointing results strongly suggest the presence of an underlying counterproductive mental pattern.

For example, you might begin a relationship believing you've found your "soul mate." For weeks, you live in bliss. Gradually, however, you notice a few faults in the other person. Focusing on the "blemishes," you become more critical. Naturally, the relationship begins to deteriorate and die. Figuring you just haven't found "the right person," you search until you think you've found your "one true soul mate," and the scenario repeats. After a few trips around that circuit, you may recognize that the props on the stage change, but the plot doesn't, and you may step back and consider your own complicity in the plot. Look for such patterns in your life.

2. Internally Held Negative Emotions

Frequent bouts of fear, anxiety, dread, apprehension, uncertainty, self-doubt, or self-condemnation can be indicators of unproductive patterns of thought. Depression, not including frank clinical depression, is yet another indicator. If you are cruising along and then notice a sudden drop in your confidence, mood, or will, see that as a red flag. Take, for example, a salesperson doing phone contacting. If he receives a harsh rejection—and that rejection is followed by an erosion in confidence and a loss of will to make the next call—his loss of confidence is due to his own unproductive interpretation of the call.

3. Externally Directed Negative Emotions

Anger, resentment, animosity, disdain, ridicule, jealousy, envy, grudge-holding, vengefulness, and other outwardly directed emotions are clear indicators of Victim thinking. A hallmark of Victim thinking is the rush to blame others for our troubles. Emotions that result in blaming or scapegoating have a Victim origin.

Another indicator is simply general irritation with humanity. If we have a hard time getting from our driveways to our workplaces without using the word *"Idiot!"* several times, we're probably in Victim mode.

4. Avoidance

If we notice ourselves ducking certain issues or procrastinating action in certain areas of our life, we are likely nurturing a pattern of Victim thoughts about that issue. Skirting issues, putting things off, or being unwilling to tackle a problem or concern is usually born of fear, which is generally spawned by a Victim-slanted viewpoint of that topic.

5. Physical Indicators

Anxious tension in the body—often manifest as the "knot in the stomach" or chronic tightness in the muscles of the upper back and neck—is a key indicator. More systemic physical symptoms also are indicative. Again, thoughts trigger neurotransmitters that orchestrate the biochemical activity in our bodies. Dour, pessimistic thoughts lead to depressed activity in the immune system. Dampened immune function leads to frequent colds, flues, and chronic low energy and can often be traced back to chronic or habitual pessimism.

6. Rumination

A ruminant is a mammal that chews its food, swallows it, but then brings it back up later to chew on it again. Cattle and camels are ruminants. Do you see why *rumination* is such a perfect term? Do you have any circuits that you ruminate on, that you run and rerun? Do you go back and relive, again and again, some experience from the past? If so, it will continue to plague your tranquility until you can discover where the "burr under the saddle" lies, reconcile the disparity, and come to peace with it.

7. Feedback from Others

Sometimes people we know and trust will level with us and let us know when we are shooting ourselves in the foot. If we squelch our defensiveness and consider what they say, we may find some patterns in our thinking worth reshaping or replacing. At other times, the feedback is not direct, and we must pick up on the clues. Some signs are subtle—like, we don't have any friends. Seriously, if we notice a pattern of distant or difficult working relationships with our colleagues and co-workers, it may be *our view of them* that is throwing up barriers. Without even knowing that we're doing it, we might be repelling, rather than attracting, support and alignment.

◆

Now that we have heightened awareness of some of the signs and symptoms resulting from unproductive thinking, we are ready to delve more deeply into our habitual patterns. We can use two other tools—The Detecting Tool and The Rescripting Tool—to discover precisely which patterns are bedeviling us and then redesign them.

The Detecting Tool

With an awareness of the leading indicators, the next step is to look for a trigger point—the moment when we first notice the onset or appearance of one or more of the indicators. A trigger point is a situation that promotes or evokes the indicators, but it is important to note that a trigger point is not the cause, just the context. The actual cause is the flow of thought we run in our head at that moment.

For example, if we're having a friendly conversation with a co-worker and notice that, as she shifts to a particular topic, we suddenly become uncomfortable and resentful, *that's a trigger point*. At that trigger point, we shifted into an unproductive flow of thoughts. This discovery enables us to detect and analyze an unproductive line of thinking.

You don't need to dive into analysis right at that moment, but you can make a mental note of the trigger point. Later, when you have a moment to reflect, you can revisit the trigger moment in your mind. Since it's a habit, you can easily cue up the trigger point and replay the specific conversation you had with yourself at that moment.

As you rerun your monologue, look for *three signals* that reveal unproductive thinking. Unproductive thinking:

1. Promotes a sense of hopelessness about the future

Does this thinking erode my confidence and positive expectations about the future? Do my opportunities seem diminished and my options limited, restricted, or non-existent? Does the situation look bleak, irresolvable, or doomed to failure? Does it seem that it's too late to remedy the situation?

2. Promotes a sense of helplessness or lowers your sense of worth or power

Do I feel weak or view myself as powerless to alter or change the situation? Does the issue seem overwhelming or too complex to resolve? Do I discount my ability to do anything on my own to better the situation? Do I see myself as trapped or "painted into a corner"? Does this thinking lead me to doubt my worth or value?

3. Promotes negative feelings toward other people

Do I feel anger, animosity, or resentment toward another person or group? Is there a villain in my story? Do I see myself as being disrespected by other people? Do I see the actions or inactions of another person as the source of my trouble? Do I consider my suffering to be due to the intentionally unjust motives of others? Am I an innocent bystander, undeserving of the treatment I receive?

◆

If you notice any or all of these three signals, then you have detected and confirmed that you have been holding a Victim point of view. Gratefully, it is only a habit—not a permanent defect or an innate character flaw dooming you to perpetual mediocrity. It's only an ineffective pattern of thoughts that you have power to change.

The only habits you and I can't change or improve are the ones we don't know exist. The Suspecting and Detecting Tools enable us to identify a bad habit and bring it out into the light of day. Once we have identified an unconstructive pattern then, and only then, can we do something about it. We can rescript it.

We address The Rescripting Tool in the next chapter.

Chapter 7

The Rescripting Tool

Awareness is power. Awareness of our ability to step outside our thinking to examine and evaluate our thoughts enables us to make significant and lasting changes. Whenever we discover or recognize unproductive mental habits, we can eliminate or redesign them using the **six steps** that constitute The Rescripting Tool.

Step 1—Capture the story in writing. In Chapter 5, we could analyze the student's essay easily and accurately because it was written. We could study the word choices and compare one sentence with another. Capturing our own mental monologues in written form gives us that same advantage. Write your flow of thoughts in as much detail as you can. Don't gloss or summarize. No one will see this work except you. Return to your trigger point and replay the thoughts you dwelt on in that moment. Capture the actual phrasing you used, and don't soften it. Write it just the way you told it to yourself at the trigger point. Take your time; be thorough and honest with yourself. Do not try to amend or modify your habitual phrasing at this point. You will do that later on. Right now, just capture in detail your current wording. You won't eradicate the weed unless you tear out the whole plant, roots and all.

Step 2—Look for Owner statements. Just as there are no perfect Owners and no complete Victims (we're all composites of both), our stories are also composites—containing both Owner and Victim elements. Owner statements need to be amplified and leveraged. For instance, the student wrote, "Not having a father really made me appreciate my mother." That's a valuable part of his background, but he downplays it by skipping right past it. He needs to expand that point and mine it for all it's worth.

His mother is an outstanding role model for him. She has not abdicated her parental responsibilities. She has set aside her personal agenda and gone to work, putting in long hours, sacrificing to give her children the best life she can provide. What a sterling example. He needs to recognize his mother's example, examine it, and emulate it. If he does, it will increase his confidence markedly as he considers his future as a parent.

Likewise, we benefit by examining *our* stories. We need to look for Owner statements and consider whether we are giving enough emphasis to them. Have we, like the student, collapsed them and stepped right past some golden elements that we could build upon to strengthen our perspectives?

Step 3—Look for Victim statements. Along with strengths, there will be weaknesses—places where we blame, whine a bit, or shift responsibility. Look for places where you depict yourself as the lone sufferer on the planet—where everyone else has it easy and you're the only one with heavy burdens—such as in the essay: "Everyone I grew up with had both a father and a mother." Look for ways in which you undermine your hope and confidence: "The future scares me because ..." Look for places where you resent someone and nurture negative feelings toward another: "I want to get back at my father somehow. I feel as if I need to, just because of the way he affected my life. It was messed up, and I don't think he had the right to do that." Some of your Victim statements may not be as obvious as these. Yours may require more scrutiny to detect. Take the time to assess your wording thoroughly. This is a vital step, so don't rush it.

Step 4—Look for exaggerated disadvantages. Are you overstating the negative consequences, making the problem seem more difficult or irresolvable than necessary? Notice Joe's tendency to do that in this statement: "I didn't have a father to teach me how to be a man, little things and big things, like mowing the lawn or dating girls." Joe is taking a fact (it is true that he did not have a father to teach and coach him), and he is inflating it with disproportionate, self-hampering significance. Many people grow up without a father to teach them. Though difficult, not having a father does not spell hopeless doom. I'm not asking anyone to turn mountains into molehills or live in denial, but in Victim thinking, you actually do the opposite by turning your mountain into Mount Everest or the entire Himalayan Range, making the scenario seem more daunting than it really is.

Step 5—Look for overlooked advantages and benefits. In preparing to redesign your point of view, look for places you might be overlooking some beneficial aspects of the situation. Ask, "How can I see this situation as actually being *advantageous*? What benefits does it offer me? What lessons or pearls of insight can I draw out of this?"

Let's go back to Joe's essay. Couldn't we make a solid case that his experience has provided excellent preparation for successful parenting? He knows what that relationship could have been like, how important it is to a child, and what a father could do to nurture and prepare a child for life. He could take those vivid perspectives and convert them into vectors of attentive parenting. Recognizing the value of simple father-to-son conversations, he could create opportunities to counsel, coach, and teach his child—passing along the lessons he wishes he'd been taught. Out of his deprivation could come great good.

Step 6—Rewrite the story as an Owner. Having dislodged ourselves from our old pattern and having considered better alternatives, we can now capture these new perspectives in writing. In doing so, we can use steps 2 through 5 as guidelines: (1) amplify the strengths; (2) dismantle the weaknesses, sentence by sentence and replace each Victim statement with a stronger, more constructive alternative; (3) tone down the disadvantages and bring them into a more realistic, accurate perspective; (4) draw out the lessons, emphasizing the benefits and advantages embedded in the experience.

Once you've rewritten your point of view, keep the rescription handy. The old habit will tend to persist, but you are now armed and ready. The moment the old flow of thoughts pops into your mind, you can recognize what's happening and intercept and halt it. When you catch yourself about to relapse into your old Victim pattern, refer to your rescription and read it through, reminding yourself and reinforcing the line of thinking you want to pursue. For a while, you may have to flip to your rescription a few times a day, but within a relatively short time, your rescription will become familiar and customary. Within a few weeks, the new version will replace the old one and become your new default mode. Just as you can rewrite code in computer software, you can rewrite code in your mental software. It just takes a little practice.

The Student's Owner Rescription

Let's take a look at the student's first rescription.

My Father

Most of my life, I have grown up without a father. At times I felt as if there were some big hole in my life, not knowing if I would ever have the satisfaction of a friendship with a man who loved and cared about me. The pain has felt almost unbearable at times. However, as I get older, I realize my father did not rob me of my life; only I can do that. I used to feel that my friends' lives were more complete than mine because they had a man in their home. As my spiritual life has matured, I have come to understand that I always had a father figure in my life—God. He never left my side, and He has been teaching me all these years how to be a man.

When my mother and father arrived in the U.S. from Puerto Rico, all they had were me, my sister, and a few possessions. Just one year later, my father chose to leave us, but my mother chose to stand strong, working from morning to night to support her children. I learned great lessons from her sacrifices—how to face adversity—how to have almost nothing but to never give up. I am in college now on a soccer scholarship, carrying on my mother's legacy of hard work and determination, with a bright future ahead of me.

Not having a father when growing up has helped me appreciate the value of a good man in a young child's life. I can be a wonderful father because I understand what a young child's heart longs for. I look forward to the future, to the chance to make a difference in the lives of my wife and children. As I learn to separate past hurts from present opportunities, I am able to accept my stepfather more and more. I realize, as I grow older, that you don't have to be someone's "blood" to love them. For example, children who are adopted into a loving family are cherished every bit as much as if they had been born there. I learn new things from my stepfather all the time, and he fills the "hole" in my life in many ways. I am lucky to have a good father figure in my life, since many young men never do, and I am most happy that my mother has found a companion who treats her well.

When I see all that my father lost by leaving us, I weep for him. One day I may choose to forgive him. I realize that he must be in pain from the choices he has made.

I guess my father has taught me many things, after all. As I get older, I see the opportunity of learning from his mistakes; I understand the tremendous value of being emotionally, physically, and financially available to my own family.

Whatever the future holds for me, I am excited with my present opportunities to keep learning all that I can, to make the most of my time and talents, and to grow into the man that I am capable of becoming.

We recognize a couple of things: (1) The rescription shows a marked improvement over his original story, and (2) it is far from perfect. Joe's first rescription still has weaknesses; it could be stronger than it is (which Joe later recognized, and hence he rescripted his rescription).

That underscores three more valuable points: (1) You don't have to author a Pulitzer prize-winning rescription for this tool to be effective; (2) there is always room for improvement, so don't settle necessarily for your first draft; and (3) even modest improvements can pay big dividends.

Chapter 8

The Intercepting Tool: Take AIM

The Suspecting Tool, The Detecting Tool, and The Rescripting Tool help us uncover and replace hidden, longstanding and unproductive thinking habits. Some of these deceitful patterns may have run in our heads for years and become so familiar to us that they now run almost automatically without check or restraint.

You may ask, "How do I avoid *forming* a Victim habit in the first place? How can I *intercept* negative trains of thought right in the moment?"

You can avoid forming a Victim habit and intercept negative thoughts in the moment by using the **Intercepting Tool.**

We have patterned this tool around a simple acronym, **AIM,** for a specific reason. When we are thrown off balance and become upset, frustrated, or angry, it's often because we've lost perspective. We have fallen into the trap of focusing on the *immediate* moment, thinking short term rather than long term. We can usually regain our poise and presence by reminding ourselves to refocus and take **AIM.**

A—Acknowledge an Annoyance. The term "annoyance" covers a wide spectrum—mild to severe. During any given day, we all encounter circumstances and events that may not exactly please us at the moment. Some are inconsequential irritations (getting bogged down in traffic), and others are very trying, gut-wrenching experiences (losing a job). Whatever the degree of annoyance, the first step in keeping our cool and dealing with it effectively is to *objectively* acknowledge that something disturbing has just occurred.

Too often we rush right past this step. Instead of looking at the situation as dispassionate observers, we decide, almost automatically, to take things personally and then leap to a series of judgmental assumptions and conclusions about who is at fault.

If we fail to acknowledge the annoyance, we will experience much irritation, frustration, and inner turbulence. Although taking a dispassionate, objective mental posture may not be our natural inclination, we can cultivate this response and gain impressive benefits. (Together we could save enough money on Maalox and other acid reflux medications to retire the national debt.)

I—Investigate our interpretations. Once we shift into an observational mindset, we can place our attention where it can do us the most good. The source of our disturbance is not the event itself but our *interpretation* of that event. Hence, on this "I-level" we can ask ourselves, "What meaning am I giving to this experience?" Say, for example, someone "steals" your parking space as you are about to park at the mall. Do you take this *personally*? Do you think the driver purposely flouted the rules of common courtesy and blatantly disrespected you? Do you dwell on this slight, letting this encounter (interpretation) upset you and ruin the rest of your day? Do you continue to relive the episode in your head, again and again, as you enter the mall?

M—Monitor Results. Continuing the observational point of view, we can look at the consequences or outcomes we are experiencing as a result of our present interpretation. Are the results what we want or not? Ask, "Do I like the way I am feeling right now? What kind of chemistry am I producing in my body? What emotions am I generating? Are these sentiments healthy? What results am I getting: Am I calm and happy, or am I upset and resentful at this moment?"

If the answer is, "No, this isn't benefiting me or anyone else," then we simply return to the interpretation, or I-level, and ask, "How else can I look at this?" Generally, it doesn't take long to come up with a different interpretation that produces something far more positive and beneficial.

As we sustain enough self-awareness to notice the onset of upsets, we can intercept a multitude of self-inflicted wounds by purposely shifting our attention to *our point of view* rather than to the event itself. Marcus Aurelius, emperor of Rome, noted, "If you are distressed by anything external, the pain is not due to the thing itself, but to your estimate of it; and this you have the power to revoke at any moment."

When you've revoked it, you will notice a marked *release of tension* in your body.

This is a Test, Only a Test

It's amazingly easy to lapse into reactive, judgmental habits that undermine our poise and serenity. When we do, we miss out on many of life's simple joys. Instead of angrily stomping into the mall, we might focus instead on the blue sky of an exceptional spring day and find ourselves smiling at people and see them actually smiling back.

If you think this discussion a bit too cheery and "unrealistic," I invite you to apply the tool. Ask yourself, "What interpretation am I giving to these words? Am I choosing to view them as sound and sensible or just plain sappy? Which choice will yield the better benefits?"

I suggest we can all benefit by applying the AIM Tool a little more often. Test it today. When you face a potentially irritating event and feel the first surge of annoyance, take hold of your thoughts, shift to an observational posture, and investigate your interpretation. Just for the sake of experimentation, do not go with your first alternative. Live a little. Take this new tool out for a test drive. Try out *several* interpretations. Play with the possibilities for a moment. You will find yourself chuckling in a moment or two—and each chuckle has therapeutic value.

Example of a Minor Annoyance

Annoyances fall somewhere on the Annoyance Spectrum between mild-and-inconsequential to major-and-heartrending. Here are three illustrations.

The first example comes from my colleague, Pat Cox:

"I'm a grandparent and I'm often asked to baby-sit for one or more of my grandchildren. One day, I was tending my two-year-old grandson who has incredible curiosity. He also is very fast and very quiet. He comes with the face of an angel and a charming smile, which he uses to his advantage. We played together for a while with his toys, but by the second hour, he was ready for some action. He cheerfully followed me into the bedroom while I went about one of my weekend chores—the laundry. I happened to notice his sippy cup was almost empty, so I left him alone for *just a minute* to fill his cup. (Did I mention he's fast?) By the time I returned to the bedroom, he was in the adjoining bathroom, holding a vacuum hose that he'd pulled from the vacuum (did I mention he's curious?), with his left hand holding one end of the hose under the bathtub faucet and his right hand on the cold water handle.

"I used the AIM Tool on the spot. I *Acknowledged the Annoyance.* Yes, this could have ruined the day and the carpet; and I did panic at first. Just seconds later, though, I asked myself to *Investigate the Interpretations.* My thinking changed almost immediately from Victim thinking to Owner thinking. My thoughts were now focused on how fortunate it was that I came back into the room *before* my grandson turned the water on and how clever he was to realize that hooking the hose up to the tub would be a great way to irrigate the carpet. Instead of being angry, I started laughing.

"A moment or two after that, giving the situation a bit more thought, I realized even if he had run the water through the hose onto the carpet, it could have easily been cleaned up, so there was no need to make a mountain out of that molehill.

"We make a choice with every situation we face during each day. Most of the time it pays to step back for a second, refocus, and take AIM."

The Third Son

Daily, we have ordinary annoying experiences. From time to time, we also encounter annoyances that have deeper meaning with more extensive implications. As the significance of the annoyance increases, so does the value of the AIM principles.

For example, a woman who participated in our seminars wrote:

"I have three sons, all grown now. Our two older sons are very intelligent. Schoolwork came easily to them, and they were always in the top of their classes. Our youngest son may be the *most* intelligent, although he has a learning disability.

"All three of our sons went to the same grade school, but the youngest son had to receive extra tutoring along the way just to keep up with the class. Our two older sons graduated from grade school and went on to a very prestigious private high school where an entrance exam was required for acceptance. Our youngest wanted the same opportunity.

"In seventh grade, his teacher confided that she didn't think our son should take the exam. She was certain he would fail it and go through life feeling depressed that he couldn't be or have what his brothers had. She knew how important this was to him.

"Following the teacher's advice and realizing how difficult schoolwork was for our son, we took him out to dinner to tell him he wouldn't be going to the same school as his brothers. We sugarcoated the conversation and then delivered our decision. His response was, 'So, you have both decided I would fail the test without giving me the opportunity to take it. I would always go through life wondering if I could have passed it. I want to get extra tutoring through the summer and take my best shot at passing it.'

"He did just that. During the summer, he worked very hard, giving up sports, playtime with his friends, television, and many other free time activities. In the fall, he took the test, passed it, and ultimately went on to graduate from that school with a scholarship to St. Joseph's University. He graduated in four years from college and continued on for his master's degree in International Marketing. He now has a successful career, a wife, and two beautiful daughters. My husband and I often wonder what would have happened if he didn't have the spirit and drive he has. It's evident in everything he does."

◆

When we Own our annoyances rather than falling prey to our Victim interpretations, we simultaneously avoid a boatload of troubles and accrue a freighter full of benefits. If this son had shifted into Victim thinking, he could have responded with, "You don't believe in me, and you never have. You've always loved my brothers more because they are smarter in school. I've always been different; I'm the black sheep of the family, and this is just more evidence." Stewing in such thinking might have taken his life down a path of self-defeating behaviors to fulfill his own prophecy.

Instead, in effect, he said, "Here's an annoyance: My teacher doesn't believe in me, and my parents are concerned." Considering various possible interpretations, he saw something beyond the "worst-case scenario." His thoughts moved to, "Why are my parents concerned, and what are they concerned about? Well, they are concerned because they love me. What they're concerned *about* is that I am not prepared. So, what can I do to get more prepared?" Choosing Owner instead of Victim, he enjoys the considerable *results* of some very constructive *interpretations*.

The Higher Road of Mindfulness

In the case of minor annoyances, such as the "stolen" parking space, shifting our thoughts to the benefits of a few extra steps of exercise can be sufficient. At other times, we need to go much deeper, as illustrated in this third example of the extraordinary results that come from taking AIM.

Jeff and Analilí Burrows had been married for two years when they learned they were expecting a baby. They rejoiced in the news and each new stage associated with it. Analilí's sister, Wendy Rojas, writes, "My sister and I live in different countries, so she would email me with the news of the development of her pregnancy. I could sense in every letter how excited she was to finally embark on the exciting adventure of motherhood. Even as a child, she had displayed great natural talent to relate to babies and little ones, always showing kindness and love to the children around her. She was born to be a mom.

"One of her early letters was filled with the joy of anticipation: 'I have been privileged to feel well all along, but today I felt queasy for the first time. It was funny ... I enjoyed it!' Another time she wrote: 'I felt the baby move for the first time today, and it was such a joyous experience!' One day in June, she wrote: 'Today is a special day. We will go to the doctor's office to get an ultrasound. I cannot wait to 'see' what my baby looks like ... I wonder if it's a boy or a girl. Will the baby have Jeff's hair? In fact, if it's a boy, I hope he looks just like his father. If it's a girl, well ... I just hope she doesn't have my nose! I will write tomorrow and let you know.'

"The next day, her email read: 'Wendy, thank you for the present you sent for my baby. I will have to save it for next time, as the ultrasound yesterday revealed that this baby, a boy, will not live. We are very sad. Please pray for us.'"

Analilí's pregnancy, from all outward indications, was normal. If anything, better than normal. She had very little morning sickness, weight gain was always within normal healthy limits, and she had no unusual fevers or illnesses that might have caused disruption in the baby's development.

Five months into the pregnancy, the routine ultrasound revealed an alarming, heart-searing fact. The baby was a normal, well-developing boy but with one serious defect. A major part of the baby's skull was missing. The cranium was virtually absent, lacking the necessary bone to protect the baby's brain.

"We could tell that something was wrong by the way the doctor reacted when he looked at the ultrasound," Analilí says. "When he turned the screen so that we could see for ourselves, we could see the form of a healthy baby from the neck down, but in the area of the brain, there was just a blur."

"The doctors called the condition *cranium bifidum*," Analilí explains. "They told us it was very rare, only occurring once in every several thousand births."

A few weeks later, Analilí wrote to her sister, "I can still feel my baby move inside me. Every time he moves, I tell him, 'Jimmy, I love you,' and 'Jimmy, I am going to miss you.'" Sadly, a subsequent email to Wendy said, "Jimmy stopped moving on Friday. The doctor said he should be born any time. I am scared. Please pray for me."

Wendy adds, "I received a call from my mother when my sister went into labor, and I boarded a plane to be with her. On the following day, we stood at the gravesite where Jimmy was to be buried, and his father, Jeff, stood up and gave some beautiful remarks, full of faith and gratitude. It was very touching."

Analilí and Jeff, buoyed by their faith in God and the support of their families, grieved without bitterness and looked forward to the future. They recognized that this event, tragic as it was, had brought the extended family closer, helping to remove hedgerows of hurt that had grown between various members of the family. Opportunities for love and service occurred that mended relationships.

"My father was such a support for us. I think he realized we really needed him," Analilí says.

"My father-in-law really stepped up," Jeff explains. "He gifted us a place to bury our child in a cemetery here locally. He helped us at a difficult time. In Guatemala, where we live, there are a lot of cumbersome legalities to overcome to bury a body—more complicated than in the United States."

Analilí's father took over all of those concerns, and baby James was laid to rest in a timely manner, in a proper way, in a fitting place.

A few months later, Analilí conceived again, but within a short time, she miscarried. About a year and a half later, the Burrows' disappointments were turned to indescribable joy when Analilí carried full term and delivered a perfectly healthy, beautiful daughter, whom they named Kezia. It seemed appropriate to name her after one of the daughters of the biblical Job, the man of trials. "I remember reading the Book of Job years ago, and I was so impressed with his story," Jeff says.

With the birth of Kezia, Analilí and Jeff thought their trials in bringing children into the world were over. Jeff continues, "We thought that we would never have to go through something like that again, but sure enough, we did. A couple of years later, we were expecting again, and just a month before Analilí was to give birth, in the very last month, we lost the baby, a little girl, because of *abruptio placentae*."

Placental abruption, the premature separation of a normal placenta from the uterus, occurs in barely one-tenth of one percent of all pregnancies worldwide. The cause is not known and is neither predictable nor preventable. In complete abrupt separations, as in this case, the fetus dies within minutes due to the complete loss of oxygen.

"This was just a tragic experience," Jeff relates. "Although the baby was stillborn, she was just beautiful. She looked a lot like Kezia at birth. She was well formed. Physically, you couldn't tell anything was wrong with her. She just didn't make it. That was hard. I shed tears, something I don't do very often."

As difficult as this loss was for Jeff and Analilí, it was compounded by another hurt. Additional pain came from an unexpected source, one that had been a great source of strength at the death of their first child. Some of the Burrows' family and friends were critical of some of

Jeff and Analilí's decisions. "It was a little disconcerting," Jeff admits. "We overheard some comments. Although it was a sensitive time and people weren't talking directly to us about it, they were questioning our decisions, 'Why didn't they do more?' And, 'Why wasn't there better prenatal care?' And, 'Why did they do this, and why didn't they do that?'"

You can imagine how stinging and painful these questions were at such a tender time. It's also not hard to visualize how easy it would be to take deep offense and build up resentment and ill will. Can there be a more difficult time to Own one's awareness than to be in the midst of a heart-rending tragedy and then be accused of negligence? It would be so easy, so typical of human nature, to be so entirely focused on one's own sorrow and pain that rising above real or perceived slights and criticisms would be well nigh impossible. Indeed, some of the most calcified and enduring family rifts are born at just such trying and vulnerable moments. Unintercepted hateful thoughts can solidify into stony walls, separating and alienating people on both sides for decades.

Jeff and Analilí Burrows experienced the impulse to take offense; the thought *did* pass through their minds, but they did not let those impulsive thoughts take over. They exercised the presence of mind to step back and take AIM. They took a deep breath and thought about the annoyance and the most useful way to interpret their loved ones' motives. Stepping out of the present, they looked forward into the future and asked, "What result do we *really* want out of this?" By working backward from the desired result they wanted, the best interpretation to obtain that result became clear.

From the powerful vantage point they created for themselves, Analilí and Jeff could see the motives of their loved ones were good. Their friends and family were not intentionally trying to pour salt into the wound; they only wanted the best for this tragedy-stricken young couple. That perspective enabled Jeff and Analilí to recognize their loved ones' comments as signs of love and concern, rather than darts of unfair criticism and second-guessing. That added even more impetus to their desire to strengthen the love and unity within the family. Being mindful, instead of resentful, allowed Jeff and Analilí to not just put on a happy face, while still harboring bad feelings beneath the surface. They were able to extend *genuine* love, and that seed germinated and reproduced after its own kind.

History verifies that hate begets hate, retaliation begets more retaliation, and genuine love begets genuine love. The increased love Analilí and Jeff extended to their family and friends was received. Then, through some form of curative emotional alchemy, the love multiplied and spread throughout the family circle, resulting in the close family ties the Burrows' had hoped for.

Because Jeff and Analilí took the higher road of mindful Ownership, two heart-rending tragedies that could have permanently divided a family, worked in tandem to heal and unite it. The first tragedy broke down old barriers and brought family members together, and the second one solidified the union.

Such is the power of The Intercepting Tool.

Chapter 9

Strengthening Others

Effects of taking Ownership only *begin* with the Owner.

Ownership radiates and recruits, affecting thinking and influencing behavior changes in people within the Owners' sphere of influence. Such positive effects occur with virtually every Ownership choice.

As our awareness of Ownership principles grows and we become more consistent and adept at applying the tools, we soon experience the benefits. Almost naturally, our thoughts turn to the people around us with a desire to help them improve and develop as well. Indeed, the question most frequently asked by participants in *The Ownership Spirit* seminar is, "How do I help another person shift from Victim thinking to Ownership?"

Believe in Human Potential for Change

It seems we all work, live, or associate with people who habitually see the negative side of any situation. To assist them, we must verify one basic requisite: a firm belief in the potential for change. Any gestures of extending help will be fruitless if we are skeptical and believe, "This person will never get it." However, if we view people as independent "thinkers of thoughts" rather than branding them as "negative," "pessimistic," or "hopeless," we sidestep the primary barrier to effectuating change: doubt.

While it may be true that many people do not change dramatically, especially in their latter years, it doesn't mean they *can't* change. One reason they rarely change is that they are not aware of the transforming power of transforming thoughts. They lack the mind management skills to see alternatives to their habitual patterns. That's precisely where an empathetic friend or a skilled leader can play such a valuable role.

Again, going back to foundational principles set forth in the Premises section of this book, we must avoid the tendency to typecast. Nobody *is* an Owner or a Victim. True, some of us have cultivated some fairly stubborn habits of seeing the dour side of things, but no one is an "incurable case." Every thinker of thoughts possesses the capability of breaking free of ingrained habits by altering the thoughts that authored those habits in the first place.

Invest Time and Attention

Victor Hugo said, "If you don't act on your beliefs, you don't know whether you believe them or not." Belief that people can change means nothing unless we are willing to invest our time and energy to assist other people in making those changes. Good intentions can override human nature, but that will require, again, a shift in *us*. We have to love people enough to lift them. We have to shift from our tendency to "just worry about me," enlarge our scope of interest, and include others, even when it's not convenient.

Most of us come across opportunities to lift others every day, yet we turn and walk away without investing any effort at all. Why the hesitation? Usually it's because we are so focused on our own interests that we don't even *recognize* an opportunity when it presents itself. When we do recognize the opportunity, we let other things get in our way. We tell ourselves that we had best not meddle because we don't want to appear self-righteous. Perhaps, we tell ourselves we don't feel justified in making recommendations to someone else because we are not perfect Owners ourselves. At times, we might think that, in order to help, we might have to confront people or make them feel uncomfortable, and we don't want to come across as hypocritical or confrontational. Whatever the reason may be, when we see traits in others that are holding them back, we often do nothing, allowing them to continue being their proverbial "own worst enemy," just hoping the other person will figure it out on his own. Sometimes, without realizing it, we even confirm or reinforce the person's unconstructive habits and even enable them.

Silence is Not Always Golden

We typically don't think of behaviors being shaped by silence, but I have come to recognize my silence on an issue can easily be interpreted as agreement or approval. Edmund Burke's famous statement, "The only thing necessary for the triumph of evil is for good men to do nothing," pertains to this subject. We do not need to be confrontational. We do need to have enough love and concern for other people to stand up once in a while and respectfully disagree with their approach, especially when that approach is not in their best interest. There have been times I have sidestepped opportunities to serve because I wasn't willing to show a bit of loving courage. Being so caught up in my own "to do" list for the day, I have passed up opportunities to serve a colleague or to strengthen my team, simply because I didn't want to get into an extended, time-eating, and potentially uncomfortable conversation.

Take, for an example, two co-workers who run into one another in the office break room. One of them has a tendency to be a little negative and down on any changes in company procedures. The person in Victim mode might try to engage his colleague in a commiseration session: "Hey, did you hear the latest? They want us to start submitting a weekly report." These words are stated in tones of exasperation and resentment. The other person might not agree with the Victim's disdain. He might actually see some value in the new reports. However, he doesn't want to get into a long debate or discussion. To get out of the conversation and back to his own agenda, he blandly comments, "Yeah, sometimes it makes you wonder what they're thinking."

The two people part company in a "friendly" manner, but was their friendship really honored? One returns to his desk feeling relieved he didn't have to put up with any prolonged complaining, while the other returns to his desk feeling vindicated in his negative assessment of the new policy. He is now more convinced than ever that management has no idea what they are doing, feeling justified in his negativity. In fact, due to the perceived agreement of his colleague, he feels more confident in spreading more cynicism in an effort to recruit more people to his point of view.

What was missed in that moment in the break room was the opportunity for the commenter to serve the complainer and to upgrade the team's Ownership Spirit. We might ask, "Did the commenter really act like a *friend* and demonstrate *genuine regard* for his colleague?" Friends and colleagues serve each other. To honestly serve one another, we sometimes have to summon the courage to say hard things in compassionate ways.

To overcome our reticence to serve others in this way, we can remind ourselves that our goal is not to convince or change the other person; we only want to offer an alternative way to look at the situation. That keeps us from thinking we have to win the debate or that it's our job to "convert our friends from their wicked ways." That mindset leads to coercive tones in our approach, and we alienate rather than serve. If we think of our goal as simply to offer a positive alternative for the other person to consider, our voice conveys more respect, and we reduce the likelihood of evoking resistance and defensiveness. All we need to do is plant a seed. It's not necessary to force anything. If the seed has value, it will sprout on its own.

What would such an approach sound like? Perhaps, again using the break room scenario, it would go something like this, "I've been thinking about this new reporting idea, too. I've decided to not dismiss it out of hand; I'm going to work with it for a few weeks and then assess its value." Or, (provided this is sincerely the case), "I wasn't too hot on the idea when I first got the email either, but the more I think about it, the more I can see some merit to what they're asking us to do. I think it might help us to..." Statements along those lines can be said simply, without any underlying agenda or manipulation. Just as our colleague with the Victim habit did, we simply share how we see the situation—but from an Owner point of view. Nothing needs to be debated or argued. If we stay away from the notion one of us has to be right and the other wrong, the conversation doesn't take on confrontational tones.

Victims bring up their negative objections hoping to recruit enough mutineers to defeat the change so they won't have to alter their comfy ways. If, however, the first two or three people they talk to do not merely nod or imply agreement, but rather respectfully disagree and offer constructive alternative points of view, the Victims will soon rethink their position.

When we can trigger some reconsideration—even just a little reassessment—in someone's pessimistic point of view, then we serve that person, stemming the flow of negativity a bit and lifting, ever so slightly, the energy of that group. If we simply allow our colleagues, friends, or family members to spread unproductive doubts and resentments, letting those ideas pollute our cultures, then we don't serve anyone. In fact, by our silence, we inadvertently enable the Victim thinkers and lend support to that position.

Chapter 10

Coaching Ownership Thinking

We now focus on a seven-step model for helping people make the shift from Victim thinking to Ownership.

The Ownership Coaching Model

Step One:
Be Authentic—Embody Ownership

Leaders who try to get by on "do as I say, not as I do," don't last long. That approach is hollow and succeeds only in the short term, if at all. Over time, who we really are and what we really think comes out. You can learn all of the world's best communication techniques and memorize perfectly worded scripts. However, if the words are inauthentic and ingenuous, the broadcast of who you really are will override your polished spiel, and you and your point will fall flat. Conversely, if you are sincerely doing your best to exhibit Ownership traits, your points will resonate and your seeds will germinate.

The first point, then, in helping people shift from Victim thinking to Ownership is to lead them by being Owners ourselves. We do not have to be perfect, but we do need to incorporate Ownership into our own thinking and behaviors. Nothing teaches "how" more clearly than a role model in action. If a picture is worth a thousand words, then witnessing someone deal with unfair, unexpected events with grace and fortitude is worth millions. As others see us take injury or insult without retaliation, or see us elevate our creative energy instead of complaining when we're faced with adversity, they will recognize the compelling value of an

Ownership Spirit. Without any compulsion on our part, they will gravitate to those traits and seek to develop more Ownership themselves.

Step Two:
Listen Fully and Deeply

Often the opportunity to contribute to someone's progress occurs inconveniently, without an appointment. With so many things on our agendas, we find it easy to be selfish, telling ourselves, "I don't have time for this conversation right now. I've got more important things to do." As strong as the magnetic pull of our "goals-for-the-day" list might be, it is often in unexpected, unscheduled moments that we have the greatest opportunity to make a difference in other people's lives. It is those times that we have to take Ownership of our attention, suspend our agenda for a while, and *focus*. The investment is usually well worth it.

A Native American proverb states, "Listen, or your tongue will keep you deaf," and could be easily translated, "Listen, or your inattention will keep us apart." Invest in dedicated listening. No real rapport can be built, no genuine understanding gained, without attentive listening. You'll never be open to my suggestions unless, and until, I "earn the right" to offer that suggestion. Listening is the passport that grants me that right to enter into your trust.

When we only partially engage in a conversation, our split attention cannot be disguised or hidden. Other people soon sense it when we're not fully "there" or only skimming the conversation. When that happens, we destroy real connection and create *disconnection*, actually widening the gap. Conversely, if we are *really* listening with fully engaged attention and not in some feigned way, the speakers *know* they are being heard, and we build genuine rapport and strengthen that relationship. Empathetic listening bridges most interpersonal chasms.

Listening has the power to transform moods and emotions. If the other person is upset or angry, fully attuned listening diffuses the hostile energy. If the other person is hurting or grieving, fully engaged, empathetic listening soothes and comforts. If the other person has a complaint or grievance, undistracted listening siphons the negative energy out of the attack.

If a colleague expresses a frustration and I'm not really listening, the emotion bounces off my shell and it rebounds back to the speaker.

The rebounding energy actually amplifies the frustration. If I openly receive what they are saying, don't overreact, rebut, or reject—and my colleagues know I got their message—something remarkable happens: their emotions subside. When they finally express their feelings, the energy is vented into the atmosphere and evaporates. A biblical proverb states, "A soft answer turneth away wrath," and the softest answer of all is listening. Calm, attentive listening invites open, productive dialogue. Two people engaged in calm, attentive dialogue build genuine, rewarding relationships. We reap rich harvests whenever we slow down, concentrate, and listen fully and deeply.

Step Three:
Respect the Person and
the Person's Right to Have an Opinion

Change only happens when people *want* to change. People change from within, or they do not change at all. No pressure or compulsion on our part, no matter how adroitly applied, will work. This reality calls for us to look inside once again. We must consider our motives carefully because they will drive our methods. If our real underlying motive for wanting to effect change in other people is selfish—to make life easier for us, make us look good, or hasten our ascent—our impact will be limited at best. Inevitably we lapse into impatient, demanding tones that will smack of manipulation. Any form of manipulation or coercion comes up short because "People convinced against their will are of the same opinion still." The more important a relationship, the less "techniques" and "skills" serve us. We must relinquish any tendency to compel. Instead, we must extend *unfeigned* love and *genuine* respect. Upon the platform of genuine respect and friendship, people can disagree without offending or alienating and can say hard things without being harsh or judgmental. The rapport of trust overpowers defensiveness and allows people to differ diplomatically.

Step Four:
Suggest Alternatives

Our goal is not to use overpowering arguments to convince people we are right and they are wrong. Our role is simply to offer a more useful alternative or two. That can be done in several ways. Often, it can be a matter of asking some open-ended questions. The so-called "Socratic Method" is a non-coercive way to help people come to their own "epiphanies." Through a series of sincere questions, we seek clarification of the scenario that seems to be troubling our friend. As the other person recounts his thinking process for our benefit, he is able to re-evaluate his logic and conclusions for himself. All this really requires is for us to shift our own posture from certain to curious, from "I already understand" to "Help me to understand."

You might open such a dialogue by saying: "I'd like to understand how you are viewing...," or, "Would you mind helping me get a clearer picture of how you see...." If I am fully engaged in the conversation, everything after that seems to fall into place. I can ask the right questions without having to rely on some stilted, prepared script.

The beauty of this approach is we don't need to advise, correct, instruct, or judge. We just have to listen and politely ask for more information from time to time. We can ask a question that invites the other person to self-evaluate: "How would you assess the results you've received from that approach?"

No matter what direction the discussion flows, people we approach in this way almost always wind up coaching themselves. By thinking about their thinking, they recognize loopholes in their own logic and see a better alternative. They do all the "heavy lifting," and our reward is often an appreciative, "Thank you, for listening. It feels so good to have someone to talk to once in awhile."

This point was confirmed to me recently when I was talking to a woman who has made a name for herself as a therapist and counselor. She said, "The first law of counseling is to never offer counsel—especially if the person doesn't *specifically ask* for it. Even then, I rarely offer it. It takes discipline to not jump in with advice. I prefer to respond with, 'Okay, but before I do, let me ask you another question.' It is far better to let people discover their own answers. Amazingly, most of the time they do."

The "Socratic Method" is not the only way to get people to consider more alternatives. With respect and rapport going for us, we can sometimes take a more direct approach. We can respectfully point out that whining and negativity are choices. When someone dumps their negativity out on the table, we might respond, "Well, I suppose that's one way to view it," or "I can understand how you could see it that way, but there are other options."

Let's look at this discussion between a mother and daughter. Notice how the daughter describes things in broad, sweeping, absolutes and how the mother redirects her daughter's thinking to see the situation as a specific, isolated event and not the norm.

Daughter: I hate math! I hate my teacher. He talks over my head, and I get lost. Besides, I'm dumb at math, and that's never going to change.

Mother: It sounds like you've had a bad day. Want to tell me about it?

Daughter: It's not just today. It's every day. I hate that class. I'm not going back.

Mother: Did something specific happen? You're usually more confident. This isn't like you.

Daughter: Today, the teacher was explaining a new method, and I was trying to follow him. I wasn't sure if I was getting it or not. So, I raised my hand and asked a question. I guess it was a dumb question because two boys behind me snickered. I was so embarrassed. I never want to go back.

Mother: I can understand why you're upset. Feeling embarrassed in front of your friends can really hurt. Are you sure the boys were laughing at you? Is it possible that they were reacting to something else?

Daughter: They were sitting behind me, so I'm not totally sure, but what else could they be laughing at?

Mother: Well, it could be many things. How did the teacher respond? Did he act like it was a dumb question?

Daughter: He seemed okay about it. He answered my question, but that's what he's supposed to do. A teacher wouldn't make a student feel dumb.

Mother: Well, what if the boys weren't even paying attention? What if they were texting each other about something that had nothing to do with you or the math class? Isn't that at least a possibility?

Daughter: I still think they were laughing at me.

Mother: Let's suppose that they were. What does that mean? What does their opinion really say about you and your goals?

Daughter: *(After a long pause)* Well, I don't know. *(Another pause)* Nothing I guess.

Note how the emotional state of the daughter changed as the dialogue unfolded. There was a marked difference in the volume, pace, and tone between the first statement and the last. The first words were tense and emotionally charged. The last responses were soft and pensive.

Without preaching, moralizing, advising, counseling, correcting, or directing, this mother helped her daughter work through an unpleasant experience by offering alternative interpretations for the daughter to consider.

Step Five:
Share Stories and Experiences

Sharing stories and experiences is another way of offering alternatives. The most honorable and respectable transformers of human behavior make their points, win people over, and induce dramatic changes in beliefs and behaviors by telling stories. Great communicators use parables, fables, and metaphors as brushes to paint new images in the minds of their listeners. Lincoln, Gandhi and Mandela, in recent eras, are notable examples of great storytellers.

Stories put the teller and the listener on the same side of the table, strengthening the relationship. When you relate a personal experience or share a story, you bypass most of the filters and defense mechanisms that block acceptance. As the narrative unfolds, the mental pictures formed by the listener are easily translated into action and behavior. In their minds' eye, listeners see the approaches and behaviors that worked and picture themselves doing the same. Such mental imagery builds hope and confidence, producing change.

Step Six:
Build Confidence through Reassurance

Most Victim statements are simply veiled pleas for reassurance. They are born of doubt and propelled by fear, the common experience of being human. Few of us are immune to the uneasiness arising from new situations or threatening circumstances. Years ago, Dr. Hans Selye recognized that perceived threats induce a "fight-or-flee" response within us. In former ages, the threats confronting our ancestors were often literal and physical. Today, most threats are intellectual and cerebral. When we feel threatened, we frequently lapse into Victim mode and resort to objecting, complaining, and criticizing.

Hence, in coaching Ownership, reassurance is a potent antidote for that fear-based, fight-or-flee response. When leaders, parents, or friends express confidence in a person's ability to deal with change and challenge, they deliver a preemptive strike against Victim responses, allay the doubts that spawn the complaints, and enable the other person to view the situation with more optimism.

Step Seven:
Commend Commendable Effort

You annihilate your credibility as a leader, mentor, or parent when you extend profuse commendation in the absence of effort. On the other hand, commending sincere and diligent *effort*, even when the *results* do not match the effort, is one of the most effective means of empowering a person to work through their shortfalls, sustain their efforts, and persist.

Years ago, I read *The Greatest Management Principle in the World*, by Michael LeBoeuf. Its central message is this: *The behavior that gets rewarded gets repeated.*

As you promote and support change in others, never underestimate the power of verbal paychecks. Whenever you see Ownership in action, praise it. Commend it. Don't overdo it, but don't be stingy either. Look for ways to commend commendable efforts, and you will accelerate progress and witness transformations that may well astound you.

In summary, the seven steps in the Ownership Coaching Model are: (1) Be Authentic—Embody Ownership, (2) Listen Fully and Deeply, (3) Respect the Person and the Person's Right to an Opinion, (4) Suggest Positive Alternatives, (5) Share Stories and Experiences, (6) Build Confidence through Reassurance, and (7) Commend Commendable Effort.

An Example: My Wife, Susan

To illustrate the model, I offer a personal story prefaced with two disclaimers. First, classic examples, like the one I am about to give, don't happen daily in the Deaton household. Second, you can't always come up with a couple of inspired sentences that will fulfill all seven points in the model. Most change is a process, not an event, and processes occur over time.

That said, here's my example: My wife, Susan, is my gift from God. Her impact on my life and the lives of our children goes far beyond measure. Her strength and wisdom have been a blessing to many people. She is tireless in her devotion to her family and friends, expressing her love unmistakably in the hours of service she renders. The total hours she has put in to helping with homework and school projects alone would stagger many calculators.

To understand the dynamics of this particular example, you need to know that Christian was born with profound, bilateral hearing loss. The way Christian has dealt with his deafness has been a remarkable example of Ownership Spirit. He is a true inspiration to me and to many others. One of his courageous choices was to be mainstreamed in the public school system. This he undertook with enthusiasm and a positive attitude. Although this route was more challenging, Christian excelled in public schools. He did extremely well socially. His outgoing, friendly-to-everyone approach crossed the boundaries of all cliques and factions. Those divisions didn't even exist as far as he was concerned. When he ran for class president of the eighth grade, he was elected by a large margin. He also did well academically, earning mostly A's and B's. However, his toughest class, by far, was English.

If you have mastered a second language, I extend my sincere respect. That is no small feat. If you have learned English as your second language, my respect for you climbs even higher. English is a challenging language. Fraught with so many quirky rules with quirky exceptions to the quirky rules, it can be a maddening language to master. When you consider that Christian can't even *hear it*, you get some idea of what a challenge English has been for him. Yet I have never seen Christian despondent or in despair. I have seen him disappointed and frustrated at times but never deeply discouraged or ready to give up.

One night, when he was in about the sixth grade, as Susan was helping Christian with his English, he learned one of the quirky rules, turned the page, applied it, and found that it worked. Then, he encountered one of the exceptions, and it didn't work. He put his pen down firmly on his notepad and said in tones consistent with his deafness, "This is sooo haaarrdd."

Susan gave a superb response. Gently but firmly, she said to him, "Yes, Christian, it is very hard." Then, after a meaningful pause, "But you can do hard things."

That statement has become a mantra around our home. I can't tell you how many times that thought has inspired me to keep battling as I have encountered obstacles.

From Story to Model

Notice the alignment between this experience and the Ownership Coaching Model. Susan had been a model of perseverance. Christian knew his mother had heard and understood what he was saying. Clearly, there was respect for his point of view conveyed in her response. She didn't make him wrong for his point of view. She didn't say, "Oh, Christian, it's actually easy. If you'd just listen to your dad's CDs you'd have a better attitude." Not only did she validate his perspective, she offered him an alternative point of view—a way to positively view himself in the context of the challenge. "Yes, it's hard, but it's not bigger than you. You are greater than any obstacle you can face, and I have faith and confidence in you."

That powerful reassurance was the exclamation mark at the end of an inspired mother's response to a much-loved son.

Section 3

Postures: Tough-Minded Ownership

"Imagine for yourself a character, a model personality, whose example you determine to follow, in private as well as public."

—Epictetus, Greek Stoic Philosopher, AD 55–135

Some people display amazing poise under pressure, think calmly and clearly when the road gets rough, and remain positive in the face of setbacks. Others do not.

As I have studied people who rise above daunting adversities—and even turn them into character-refining, soul-strengthening experiences—I have come to recognize the value and power of a certain set of mental approaches, attitudes, or postures. When braided together, the five elements introduced in this section form a potent mindset, *Tough-Minded Ownership (TMO)*.

TMO makes a real difference when people encounter unexpected turbulence and severe headwinds on their personal flight plans. Without it, they struggle. With it, they display extraordinary measures of courage, grit, resilience, and creativity.

Being *tough-minded* means *facing facts and difficulties with strength and determination.* Tough-minded people deal with reality. They don't discount difficulties or deny them, but neither are they intimidated by them. They seek solutions, bolstered by a rational optimism that, "Where there's a will, there's got to be a way." Their mature Ownership of reality, and of the problems they face, enables Tough-Minded Owners to persist long enough, delve deep enough, and push their analytical thinking far enough to reach the solutions required to prevail over formidable challenges.

Five mental Postures make up the core competencies of TMO and separate the people who triumph in the face of adversity from those who do not. Tough-Minded Owners: (1) Decide to be Undaunted by Difficulty, (2) Divide in Order to Conquer, (3) Heighten Their Creative Efforts, (4) Redirect Negative Trains of Thought, and (5) Alter Circumstances by the Force of Their Commitments.

In this section, we will explore each of these five postures in chapters 11 through 15.

Chapter 11

Tough-Minded Ownership: Posture 1

Posture 1:
Tough-Minded Owners Decide to be Undaunted by Difficulty

We become Tough-Minded Owners by *deciding* to become Tough-Minded Owners. We become undaunted by difficulty by *making up our minds* to be undaunted by difficulty. Obviously, this decision means little unless we are able to sustain it and translate it into how we act, respond, and behave.

So, what can we do to arrive at a decision so fixed and so firm that we abide by it, no matter what? What can we do to make that decision such a part of our behavioral DNA that we don't discard it at the first hint of opposition?

The roots of Tough-Minded Ownership grow in the soil of healthy perspectives about the fundamental premises of life. If we choose to believe life is all about comfort and recreation, then every bump of the road seems to be unfair, unwarranted, and disturbing and tough-mindedness will not flourish.

Tough-Minded Owners see life more as a university than a carnival and recognize the difference between fulfillment and fun. As we awaken to the fact that we derive deeper joy and satisfaction from growth and development than from entertainment and diversion, we then become more willing to engage in the substance of life.

No one comes into this world with a perfected set of Ownership traits. As newborns, we are the very antithesis of strength and independence. We are entirely dependent on, and very demanding of, others to supply our needs and wants. To go from an infancy of utter helplessness and dependence to an adulthood of mature self-reliance and independence constitutes the fundamental format of our existence.

To achieve substantial measures of mature independence, nuggets of *factual* knowledge do not suffice; the acumen we need is *experiential*. We have to acquire traits and assimilate attributes rather than store quantities of facts in a database. We have to *become* something, rather than be *acquainted* with something. That type of experiential knowledge can't be granted; each one of us must gain it on our own. Since, by definition, experiential knowledge can only be gained through personal, individual experience, we could make the case that life itself is a school set up for that purpose: the imparting of invaluable, indispensable lessons through the medium of experience.

Although many of us fervently desire and seek a life of unruffled ease, it seems that life won't hear of it or cooperate. At every turn, we encounter disruptions and obstacles that cause us to work on our surmounting skills. In the words of comic genius, Gilda Radner, "There's always something."

One memorable introduction to this truth came for me years ago when I read Dr. Scott Peck's book, *The Road Less Traveled*. It begins with a three-word sentence: "Life is difficult." Acknowledging that fact gets us past a major "roadblock"—pretending life is supposed to be smooth and easy, when it's not. The road is rough and rather steep. Like it or not, we are all matriculated in the institution of higher learning known as The University of Life, where we have only two choices: drop out or major in Tough-Minded Ownership. Cavett Robert, founder of the National Speakers Association, said, "The road will never get easier; it is up to us to become stronger."

Once we accept the premises, "Life is difficult," and, "It is up to us to become stronger," we gain an orientation toward the exams meted out by the University of Life that not only eliminates all the hand wringing and "why-me-ing" but actually serves as a tool to help us maximize the value of the coursework.

Examine Your Perspectives

What *is* your philosophy about life and the challenges inherent in it? What do you say to yourself when something unfair and painful happens? What perspectives do you fall back on in those moments, and do they help you or hamper you? Overall, how do your current perspectives work for you—are you getting the results you truly want?

When I'm faced with challenge and adversity, I say to myself a simple phrase that bolsters my resolve: "Life is a university, and this is a test. I am capable of getting an 'A' on this exam, and with God's help I am going to do just that."

We are all free to choose our beliefs, of course, and each of us is entitled to our opinion about the "meaning of life." However, each opinion generates its own set of results, and the results speak for themselves.

For instance, when Joe, the student who wrote the essay we discussed earlier, engaged in Victim thinking, he portrayed himself as *the lone sufferer on the planet* whenever things didn't go his way. Essentially, he was saying to himself, "This is not the way life is supposed to be. It's supposed to be easy, and that's exactly the way it is for everybody who had a dad that stuck around and taught them all the secrets to success. I didn't have a dad who did that. I'll never be able to succeed, and it's not my fault. My predicament is someone else's doing, and that is so unfair and wrong. There can't be a God, or such unjust things wouldn't happen to innocent people like me."

I am sure you recognize the Victim mindset Joe has authored and can see the results it generates. It does not change or improve one thing. It only deepens the agony and prolongs the paralysis. It leads to discouragement, despair, and dissipated energy. So, *what is* a strong Owner-based replacement for that mentality?

If portraying myself as the lone sufferer is patently ineffective, then it's probable that a more powerful alternative lies in the opposite direction. Could it be that I am *not* alone and that *everybody* has their share of problems and adversities? Could it be that, although no two of us have exactly the same set of difficulties, everybody has their share? Personally, the response that works best for me is to say "yes" to those questions and to accept that we *all* have our challenges and *nobody is exempt*!

That conclusion immediately takes the energy out of the "poor me" drivel and prevents me from playing the "lone sufferer" card on myself, reminding me to pursue more productive lines of thinking.

A Powerful Alternative

During my collegiate studies, I came to appreciate, almost reverentially, how much the patterns of nature have to teach us. For example, I point to one of the most prominent, pervasive, and universal Laws of Nature, one that applies to every living species, from plants to animals, including human beings: *Living things are strengthened by struggle.*

Most of us witnessed this law as children, although we tend to forget it as adults. As a school child, you may have had an experience similar to mine of scooping up a caterpillar and hosting it in a glass jar. We punched a few holes in the lid, threw in some fresh green leaves for meals, and proudly took our guest to school. The teacher said, "Ah, now you're going to see one of nature's sublime miracles—the birth of a butterfly." She told us to keep feeding the caterpillar and promised it would undergo an amazing transformation. After it had progressed all it could as a caterpillar, it would spin itself into a chrysalis. "Then," she explained, "it will break out of its chrysalis and emerge into the world as a gorgeous new creature, totally transformed from its original appearance as a caterpillar."

So, we followed her instructions and waited anxiously for the day when the butterfly would emerge. One day, the teacher's prediction came true. The chrysalis began to pulse and move. Then it cracked open—not all the way, just a bit.

At that point, our teacher told us to be patient. She urged us to be wise and refrain from breaking away any part of the chrysalis. "If you try to help the butterfly too much," she said, "you'll interfere with nature's way, and the butterfly won't survive; it will die. To be a strong adult, it must make its own way out of the chrysalis. It has to gain strength by struggling."

Confirmation from the Biosphere

In Arizona, just outside of Tucson, stands a vivid validation of this principle of gaining strength through struggle. Biosphere 1 was a well-intended project conceived and constructed for the purpose of studying the complex interrelationships of life forms within a closed system. The intent was to create a perfect, self-perpetuating environment capable of sustaining life in remote places like outer space.

Although Biosphere 1 was considered by some to be a failure, it did provide some valuable lessons. When the trees in the Biosphere attained a certain height, they started tipping and falling over. Why? There was no *wind* in the perfect environment.

In essence, the Biosphere re-corroborated the universal law of nature: living things are strengthened by struggle. It illustrated that, for a tree to attain its full adult stature, it has to develop an expanded root system and trees develop expanded root systems in response to the winds, gales, and typhoons of life. Even the breezes exert a beneficial effect. Without those forces, trees have no stimulus for increasing their strength, and they fail to achieve their maximum height and full potential.

An Analogy to Ponder

Analogous to the winds and gales acting upon the trees are the adversities we encounter in business and at home. When viewed from this perspective, these seemingly *opposing* forces are actually beneficial necessities that help us attain our full stature as leaders and as human beings. We might even esteem them as irreplaceable and indispensable. Without opposition in our lives and the opportunity to battle against it, none of us could become who and what we are capable of becoming.

Each of us needs to send out our roots. We gain strength by driving them deeply into the soil of healthy perspectives that are more nutrifying than the lame "why me" monologues we often create in our heads. The better question is, "Why *not* me? Am I not entitled to the same growth experiences that have molded and shaped the character of people I admire?" One such person on my respect list is Spencer W. Kimball. This stalwart leader of my religious faith, though he faced extreme physical challenges throughout his life, was known not just for his *willingness* to take on challenges but his *eagerness* to do so. His roots drew strength from the perspective that God had a high and noble plan for his life, and one of his self-motivating slogans was, "Give me this mountain." Rather than settling for conquering a modest hill or two, this man wanted to breathe the rarified air of standing atop the highest peaks possible. How much more powerful were the results of his leadership that issued from his "give me this mountain" mentality than would have been achieved out of "give me this molehill."

Are the difficulties and disappointments that confront us just bad luck and bad news? Are they *really* just cruel and unusual punishments from some fiendish being, out to defeat us and make us miserable? Do those perspectives provide the richest soil for our roots to draw strength?

Even if it *were* the case that the gods of Olympus were capriciously toying with us mortals, as portrayed in the ancient mythologies, would pining about our punishments be the most practical, useful way for us to reconcile their meddlings and deal with them? We still have the power to think and choose how *we* view those occurrences. We would fare better operating from the mindset that we are being challenged rather than punished.

It's Not About Adversity

While we all can chuckle at Elbert Hubbard's quip, "Life is just one damned thing after another," to Tough-Minded Owners, life is not about struggles; it's about *increasing strength and capacity by working through struggles.* That subtle distinction makes a monumental difference.

Drawing upon those powerful perspectives, Tough-Minded people become undaunted by difficulty by *making the decision* to be undaunted by difficulty. Knowing they will face their share of challenges, they are seldom surprised by trouble. It's not that they are out there *looking* for trouble, *hoping* things will get tough. They just know the curriculum of life presents an array of experiential lessons and tests, and nobody is exempt. Hence, by making agreements with themselves about how they will respond and act when trouble occurs, they cultivate the proverbial grace under pressure that gives them the steadfast inner strength to persist and prevail.

Chapter 12

Tough-Minded Ownership: Posture 2

Posture 2:
Tough-Minded Owners Divide in Order to Conquer

The second posture of Tough-Minded Ownership becomes the prime strategy in passing the courses meted out in the University of Life. If we were to formalize an Owner's credo, we might say: Life is not about obstacles; it's about gaining skills to consistently overcome obstacles. Life is not about problems; it's about becoming proficient problem solvers. Life is not about adversity; it's about learning to be poised and creative—not in spite of, but in the very process of developing character through surmounting adversity.

When we think life is supposed to be easy, it alters our posture in how we address obstacles and problems. We get very impatient and petulant when anything disrupts or slows down our joyride. Any impediment, be it events or people, is simply intolerable. Delays and detours, which were not supposed to occur in the first place, must be vaporized immediately so we can hurry back to how life was supposed to be all along—cozy and effortless.

This "Life's One Big Amusement Park" mentality spawns disadvantageous effects. First, we become obsessed with the quest for quick fixes and instant solutions. We convince ourselves we can simply *attract* all the good things in life by nothing more than a fervent wish. Following that line of thinking, we also fall prey to every get-rich-quick scheme that comes along, believing we are entitled to wealth without work.

This same mentality exerts its enfeebling effects on how we view the role of government, and it results in the dumbing down of our political dialogues. Our fix-it-for-me-quick mentality does not permit us to tolerate much ambiguity or complexity, which real issues often entail. We demand bottom-line, black-and-white answers, and we want them as fast and as sweat-free as possible. Negative campaign ads work because we don't want to delve into the hard work of sifting through the *issues* for ourselves. "Just tell us who the good guys and bad guys are so we can vote for the least bad one," we say, "and hurry will you. I'm late for my tennis lesson." Hence, we wind up with inane, rehearsed, sound-bite "debates," and we generally vote for the candidates who promise us the greatest number of programs with the lowest taxes, inexhaustible social security benefits, and self-cleaning pets.

The Bane of All-or-Nothing Thinking

Our fixation upon instant gratification and quick, easy solutions generates one more deleterious side effect: It virtually locks us into *all-or-nothing thinking*. "If it can't be done with a snap of the fingers, then it probably can't be done at all," our all-or-nothing voice tells us. "Or, if it can be done, but it's going to take a lot of time and some real effort, well then, count me out. Let's get somebody else to do the heavy lifting; I might break a nail."

A common philosophy of our day declares, "I want it all, and I want it now." While that may not sound like a Victim statement, neither is it an Owner statement. Tough-Minded Owners, in all the best senses, certainly want it all—they work for complete solutions to their problems, and they labor for the highest pinnacles of success and self-development they can attain, but they do not have to have it *all* right *now*. They are willing to achieve their ultimate ends in incremental steps if necessary. They divide in order to conquer.

Significant goals encounter resistance. The higher and more worthy the goal, the greater the opposition that will confront it. That, too, is a law of the universe. Tough-minded people sense that law, and they recognize that nothing meaningful is ever attained without paying the price.

Down deep, we know formidable opponents are seldom, if ever, defeated with one lucky punch. Tough-Minded Owners quit kidding themselves. Knowing that achieving victory in truly worthwhile endeavors requires time and hard work, they prepare themselves for battle and learn to employ the best strategies possible.

The Boon of Divide-and-Conquer Thinking

The most successful strategy in warfare is also the oldest. "Divide and Conquer" was time-proven wisdom even before Alexander the Great. Military leaders who first discovered the effectiveness of this approach may have derived their epiphanies by observing the successful patterns of nature. Wolves take down moose and elk that are more than twice their might and size. Lions are considered the king of beasts because, despite their lesser weight and stature, they can subdue large animals, including elephants, the world's largest land-living species. Even with their size and strength advantage, elephants attempt to further maximize their defense against attack by traveling in herds. Yet, even that added measure does not thwart the prides. Lions still feast on elephant meat by employing one instinctual tactic: They divide in order to conquer. Lions stalk the elephant herd patiently, observantly searching for weaknesses. Then, after they select their quarry, they create confusion and panic, disrupting the unity of the herd. Amid the chaos, the lions separate their targeted prey from the rest of the herd. The end result is sure and inevitable.

Divide in Order to Conquer: General Washington

When Tough-Minded Owners are beset by daunting difficulties, they rivet their attention on formulating their battle plan, which involves exerting faith in the divide-and-conquer approach. They may not see an entirely detailed plan at first, but they know the outcome they want, and they can see an intelligent first step. So, they get to work on it.

How did Washington win the American Revolutionary War when he was facing the greatest, best trained, best equipped military opponent of his day? In terms of a comprehensive war strategy, Washington probably wasn't sure of anything, but he knew the final outcome he wanted, and the first thing that made sense was to kick the British out of Boston. Rather than being overwhelmed with the enormity of the task he was charged with, he concentrated on the most obvious constructive thing he could do and focused on winning that battle.

At the outset of the war, and all along the way, wittingly or not, Washington used and revalidated the divide-in-order-to-conquer strategy. Setting his mind to work on how he could possibly get the British to give up their occupation of Boston—when they were deeply entrenched, well-armed and fortified, and comfortable spending the winter of 1775 in front of the warm hearths of the city—Washington began by identifying and sorting through his options.

He knew he needed artillery. "Where do I get enough artillery to make a difference in this situation?" he asks himself. There were 58 heavy mortars and cannons at Fort Ticonderoga, but that was more than 200 miles away. "It would be almost impossible to move artillery that heavy in this wretched weather; so, that won't work," says the Victim voice. "We'll just have to wait until Oppenheimer invents the atom bomb so we can blow London to smithereens."

The Owner voice rebuts, "It won't be easy, but moving artillery is the best option we have. The fact that it's difficult will work to our advantage. The British know the guns are at Ticonderoga, but they won't believe we could ever get them here during the winter. They won't even have any spies watching for that because they're all cozy in front of their fires thinking nothing could happen until summer. So let's pay the price, buckle down to the task, and do whatever it takes to drag those cannons through the snow and mud and get them here, the sooner the better."

The Victim voice retorts, "I figured you would come up with some unrealistic, ridiculous, hair-brained idea. You Owners are so wrapped up in your Wonder Woman complexes, you actually believe you can do anything you set your minds to. Do you realize most of our men don't even have decent coats or boots sturdy enough to make that trek? Get ahold of reality, man—you're delusional."

On January 24, 1776, Henry Knox, former resident of Boston, solved the first problem. He led a task force of patriots in dragging 60 tons of artillery from Fort Ticonderoga, in upstate New York, to Cambridge, Massachusetts, despite unspeakably brutal weather conditions. That mountain conquered, Washington turned to the next—getting those heavy guns into position without the British detecting.

On March 5, 1776, the British rolled out of their comfy beds in Boston to discover 58 pieces of heavy artillery trained on them from atop the strategically advantageous high ground of Dorchester Heights overlooking Boston and Boston Harbor.

Stunned, British General William Howe, taken completely by surprise, wrote, "It [the work of just getting the cannons from Cambridge to the top of Dorchester Heights] must have been the employment of 12,000 men. The rebels have done more in one night than my whole army would have done in a month."

After one failed attempt to dislodge the patriots from their vantage point, General Howe abandoned Boston. On March 17, 1776, nearly 10,000 redcoat troops boarded ship and sailed out of Boston Harbor. Having worked out an agreement with the vastly superior army, Washington did not fire on the retreating British in return for their agreement to not burn Boston to the ground.

Joe Hernandez

One man. One team. One opportunity. One daunting uphill climb. Such are the ingredients in one of my favorite examples of the divide-in-order-to-conquer component.

Much has been written about the sizeable hurdles inherent in moving and motivating large organizations through the process of change. *Getting Elephants to Dance*, Rosabeth Kanter's apt title, colorfully captures the magnitude of the task. Energizing and redirecting large multi-departmented behemoths, staffed with hundreds of people (who almost reflexively resist change), amounts to as big a challenge as any.

Take all of those dynamics and then season that "chili" with the cayenne pepper of union unrest on the heels of an acrimonious strike. For good measure, toss in a heaping dose of rigid governmental regulations, along with the constant oversight placed upon a regulated utility. Finally, set the table with a companywide culture of indifference toward customer service, resulting in dramatically declining revenues. Form a mental picture of all of that, and you'll have a pretty good image of the elephant Joe Hernandez was asked to bag and swallow.

The company Joe worked for had not secured many big revenue deals. In fact, the win rate was dismal. Worse yet, there was no process in place to determine whether the contracts they *did* win were even profitable after they were inked and implemented.

Upper level management decided enough was enough. They said, "We need to build better solutions, increase our win rate, and ensure these projects make money." That decision led to the forming of a brand new, "never-been-tried-before" team within one department. Joe Hernandez was selected to head the Strategic Opportunities Response Team (SORT). He began with no model, no precedents, no strongly defined guidelines—just the mandate, "Form an organization that will win more business, and make it profitable."

The corporate environment is as treacherous as a minefield. One wrong step and your career can be detonated. Hence, people play their cards very guardedly. The unwritten, but well-understood, caveat is: Stand out just enough to be mildly noticeable, so people know you exist and that you are making some contribution, but make no waves. If you do, you are likely to make enemies, and that can seal your fate. Like the biblical Uriah, soon you'll find yourself on the front lines in need of support, and your enemies (disguised as loyal colleagues) will withdraw, and you'll come to a bitter end as you discover that you're fighting the battle alone.

Joe Hernandez was fully aware of all the perils and risks associated with taking full Ownership of this new team's mandate. He faced a significant Owner/Victim choice. A Victim might see a no-win scenario. If SORT fails or the political skirmishes just get too hot and volatile, all upper management needs to do is blame and fire Joe. Joe's record would be damaged, but management would move on untarnished. If, conversely, SORT succeeds with flying colors, there's no guarantee that Joe's pains or risks would even be acknowledged, let alone rewarded. A Victim in Joe's position would likely, therefore, venture forward cautiously and tentatively.

Joe didn't allow himself to go there. Assuming a Tough-Minded Owner posture, he chose to trust the leaders who had selected him, exercised confidence in his own ability to figure it out, and energetically concentrated on how to take down an elephant that large.

Right away, Joe faced some fairly hefty decisions, such as "Where do I start? What should this team look like? How will it function? What metrics will we use? What resistance are we likely to encounter? Can we think our way beyond the obvious obstacles and anticipate some less obvious ones, troubleshooting or even preempting them before they get in our way?"

As he wrestled with these questions, Joe became keenly aware that several obstacles were likely to arise from the project within the project—the human element. He also saw there would be no way to skirt or ignore that element. Nothing resists change like a mind set against it, and Joe could sense, from the outset, that major change was the essence of this new undertaking. He had been asked to lead an effort that would alter people's comfort zones—SORT needed to make a companywide impact if it were to have any meaning at all.

Bearing all that in mind, Joe used a process called "visioneering." In our seminar, Joe had learned that breakthrough ideas can be generated by intentionally focused visual imagery, and he used that methodology to "create" the structure of his team. Realizing that the SORT team would have to have expertise in a broad array of areas—regulatory analysis, technical analysis, sales analysis, financial analysis—he began to envision the make-up of the team and the specific players who could fulfill those roles.

Once the team was formed, members worked together to create mental models of how this new team would have to work in order to meet their challenges. They realized most of the big contracts would be unique, one-of-a-kind deals that would involve practically every division and function. Flexibility and cooperation from every department would be crucial. People would have to do things they weren't accustomed to or mentally inclined to do.

SORT foresaw the potential reluctance and push-back. The company would have to take some calculated risks—push its norms—even push the regulatory norms. Seeing they would have to defend those positions, SORT prepared. They collected the statistics and organized the data so they could present solid, fact-grounded explanations of how they could make the changes work. Obviously, not everything went smoothly, but by overcoming one objection after another,

SORT made steady headway. When they encountered a setback, they remembered what was at stake—they were creating a new way for the company to compete that would lead to huge revenues and profits.

Keeping *that* vision in their mind helped them persevere when things got turbulent. Because they had prepared for the push-back that accompanies change, they refused to be surprised or intimidated when their motives were misconstrued. In every meeting a SORT member attended, they continued to make their case for why the new flexibility was imperative. Sticking to the conquer-by-dividing strategy, they learned to deal with each objection in specific terms with specific facts, rather than letting the opposition try to defeat the change movement with blanket generalities like, "This just won't work for our department," or "Our department has never done *that* before." By inviting the objectors to get specific, SORT could counter with specifics, again conquering the resistance by breaking it down.

Within months, they started tallying the victories. The win rate on big projects soared—going from 5 percent to 74 percent within nine months. The following year the company captured 86 percent of all new business it went after and booked three-quarters of a billion dollars of revenue—income that, in the past, would have largely gone to its competitors.

The confidence level of the front-line sales teams climbed to new heights. Salespeople went into every presentation knowing they could make big promises and the company could fulfill them—something they couldn't do just two years prior.

Change can be achieved on any level by starting from rather modest beginnings—a change in thought and the cultivation of a new posture or approach. Often we become intimidated by big challenges because we look at the mountain as a mountain, rather than a series of steps. We drastically underestimate that power of a committed mind and our ability to be tough-minded thinkers of thoughts and to find ingenious solutions to enormous challenges—one step at a time.

Chapter 13

Tough-Minded Ownership: Posture 3

Posture 3:
Tough-Minded Owners
Heighten Their Creative Efforts

The primary distinction between Owner and Victim comes down to the mental postures we assume in moments of crisis and uncertainty. In those telling moments, do we panic, fret, and let our thoughts run wildly to unproductive monologues? Or, do we take control of our inner faculties and govern our thoughts in such a way as to channel the emotional energy into creative thinking, problem-solving, and action?

Learning to harness our thoughts and emotions is an aptitude that can be developed, a skill that can be acquired, and an option that can be turned into a habit. It can even become so ingrained as to be our *typical* response, if we are willing to cultivate that posture.

Soichiro Honda

A prime example of overpowering prodigious opposition through sustained creative effort is Soichiro Honda. Honda was the creator and driving force behind the company that came to dominate the world motorcycle market and carve a respected niche in the global automobile industry. The saga of this ultra-pragmatic, results-oriented leader

109

is a study in the third component of Tough-Minded Ownership—intentional heightening of creative effort.

Casual observers have attributed much of Honda's success to the luck of propitious timing, linking Honda's rise to the momentum of Japan's post-World War II reconstruction. In reality, the opposite is true. Honda's rise was a major contributing factor in the recovery of Japan's decimated post-war economy. Far from being the beneficiary of governmental support, the Japanese hierarchy was Honda's most formidable obstacle. In actuality, Honda's amazing ascent to global respectability and success constitutes one of the greatest examples of business indomitability in history.

A former bicycle mechanic, Soichiro Honda began with nothing. He had no financial resources of his own to begin with and no viable way of getting any financial backing. He had no reputation, no influential family legacy, no inside connections. He didn't even begin with much of an education. He achieved his dream by applying extraordinary effort to *developing* his creative ingenuity. Though considered a creative genius by many of his close associates, Soichiro shunned the idea that he was *gifted* with genius. He attributed his innovative breakthroughs to intense concentration on his projects and an eager willingness to learn from his failures. Honda would stay with a project until he had perfected it, analyzing each failure through a disciplined application of trial and error. In effect, akin to building a muscle by exercising that muscle, Honda heightened his creative genius through tireless creative exercise.

The demands thrust upon his ingenuity and resourcefulness right from the start were huge. Almost from the outset, he faced opposition from the Japanese establishment—a formidable alliance of entities who looked upon him as a maverick and an affront to the traditional Japanese system and way of doing business. That opposing coalition consisted of the already established manufacturing companies in Japan, coupled with the traditional power structures and influence brokers behind those companies. On top of that was layered governmental and bureaucratic opposition, including the Japanese Ministry of International Trade and Industry itself. This agency held control of the permits and natural resources Honda would need to commence his enterprises and compete.

All of that is just the homeland side of the equation. In time, as Honda moved into the global markets, he would have to figure out how to defy the intense competition from the largest, most well-entrenched automotive leaders in the world. Eventually, the biggest names in the industry, all of the highly respected, well-established manufacturing giants of Europe and the United States, would lose sizeable chunks of their market share to the relentlessly applied creative effort of the diminutive man from Komyo, Japan.

In an article profiling "the greatest innovators of the past 75 years," *Business Week* magazine paid tribute to Soichiro Honda with these words:

> Not only was Honda ostracized from polite Japanese business circles for most of his career because of his unusual management techniques and aggressive marketing style, but Japanese bureaucrats tried to block Honda's growth more than once. It wouldn't be overstating the case to say that when the fuel-efficient Honda Civic took the U.S. by storm in 1972, there was likely as much tangible resentment in Tokyo as in Detroit.

Honing the Creative Edge

Leaving his father's bicycle repair shop, Soichiro Honda studied mechanical engineering and began tinkering with engines in his own tiny workshop. Focusing on pistons and piston rings, he came up with some innovations he intended to sell to Toyota, Japan's leading automobile manufacturer. Over a two-year period, Toyota rejected Honda's designs again and again. Undeterred, he continued to work and rework his designs, persisting until he won his coveted contract from Toyota. That small victory was the match that lit a fire. To Soichiro, it meant he could achieve lofty goals by focused effort. Innovative ideas would come to him as long as he was willing to persist. In his mind, that single concept opened a vast panorama of exciting possibilities.

Lifting his sights to goals beyond the design of engines themselves, Honda soon focused his efforts on doing something about Japan's dire need for low-cost, fuel-efficient transportation. His bicycle background, combined with his work with engines, led to his idea of building bicycles powered by small motors (primitive motorcycles); but to have any impact, he would need a sizeable lump of capital.

Conventional sources were out of the question. Soichiro was a nobody with no experience, no collateral, and no credentials.

After due consideration of those realities, instead of foregoing the idea, Honda elevated his creative effort. "There had to be a way somehow. What could he do to raise money?" Those thoughts dominated his mind until a possible, albeit tenuous, solution dawned. Soichiro began writing to hundreds of bicycle shops, soliciting funding from his would-be customers and dealers. As expected, most of his letters went unanswered or were rejected, but some were not. Honda just kept writing letters. Eventually he wrote more than 17,000 of them, until he obtained sufficient capital to get into production.

Once Honda got going, Soichiro's positive posture toward failure proved vital. He refused to be intimidated by his products' weaknesses; he analyzed them and learned from them, ever pushing his creative effort to come up with answers. That mindset began to pervade his company. "What we learn through failure becomes a precious part of us, strengthening us in everything we do. Let the tough things make us tougher," was one of Honda's incitements to his workers. Leveraging trial and error and the will to promptly make corrections to eliminate the sources of errors, Honda motorcycles steadily gained a respected reputation for reliability and economy. Honda observed, "Success can only be achieved through repeated failures and introspection."

Because he was working outside of the traditional Japanese system, he incurred continual resistance and opposition from people of influence. For that reason, at first he had a hard time attracting new college graduates to strengthen his rapidly expanding organization. Honda conquered that mountain by coming up with a new, open, more respectful, more participatory work environment. This "style" of leadership was revolutionary, especially in the Japanese culture of the time, and it worked. Honda attracted more than his share of Japan's best and brightest graduates, and they flourished in his energetic, innovation-oriented, have-no-fear-of-failure company culture. "We only have one future," Honda reassured them, "and it will be made of our dreams, if we have the courage to challenge convention."

By 1959, the Honda brand was dominating the motorcycle market in Japan, experiencing phenomenal growth. That year, Honda sold just under 300,000 motorcycles. By the end of 1961, they were selling more than 100,000 motorcycles *per month*.

With sales and production booming in Japan, Honda turned his attention to breaking into the motorcycle market in America. Almost immediately, Honda was slapped with challenges on two fronts. First, again motivated by jealousy, Japanese bureaucrats threw up roadblocks to impede Honda's foray into the U.S. market by restricting the capital investment Honda was allowed to make. The second obstacle was even more galling to Soichiro. Honda motorcycles did not perform well in America and were immediately branded as inferior in quality. American cyclists demanded much higher performance than Honda's Japanese customers. Americans drove their bikes harder and at much higher speeds. The first Honda cycles in America were blowing head gaskets and throwing clutches right and left.

Not wasting time thinking, "Oh no, we're ruined. We've blown our first impression in America, and it will take us years to recover," Honda and his people responded with immediate and intense concentration on revamping their motorcycles. With mind-boggling speed they re-engineered their designs, re-tooled their production lines, and got back to market with excellent, high-performing cycles. By 1963, barely three years after their initial debacle, Honda was the top-selling motorcycle brand in the United States. "Success represents the one percent of your work which results from the 99 percent that is called failure," Honda states.

Now that Honda has become a household name and one of the best known brands on the planet, you know how the story ends. Honda dominated the world motorcycle market, producing the highest selling motor vehicle in history, the Honda Cub. From there, Honda moved into the automobile business, and today Honda automobiles are revered the world over for their reliability, longevity, and resale value. The same holds true for Honda's ATVs, watercraft, and yard care products.

Soichiro did it. He fulfilled his dreams. Nobody handed him one iota of his success; he earned every particle of it. Of the myriad obstacles he surmounted during the course of his career, I have highlighted but a few. Honda's mindset and methods epitomize Tough-Minded Ownership—a sterling example of all five of the mental postures.

His story could be placed in any one of the five chapters as a classic illustration of that particular posture. As I studied his life and marveled at his traits, I realized that of the five postures he mastered, the honing of his creative edge stood above the rest. Whenever he was faced with challenges, he heightened his inventive effort, building innovative muscle in gradual steps until he became a creative ironman.

Eventually, he became so confident in being able to call on his ingenuity at will that he even welcomed the challenge of his competition because it provided creative stimulus for him and his team. "I've never refused competitors' visits to our factory. I've welcomed them at any time, because I am willing to jump to new innovations when they try to follow us."

Chapter 14

Tough-Minded Ownership:
Posture 4

Posture 4:
Tough-Minded Owners
Redirect Negative Trains of Thought

When faced with adversity, tough-minded people like Honda don't drop out; they dig in. How do they do so? What mental steps do they use? *They focus on what they want, not what they fear.*

Disciplining ourselves to focus first on the results that we want is the answer. Intense concentration on our goals overpowers our qualms, fears, and doubts. Our passion for our goals quickens our creative centers, triggering bursts of inventive illumination. The vision of our desired results is so sensory-rich and emotion-laden that we simply *must* have our goals, leading us to probe and persist until we find a way to demolish whatever blocks our progress to our goals.

The ability to maintain undistracted focus on the target or the task at hand is *the* fundamental discipline that differentiates champions from also-rans. In every activity—from salesmanship to marksmanship, from diving to gymnastics, from prayer to public speaking—distraction, preoccupation, or wavering is the bane of human achievement. Single-minded focus, being in the zone, laser-like concentration is the boon. Truly, as the Bible records, "A double minded man is unstable in all his ways."

The mental discipline of focusing on what you want, not what you fear, does not come naturally. It can—and must—be developed if you are to enjoy the full benefits of Tough-Minded Ownership. Our natural tendency, when we encounter opposition, is to equivocate or rush outright to worst-case scenarios and dwell on them. Fixated upon the horrors of the impending doom, we get mired in doubts and fears. By feeding them with our negative attention, they grow heavier until our faith and resolve capsize.

Although we are constantly aware of a kaleidoscope of peripheral stimuli, the fact remains: We can only think of one subject at a time. Sometimes we think of our "lateral or peripheral inhibition" as a limitation, but this property can be leveraged to our advantage.

A Beautiful Mind

The movie *A Beautiful Mind* puts this point across in stunning fashion. For the first third of the movie, you think you are watching a story about espionage and code-breaking. The movie is actually about schizophrenia, and it's based on the life of a Nobel Prize Laureate, John Nash, of Princeton University. The filmmakers help us appreciate, to some degree, what it's like to be afflicted with a mental disorder wherein one experiences images that seem real but are not.

As the movie progresses, we come to discover that three of the characters we thought were real are only fabrications of Nash's diseased brain. They are not real people. To Nash, they seem real, but they're only figments of a schizophrenic mind. Eventually, Nash comes to recognize he is being deceived by his own brain—that he's afflicted with a condition that spawns false images and erroneous trains of thought. Once he comes to grips with that fact, he then learns how to distinguish the figments from actual events, and through his conscious awareness, he gains the upper hand on his illness.

This story is a powerful illustration of the "thinker of thoughts" concept. Nash's higher self—his thinker of thoughts—takes control of his life by learning to analyze itself and separate the real from the surreal.

Herein lies a lesson for us all. In a sense, Nash's dilemma is also our dilemma. His case was more severe, of course, but we are all a little schizophrenic or double-minded. We float in and out of productive mindsets, confident one minute, self-doubting the next. We're all plagued with "erroneous images" and counterproductive thoughts that sabotage our performance.

As the movie concludes, we see Nash walking across the campus, talking to a colleague, and explaining how he has gained ascendance over the fictitious images and negative trains of thought:

Nash: They're not gone and maybe they never will be, but I've gotten used to ignoring them. I think, as a result, they've kind of given up on me. I think that's what it's like with all our dreams and our nightmares—we have to keep feeding them for them to stay alive.

Colleague: They haunt you, though.

Nash: They're my past. Everybody's haunted by their past; but like a diet of the mind, I just choose not to indulge certain appetites.

Zing! That's an insight to chisel in stone—"That's what it's like with all of our dreams and our nightmares—*we have to keep feeding them for them to stay alive!*" The patterns of thought that impede our progress exist, and continue to plague us, *only as long as we feed them* by entertaining them, dwelling on them, revisiting and rehearsing them. The way to defeat them is to starve them—to deprive them of life—by putting our focus and attention on something more worthy and productive and keeping it there.

Strengthening Our Strengths

We weaken our weaknesses and we strengthen our strengths by how we direct our thoughts and where we fix our attention. Whatever we dwell on grows larger and gains strength—be that our goals or our obstacles. When people like John Nash and Soichiro Honda encounter failures or obstacles, they refuse to let their minds dwell on anything but what can be done to overcome them. They are not oblivious to the threats, they just know if their eye is single to finding a solution, the harms are not likely to materialize. They recognize negative rumination is not just a waste of time, it's a trap: *The more you try to avoid something, the more you tend to attract it.*

This principle is oft illustrated in sports. After gaining a lead, the surest way to lose it is to start playing not to lose. Any coach can tell you there's an entirely different spirit about a team when it's playing the game to win versus when it's playing not to lose, and the results confirm it. As soon as a team shifts into the "not losing" mode, they give life to losing, and soon their lead begins to dwindle away.

Honda's rapid and impressive recovery from the quality debacle when they first hit the American market was due directly to how well they applied this principle. They immediately and entirely immersed themselves in fixing the problem, and they spent no time dwelling on the negative publicity. By this stage of Honda's development, this posture had become an ingrained discipline. Honda and his people had practiced this "technique" for so long that it became an integral part of who they were and how they worked.

Tough-Minded Owners derive an additional benefit by developing this discipline: they banish worry from their lives. Since their minds can only focus on one thing at a time, they cannot work and worry at the same time. It's either one or the other. The brilliance of Roosevelt's, "We have nothing to fear but fear itself," hinges on this principle. Tough-minded people focus on their destinations rather than the deterrents. By doing so, they exclude most of the angst and pain that would otherwise plague them.

An acquaintance of mine once talked with me about a mutual friend. He said, "He never seems to worry. He never gets rattled when things go crazy in his life."

My response was, "That's because he is so immersed in finding and implementing solutions, he has no space left in his brain to worry with."

Redirect, Rather than Repress

Here's another secret to mastering this concept. Whenever you catch yourself dwelling upon unproductive topics, redirect those thoughts rather than trying to repress them. Repressing thoughts—trying to not think certain thoughts—trying to stifle trains of thought by endeavoring to not dwell on them, proves to be a trap. Trying *not* to think a negative thought backfires on us every time; it actually *heightens* our attention on that image. That tactic is another version of playing the game not to lose, and it simply does not work. The undesired thought still remains the locus of our focus. If I'm trying not to think of chocolate cake, I am still thinking of chocolate cake, and the temptation still entices.

Redirecting, not repressing, is the answer. Redirecting—shifting your attention to an alternative topic—*works* with the one-track property of our minds. To teach this point, one of my mentors used the analogy of irrigating a field. He said, "If you just turn water onto an unfurrowed field, the water runs everywhere and you waste your resources. For water to do the most good, you need to give it a place to flow. You cut furrows in the field so that water has a place to go, and you can direct it where you want."

Worthy, exciting, meaningful goals are effective furrows for the flow of our thoughts. The moment we recognize that negative impulses have hijacked our train of thought, we can switch to the track of our predefined goals. You might try a simple little technique I use when I catch myself dwelling on fears, worries, doubts, grudges, or any useless thought. Rather than berate myself, I say, "Oh, that reminds me that what I want to make happen right now is..." Then I hit the play button on the "DVD player" in my head and run the mental movie of my current Power Goal.* Within moments, the negative figments have lost their grip, and I find myself thinking of ways to move closer to my goals.

Another Way of Redirecting

Another productive way of redirecting thoughts is to give yourself a creative challenge. Even if it's just hypothetical, take on some above-average premise, problem, or project as though it were real, and challenge yourself to devise a workable plan to resolve or accomplish it.

Working through big challenges in your mind is an effective way of redirecting your thoughts and a great way to strengthen your creativity machinery. Creativity, like any faculty, improves through

---

*See *The Book on Mind Management* for more insights on strengthening mental discipline and achieving superlative goals.

exercise, and exercising it prepares you for times when you need to work through those hypothetical examples for real.

I saw this firsthand at a semiconductor company's leadership conference held in Chengdu, China. After my part on the program, the CEO stood up to give the closing address. He wanted to conclude this multi-day conference by having his leaders take Ownership of a more energetic, innovative approach to customized product design and customer service. He achieved his purpose—and it was electric.

After describing the traditional way of looking at semiconductor production and customer service, he presented a hypothetical scenario, challenging the company leaders to open up their creative throttles and elevate their commitment to on-time delivery of customized products. After expressing his confidence in them and their ability to accomplish big goals, he threw down the gauntlet. "I'd like you to *really* think about something," he said. "What if every one of us agreed to this commitment: *We give our customers perfect products—on time—or we give them the products for free?*" A thunderous silence followed. After a long pause, he asked, "Are you up for that? Are you willing to take that on? What if we took that on as though it were a matter of life or death and made an all-out commitment to give our customers perfect products, on time, or the products were free?" Again, he made an emphatic pause, allowing his team to absorb the premise he was presenting.

Then, to underscore that he wasn't kidding, he began addressing specific team leaders by name, asking each of them, "Are you up for that?"

Since they had all just participated in my four-hour presentation on *The Ownership Spirit,* I was hoping that no one was thinking, "We can't do that! There's too much beyond our control. We're already working at full capacity. Customers are fickle, and they change their minds. We're not geared up for that. It's impossible." Instead, I was counting on most of them saying to themselves something like, "Now *there's* a challenge! If we could pull that off and be that nimble and responsive, why would customers go anywhere else? We'd really have to step it up and break the mold of how we are doing things. If we did, it would be a fantastic coup and we'd slay the market!"

Just how many of them did take the Owner posture, I cannot say. What I do know is within 18 months of this meeting this company dramatically altered its reputation from being a smug, product-centric company to a flexible, customer-centric company, and they garnered more than 20 industry awards for customer service excellence.

Chapter 15

Tough-Minded Ownership: Posture 5

Posture 5:
Tough-Minded Owners Alter Circumstances by the Force of Their Commitments

How often do we let circumstances drive our commitments and determine our outcomes? We rarely even notice how frequently it happens. We become so hypnotized by our own rationalizations we hardly ever notice how prone we are to creating an excuse as a substitute for execution. It sounds something like this: "Well, we wanted to increase productivity by 50 percent, but the value of the dollar slipped against the yen and the euro, and the stock market jittered and coughed. Now we have global warming, and El Niño put down a lot more rain in the Gulf than we expected. On top of all that, the Yankees lost the series again, and that's why we didn't reach our goal." We often put more energy into *justifying* why something didn't work than in *analyzing* why it didn't work and learning from it.

The most subtle and insidious form of Victim thinking is when we depict ourselves as hapless warriors who put up heroic efforts but who were, in the end, defeated by such overwhelming circumstances beyond our control that even Superman could not have prevailed. Taking that approach doesn't make us bad people, but we are capable of better. As we pursue our course to develop Tough-Minded Ownership, we need to fight that mentality.

Without awareness, we can get so sloppy in our commitments that we end up just following the path of least resistance and accomplish nothing. Every time we set a mark, then work through adversity and achieve that mark, we gain strength. Conversely, every time we make a commitment, but let circumstances get in the way and give in without struggle, we lose strength. Tough-minded people recognize the incomparable power that emanates from consistently keeping commitments. The more consistent we are, the more power we acquire. Eventually, we refuse to tolerate excuse-making. We see that an excuse is an excuse no matter how valid or plausible—a paltry substitute for execution and achievement.

The annals of human history are filled with examples of people who changed the course of events, practically turning rivers upstream, by the force of an indomitable inner commitment. As one example, I offer the story of a dedicated pioneer in the field of open heart surgery, Dr. Russell M. Nelson.

Open heart surgery is so common today that we hardly give it a second thought. Not too long ago, my good friend and brother-in-law underwent a sextuple bypass operation. Most of the family approached it with the attitude of, "Oh, well, he'll be up and around in a couple of days," but for the doctors who pioneered those techniques, there's much more to the story.

Imagine the responsibility doctors must feel when they hold someone's heart in their hands? Imagine how you would feel if things didn't work out. In his autobiography, *Heart to Heart*, Dr. Nelson recounts a painful stepping stone moment he encountered in the discovery process. After one couple had already lost their first child to heart disease before doctors ventured into this new field of surgery, their second child also succumbed to congenital heart disease, despite Dr. Nelson's ardent efforts to save the child's life through open heart surgery.

A few years later, the same couple came to him with their third and last child, who also was dying from congenital heart disease. Dr. Nelson operated on the child, but she died later that night. He was devastated. As he drove home from the hospital, tears coursed down his cheeks; he was totally inconsolable. When he arrived home, he said to his wife, "I'm through. I'll never do another heart operation!"

He did not go to bed or sleep at all that night. Specters haunted him mercilessly. Like burning arrows through his heart, the faces of two parents, now childless, inflicted excruciating pangs. Even more poignant were the images of the smiling, hopeful faces of those blue-lipped children, plaintively looking at him—beckoning for his help to heal them. Every nightmare of a compassionate physician had seemingly come true in their most soul-wrenching form. He said, "Words cannot describe my feelings: pain, despair, grief, tragedy—these characterizations only scratch the surface of the torment raging in my soul, which caused me to determine that my failures and inadequacies would never be inflicted on another human family."

As dawn broke, his wife came to him and said, "If you quit now, someone else will have to make your mistakes all over again. Isn't it better to keep trying than to quit now and require others to go through the same grief of learning what you already know?"

Dr. Nelson later wrote, "Her compassionate wisdom was not only for me, but for those whom I might serve, if I could just work a little harder, learn a little more, and strive further for the perfection that was demanded for consistent success." Setting aside his own personal wounds and concerns, Russell Nelson dug down deep into the vault of human emotion and *chose* courage. Courageously he went back to the hospital. Courageously he studied, pondered, and delved deeper into the secrets of cardiology. He tenaciously kept persevering until he achieved a breakthrough. Other breakthroughs followed, and the success rate for these medical miracles rose until, today, we take them virtually with the same gravity as tonsillectomies.

How many great businesses, how many ingenious inventions, how many breakthroughs in science, and how many ways of delivering service exist today because someone pushed fear aside and took Ownership of a dream or idea with sufficient determination to see it through? All of us, countless times each day, are beneficiaries of people who have persevered—people who assumed a posture of Tough-Minded Ownership and took steps into the uncertain future that had intimidated others.

Personal Experience

Sometimes, we are presented with consequences so dire that we cannot allow ourselves anything short of our utmost efforts. In such instances, excuses and rationalizations are so untenable that we force ourselves onward, unwilling to rest until we have searched every alternative and explored every avenue, battling forward until we are satisfied that we have done everything in our power to solve the problem or reduce the damages.

Such is one of my personal experiences.

To continually nourish and strengthen an Ownership mindset, I've made a habit of carrying an *empowering idea* with me—a story, a thought, a scripture, a quote—something that inspires me and bolsters my resolve to live what I believe and teach. It hasn't always been the same idea. I try to keep it fresh by updating it from time to time.

One summer, after much introspection, I laid aside a former empowering idea in favor of one dealing with the priceless value of adversity.

I had seen that the major trials of my life turned out, in the long run, to be my most cherished experiences. When they were happening, I didn't like them at all, but in the aftermath, as I could see the strengths gained, the perspectives honed, and lessons learned, I had to say without hesitation, "Those were the golden moments." Those were the experiences I wouldn't exchange for all the proverbial wealth of Solomon.

As that realization crystallized, a question followed, "If times of adversity turn out to be the golden moments, and you gain so much from them, then why do you whine and complain so much when you're in them? You're usually grateful for them *afterward*, especially if they work out all right. If you were really growing in your Tough-Minded Ownership, you could learn to be grateful for those experiences *right at the time they are happening.* If you did so, how much more could you learn from them? How much more power could you access from within and from God? How much better might your experiences turn out? If you could get past your own self-concern, you could be of greater support and assistance to the people who are involved in the experience with you." As I entertained those thoughts, something gelled. I began to write a flow of thoughts that came to me as a priceless epiphanous insight. After a bit of refining, it wound up being three paragraphs long, and the last sentence summarized it all:

Every challenge is good news—every obstacle a gift—every conflict an opportunity to exert, access grace, and gain strength.

That summer, I began reading that statement daily. I wanted to embed that idea so deeply into my thinking and conduct that it would be part of my very being, so much a part of me that, even under duress and pressure, I would not forget it and lapse into Victim thinking.

One day, after teaching a local seminar, I checked my phone messages. Among them was a terse, ominous-sounding message from my wife, Susan. "Dennis, we just received Timothy's medical report on the MRI. It's not good. You'd better come home right away."

Timothy was our tall, handsome, athletic, 16-year-old. He'd been fit and healthy all his life. His only health complaint was that he was having difficulty breathing through his nose. For a while, we assumed he had chronic allergies that are common in Arizona. We gave him antihistamines. For a time, they seemed to help. When it became clear that antihistamines were not the answer, we took him to an ear, nose, and throat specialist.

Upon examination, the doctor noticed a mass of unusual tissue located near the back of Timothy's nasal passage. He said, "It looks somewhat like a polyp. If Timothy has polyps, you won't have much to worry about. We can take care of them with a simple in-office procedure. However, as a precaution, I'd like to run a few tests and get an MRI."

We'll be ever grateful the doctor took that precaution. It turned out Timothy was afflicted with something far more serious. Had the doctor cut into what he thought was a polyp, Timothy would have bled to death within minutes.

We had been waiting for the MRI report for a couple of days. When I received Susan's message and heard the concern in her voice, I raced home. As I entered the door, I felt a very somber tone in the air. Timothy was ashen, and Susan looked like she'd been crying. She handed me the report, and I began to read that the mass inside Timothy's head was not a polyp, but a huge tumor, probably an angiofibroma (vascular tissue that's gone berserk). The tumor had originated in the center of his head and was spreading in all directions.

Angiofibromas are not the kind of cancers that send out satellites to other parts of the body. They do their lethal damage by expansion, first encroaching on and then destroying vital healthy tissues and structures. This thing was large and had apparently been growing for several years. Now time was of the essence. If the tumor wasn't dealt with promptly, Timothy would soon lose his smell, sight, and hearing, and eventually suffer paralysis and death.

As all of this coalesced in my consciousness, I began to recognize an old software program trying to impose itself on my thinking: "Why us? Poor us. What have we done to deserve this?" But just as I was about to go down the Victim's path of fear and self-pity, my empowering idea popped into my mind: "Dennis, could this be one of those golden learning lessons in the making? Can you believe that this challenge is good news—that it's a gift—an opportunity to exert, access grace, and gain strength?"

I paused for a second, dug deeply, and decided that the answer was, "Yes, I can believe it, because I choose to believe it." In that moment, I was able to get ahold of my thoughts and channel my emotions. Then and there, despite all my gut-wrenching concerns, I chose to view the situation as a God-given opportunity to grow in faith and gain strength. I was able to look upon that challenge, no matter how it might turn out, as a blessing, not a curse. At that instant, I was able to move to a posture of profound and sincere gratitude for this trial, and that state of gratitude never left me. It sustained me and my family through the entire experience.

I was not alone in that kind of thinking. I am blessed with a wonderful wife, a rock of courage and strength. Timothy and our other children also share our strong spiritual convictions, as does our extended family. Together, we rallied our faith and we made some promises to each other: "We're going on the offensive with this thing. We're going to learn everything we can about complicated brain tumors, angiofibromas in specific. We need to educate ourselves, since we are going to be talking to a lot of doctors. We need to be able to ask the hard questions and find out who knows their stuff. We will leave no stone unturned, and we won't stop searching until we're sure that Timothy is in the very best hands—the doctors best equipped to deal with this case. With God's help, we will get that done, and then we can be at peace and know that the rest is up to Him."

From that point we moved forward, doing our best to do what we had said we would do. We searched all the medical information from every source available to us. Susan led the search for the doctors, following up on every lead. We pushed past roadblocks and discouragements. The first several doctors we consulted—physicians with impressive medical credentials—told us we were too late, that Timothy's tumor was inoperable. One respected specialist said, "This tumor is far too advanced for any hope of a cure. You shouldn't even think of attempting a surgical intervention on a tumor this complicated. He'll be a vegetable, if he doesn't die on the surgical table. Just take him home and let him enjoy life for the few months he has left."

We got Timothy's case in front of surgical teams at some prestigious medical schools. At one of them, we got a slight glimmer of hope. The lead surgeon said, "We think a limited surgical intervention is still possible. We would have to make an incision down the middle of Timothy's face. He'll have a lifelong scar, but cosmetic surgeons can do a lot with them. We think we can get enough of the tumor to slow it down, maybe we can get it all." Although we were appreciative of the hope, we still did not feel like we had found the solution.

We didn't relent; we pushed ahead. Time was of the essence, and we were not about to quit until we all were completely satisfied we'd done everything in our power to find the best team of doctors with the best approach. We were willing to go anywhere, but as it turned out, the best team for Timothy was right in our own backyard.

Dr. Robert Spetzler

Through a quirky conversation Susan's sister had with a woman in the line at a grocery store, we came to hear about Dr. Robert Spetzler, an eminent neurosurgeon at Barrow Neurological Institute in Phoenix, Arizona. As we followed up on this lead and learned more, we became ever more impressed that Barrow might have the answers we were searching for, and the clouds seemed to be parting a bit.

Just getting enough medical momentum to get Timothy's case in front of Dr. Spetzler was a saga in itself, but we succeeded. On a Tuesday afternoon, we sat in a room with Dr. Spetzler and one of his colleagues at Barrow and were told that this amazing team of dedicated neurosurgeons had recently developed a new technique. After reviewing Timothy's records, he said he was confident that he and his team could remove the tumor. Without minimizing the risks, Dr. Spetzler then described in detail the operation the neurosurgeons proposed to perform. By removing Timothy's face and sectioning the cranium, they could obtain sufficient access to the seat of the tumor to close off the exaggerated blood supply characteristic of this tumor and then remove it.

When Dr. Spetzler described the detail of the operation, my mind raced back to my dental training at Washington University in St. Louis. The first thing we were taught was to take the *least* invasive approach to medical intervention. The operation Dr. Spetzler was proposing was so extensive and dangerous and so drastically invasive, I was stunned and repulsed. As I pictured each phase of the procedure happening to my dearly loved son, my first inclination was to recoil and say, "No way."

As we drove away from the Institute that afternoon we were a humble and subdued trio. It took us a few days of prayer and pondering before we became comfortable with the decision. We knew we had been given a chance for Timothy to be completely cured. What more could we ask? Timothy, too, felt like his prayers had been answered and that he could put his life in Dr. Spetzler's hands.

A few weeks later, on a Friday, Timothy underwent an incredible 14-hour operation in which an extremely talented medical team, headed by Dr. Spetzler, took Timothy's head apart—literally—removed the tumor, and put him back together. When Timothy came out of the operating room, he was not nearly as distorted as we thought he might be. The swelling of his head was fairly modest. On the following Monday morning, the swelling crested and began to recede. By Thursday, when Timothy was released from the hospital, he was looking very much like himself. Over a period of six months, two more procedures were performed. Today, Timothy is a perfectly healthy, married man, with a beautiful wife and a handsome son. All of his faculties are restored, including the sense of smell, and there is not a single scar on his face.

The thoughts that came to me that summer were upheld and validated. This challenge, despite its gut-wrenching portent, did turn out to be good news. We do see it as a great and supernal gift. It was indeed an opportunity to exert, access grace, and gain strength. We grew stronger as individuals and as a family. Our family, extended family, friends, and neighbors of many faiths and creeds grew closer. Everyone's faith in God and in His power to lead us to answers and to heal grew by leaps and bounds. We look on this experience with great gratitude and reverence as one of the most significant blessings of our entire lives.

The Graduate Level: The Posture of Gratitude

Does the statement, "Every challenge is good news—every obstacle a gift—every conflict an opportunity to exert, access grace, and gain strength," hold true in *every* case and instance? Maybe not, but that doesn't negate the fact that it's an extremely powerful platform to be standing on as we face the ups and downs of life.

I am keenly aware that not all stories have happy endings. Sometimes we can do our research, work relentlessly, resist discouragement, and exercise faith and, in the end, miracles do not happen and things do not turn out the way we would like. In such cases, does that mean we did something wrong? Or, if things work out "better" for someone else, does that mean they did something more right? No, emphatically not.

Exercising Tough-Minded Ownership does not guarantee that every poignantly challenging experience will turn out to our liking. It *does* guarantee the way we will experience the experience and it *does* determine the degree of strength we will leverage in those trying times. Looking at adversity as a punishment, as perverse bad luck beyond our control, or as something we have somehow brought upon ourselves, markedly diminishes our internal energy, and our will to act weakens. However, looking at adversity as a gift, as an opportunity to grow and gain moral muscle, strengthens our will to act and to rise above circumstance.

Admittedly, in many situations, shifting from resentment or despair to genuine gratitude is asking a lot. Especially right in the moment, it can be very difficult to see any good coming from a heart-rending trial. (Sometimes, even the passing of time does not help.) Yet, it is right in the throes of such personal crucibles that the opportunity for dramatic growth in character and fortitude reaches its zenith.

If, in those emotionally charged moments, you can bring yourself to look for the gold and sincerely ask yourself, "What am I being taught through this experience?" I can promise you, without exception, you will come upon life-changing insights—the kind of breakthroughs that can only be obtained by a willingness to be schooled by the headmaster's curriculum in the University of Life.

Section 4

Portraits:
Ownership in Action

_____

"There is no teaching to compare with example."

—Sir Robert Baden Powell

The portraits in this section are true accounts of people who have put the Ownership Spirit into practice. The portraits largely speak for themselves. Yet, because of *The Othello Principle*, they speak to each of us in different ways. As you read these examples of Ownership in Action, you'll have occasional flashes of application insight come to mind. Something will click for you or prompt you to take action and apply that insight to your own situation.

I urge you to respond to those flashes by capturing them in writing. Your list of insights will be of considerable value to you. I encourage you to refer to it regularly over the next few months. Spaced repetition is an effective way to convert principles into practices.

Other promptings will come to you as well. One of the portraits might remind you of the needs or situation of a friend, co-worker, or loved one. A great way to introduce them to these principles and life-affirming accounts is to share this book or direct them to my websites and blog where I provide ongoing insights and support to translate the Ownership Spirit into working reality. Visit www.QumaLearning.com, www.OwnershipSpirit.com, and www.DrDeatonSpeaks.com.

Your current personal list of insights will take precedence for now. However, over time, as you become proficient at applying your ideas, your list will need to grow to keep pace with your progression. Because we are all on different levels, facing different things, at different times in our lives, something that may not mean much to you now might make a world of difference later on. By rereading this book periodically and renewing your list of insights, you can continue to draw power from the principles and tools.

All of the accounts you are about to read are true and the quotes authentic. Most of the names are the actual names of the people involved, but some are not. Due to the sensitive quality of some of the events and situations, anonymity and confidentiality are warranted for obvious reasons.

Chapter 16

Terry Sutter

"You ought to be a mechanic," were words Terry Sutter heard with some frequency as he grew up in suburban St. Louis, Missouri. Ever fascinated with how and why things worked the way they did, he was constantly taking things apart and putting them back together. Around the house, clocks, radios, and small appliances seldom escaped his explorations. Seeing his aptitude, his family encouraged him to attend a vocational high school and learn a trade, which he did. "My father also taught me a strong work ethic," Terry said.

After graduating from high school, Terry attended a two-year vocational program at a technical institute and went on to work for a heating and air conditioning company. Before long, he carved himself a niche as a bright, reliable technician. Equipped with a truck, all the tools of the trade, and a perpetual list of service calls, Terry had pretty much settled in for a reputable, comfortable career.

Although Terry had attained the career he had envisioned for himself, something did not quite seem complete or settled. Something seemed to beckon him toward another path.

On one of his service calls, Terry encountered a group of young engineers and was immediately impressed with them. They were intelligent, sharp, and had an air about them that intrigued Terry. The thought of going to college and learning a profession flashed ever so briefly through his mind. That seed germinated for a while, until one day he was driving past Meramec Junior College. He says, "For some reason, I pulled into the parking lot."

As he inquired into enrolling in college, Terry was a little surprised when the registrar actually tried to talk him out of it. Pointing out that most of Terry's educational background was not relevant to a college degree, the registrar told him that essentially he'd have to go back and redo the last two years of his high school education.

Terry enrolled anyway. As he pursued his curriculum, which included a lot of math classes, Terry signed up for a chemistry class, and he loved it. His natural hunger to figure out how things worked was now piqued on a higher plane, and new vistas began opening up in his self-expectations. Before long, he found himself far more excited about going to chemistry class than going to work, and he aced all of his tests. One day, the instructor cornered Terry and said, "What are your plans? You're bright and have great math skills. You should really think about quitting work, going to school full time, and becoming a chemical engineer."

Terry recalls, "I went home and told my older brother about what the instructor had said. At first, he almost fell out of his chair, and we both started laughing. No one, not even myself, had ever looked at me as a serious student, but to his credit, my brother came around and was incredibly supportive."

With that boost, Terry followed the instructor's recommendation. He graduated four years later from the University of Missouri with a bachelor's degree in Chemical Engineering and followed that with a Master's Degree from Texas A&M.

After college, Terry worked for Pennzoil. When his wife, Amy, decided to further her business education at the University of Chicago, Terry started looking for a new job in Illinois. "At that point, I had no idea what a headhunter or recruiter was. All I knew was that I needed to get a job in the Chicago area, and I got a copy of the *Chicago Tribune* and began following up on the want ads."

One day, Terry received a call from a recruiter who asked for a résumé, and he complied. A few weeks later, the recruiter called with a lead. Something in the conversation hoisted a red flag, and Terry got the feeling that the recruiter had taken liberties with his résumé. "When he faxed me a copy of what he had sent out, I found that it was filled with things that weren't true."

Terry immediately called Morton Thiokol, the company that had expressed interest in him. He had no contact name or number. He just called the general number for the human resources department. A man answered the phone and Terry proceeded to tell him who he was and what had happened—that there were a number of inaccuracies on the résumé. As fate would have it, the person on the phone happened to be the very person who was responsible for filling the position. He said, "Amazingly, I happen to be looking at your résumé right now."

The man asked Terry to fax over a copy of his *real* résumé, which he did. About a week later, the man called. After a series of interviews, Terry wound up being hired as a capital project engineer in Morton Thiokol's central engineering department.

Along with this position came many opportunities to learn, grow, and further his career. Terry took ownership of all of these opportunities and made the most of them. When further education was offered, Terry seized it. Working hard during the day, he also worked hard at night going to school. His drive and talent became ever more evident. Terry caught the attention of the leaders above him, and he was soon promoted to be the manager of capital planning for the Specialty Chemicals business. In that position, Terry worked closely with Tom Russell, a strong leader who became a mentor.

Tom offered Terry two crucial pieces of advice: First, "If you want to sit in the highest chair, get all the experience you can, in as many areas as you can, so that no matter what comes at you, you have some background and a feel for what's happening." Second, remember, "Things are never as bad as they seem to be." Terry reflects, "I have done that, and I want to tell you, it gives you an unbelievable amount of confidence when you're sitting there in the decision-maker's chair and things are flying at you."

One day, Tom Russell, who had just been in a meeting with Morton Thiokol's president, walked into Terry's office and said, "You wanted a business. Well, you got one." Terry was made the general manager of what was called the Morton-Yokohama joint venture. Along with that good news came some sobering realities: The business had been losing money for years. Terry recounts, "I remember the COO of the company, telling me, 'This thing has lost money since Morton started it. We don't want to put any more money into it. By the way, this business makes terrible quality products, and we want you to figure something out.'"

Facing the proverbial "it was the best of news; it was the worst of news" situation, Terry had one of those Owner/Victim choices to make. He took Ownership—wholeheartedly. "I've never put more energy and effort into any role I've ever had. I was so excited I couldn't stand it. We had a big problem. We had built a plant that we had probably tried to save a little too much capital on, and we made bad products on a regular basis.

"I remember being in my first commercial meeting. We were at a Toyota plant in Georgetown, Kentucky, with the production team. There must have been about 20 Toyota engineers in the room. Not only did they tell us we were one of the worst suppliers in the whole plant, they had data to back it up!

"Now, I had never been a salesperson, and I had never been in front of customers, but I stood up and said to them, 'First of all, I want to thank you for not throwing us out. As I look at your data, if I were you, I would have probably thrown us out, but I can tell you that we won't need to have this meeting again.' I made some firm commitments to them about improving our quality, and I went back to the plant."

Terry kept his word. Without putting any more money into capital improvements, he and his team were able to fix the problems. Within six months, the business was consistently turning out top-quality products. A year later, it received one of Toyota's highest quality supplier awards. Toyota told them they had never seen a supplier turn around so completely so quickly.

From there, it was not long until the Morton-Yokohama joint venture turned the corner and become profitable for the first time in its history, and Terry was ready to be challenged with something else.

Along came an opportunity to join Allied Signal. He had met a man named Paul Norris, who had made a strong impression on Terry for a number of reasons. Paul was extremely bright, focused, and astute in his judgments. Circumstances led to a job interview with Paul for a position with Allied Signal. Terry walked out of that meeting feeling like he had completely bombed. For every question Paul asked, Terry would give his honest opinion, and Paul would have the opposite point of view. The two didn't seem to see eye to eye on anything. After the interview, Terry told Amy he was almost positive he wouldn't get the job.

To Terry's surprise, he was offered the position, having demonstrated in the interview what Paul was really looking for: someone who could think, not collapse, under pressure and stand his ground in the face of criticism and rejection.

It was a good hire for Allied Signal. Terry held a number of very responsible positions during his tenure there, both before and after the merger with Honeywell. By the time he moved on to another opportunity, he was President of Honeywell Industry Solutions, a $1.5 billion division. In every position he has held, Terry has been known as a people-oriented leader, one who believes strongly in investing in the employees* and trusting them to own their areas.

When Terry took over as president of Industry Solutions, he held "town hall" meetings to meet the people and gauge the pulse of the team. In one of them, a woman asked what the division strategy was going to be. Terry responded, "I have no idea at this point; I don't even know where the bathrooms are. You are all going to be very disappointed that I'm not going to walk in here in the first week and tell you all what you're doing wrong and what the right answer is. What I *will* tell you is this: As a team, we are going to go through a process. I have a lot of clarity around where I think we ought to be, but we are collectively—*as a team*—going to figure out how to get there." You can imagine the positive impact that had on that division.

Shortly after Terry left Honeywell to join the executive leadership of a $40 billion company that was in need of a turn-around, he and Amy were presented with a new opportunity to exercise Ownership.

At about age four, the Sutter's oldest son, Graham, was diagnosed with a heart murmur, known as "left pulmonary stenosis." At first, this was not considered a grave concern. It simply meant that Graham would have to be monitored by a cardiologist, involving an annual checkup and electrocardiogram.

At this time of tremendous professional demands on Terry, working day and night in his new position, 11-year-old Graham had one of his annual checkups. The cardiologist broke some alarming news. She had

---

*I first met Terry Sutter when, as President of Honeywell Industry Solutions, he led the division-wide roll-out of *The Ownership Spirit* training for all Industry Solution employees.

found an anomaly involving one of the arteries in Graham's heart. This serious defect put Graham's future, even his very life, in question. Surgery was an option; however, at the time there was no consensus among cardiologists about how, when, and what type of surgery was best.

"When you are facing a life-and-death decision involving one of your children, it obviously weighs heavily on your mind," Terry continues. "You talk about Ownership; we *really* had to apply it then. When you are facing something like this, it is easy to have some dark days."

At this same time, as Terry and Amy were desperately trying to gather critical information to make the momentous decision regarding Graham's surgery, Terry's mother became gravely ill and slipped into a coma. Terry's father called and informed him that his mother was in intensive care and unconscious. Terry spent the next week with his father and brother as his mother passed away. Although his mother had been ill for quite some time, Terry's father was totally unprepared for the passing of his wife. He was completely devastated. Terry stayed by his father's side, supporting him during this very difficult time.

When Terry returned, he and Amy resumed their intense search, throwing all their energy into finding the best information possible to make a decision about their son. They read countless articles, visited some of the best-known hospitals and clinics in the United States, and communicated with some of the most renowned specialists in the country.

Eventually, the Sutters found a doctor who could explain what the real issues were and what kind of surgery could be done to address them. Most importantly, this doctor confidently offered them a promising prognosis. "This is where Ownership really comes in. I have always been, almost by DNA, an optimistic person; it's just a better place to live, but when the doctor starts talking about opening your son's chest up, inducing a full cardiac arrest, and tells you some kids just don't come out of that cardiac arrest when they try to resuscitate them, it's not an easy decision to make.

"I kept trying to focus on one thing: We had visited all these hospitals and seen a lot of families with tough situations. I said, 'Look at all these children. There are a lot of families who have children who don't have a path forward, who don't have a prognosis. We have a prognosis. We have a surgical path. Furthermore, we have identified someone who many agree is the greatest pediatric cardiac surgeon in the world, and he's looking us in the eye and telling us he can fix this and that we can expect to have Graham restored to a full, normal life. That's the path we have to take.

"I'm telling you, that's the one thing you have to keep telling yourself every single day—at work or wherever. I've had some pretty dark days at work. I think back to the surgery and what could have happened. But you just have to keep bringing yourself back to that path forward." The Sutters decided to go ahead and the surgery was performed. After the surgical repairs were made, it came time to resuscitate Graham. The 12-year-old responded and successfully survived the surgery.

The path to full recovery was not without its bumps. There were many complications. Within two or three days of the surgery, fluid started building up around the heart. Called "pericardial effusion," this condition is not uncommon after surgeries like this one, but Graham's effusion was more severe than most. For the next couple of months Graham's condition remained a concern. There was a two-week period during which he had to go back to the hospital daily with the distinct possibility that he might have to be taken back into surgery. For the Sutters, the mental burden during those times was extremely heavy. Gradually, the effusion problem improved, and after much longer than the usual three-month recovery period, Graham Sutter was given a clean bill of health.

The once fairly contented heating and air conditioning technician had come a long way. Had someone foretold Terry how far he would go in his career at the time he was driving around Missouri in his service van, he probably would have deemed that person a raving lunatic. Yet, the story is true: Terry went from one degree to a greater one, and he did that again and again, propelled by a confident willingness to stretch and try something "a little out there," as he puts it.

In summarizing Terry's life, it is hard not to make it sound like everything fell into place, virtually without effort. Each step has been fraught with perils and distinct potential for failure and embarrassment. Many times he had to dig down, swallow his qualms, push back his fears, and proceed with faith and hope that things would work out. The successes were not unmerited arbitrary strokes of luck or fate. Rather, they were the gifts that accrue when any individual melds a positive Ownership mindset with the corresponding work and effort.

Chapter 17

Kristy Malone

"My philosophy has always been, 'If somebody else can do it and survive it, so can I,'" says corporate business *leader*, now turned business *owner*, Kristy Malone. "I look at risk as an opportunity; I really do." She continues, "I am an extreme skier. I am not in as good of shape as I used to be, but eight years ago when we were in Colorado, I put my skis over my shoulder and hiked for 20 minutes to go out of bounds and ski something that had just been avalanche blasted. I have done a bungee slingshot ride. I love roller coasters. Now that I have kids, I am trying to be a little more sane, but I have grown a lot and enjoyed more of life, I think, because I was willing to take a risk now and then. You have to take ownership for your own growth in life, and that comes from making decisions—sometimes taking a risk—and then owning the outcomes of your decisions and learning from them."

As Kristy has followed that philosophy and enjoyed resulting success and recognition, she has been invited to share her insights with others, including teaching a class on Leadership Ethics. One of the points she stresses in her class is something she lives and embodies: "Bad decisions don't define you, unless they are catastrophic. Take accountability for your actions, and move on. It is how you handle the outcomes and aftermath of those decisions that defines you."

Raised an Irish Lass

Kristy Malone was born and raised in Pennsylvania, an only child, by parents who were proud of their Irish background. "I did a lot of Irish-centric things," she explains. "I raised Irish Wolfhounds, did

Irish dancing, and traveled with my family back to Ireland. A lot of my upbringing was centered around my Irish heritage."

As she grew up, Kristy demonstrated a strong competitive quality. She won medals in Irish dance. She was a skier and a competitive swimmer, winning more than her share of blue ribbons and honors. Never limiting herself to any one area, Kristy ran track, played softball, and loved horseback riding. "I'm a real animal lover," she adds.

Kristy also applied her competitive drive to her academics. She was an honor student and was enrolled in gifted programs through school. In addition to traveling abroad, the family spent vacations at their condominium in Vail, Colorado. "We were a big skiing family. Most of my really happy vacation memories were out in Colorado," she says.

This sunny picture had one dark cloud. "My father was an alcoholic. He was very functioning and successful but, nonetheless, a very heavy drinker," she recounts. "That certainly had an influence on me when I was growing up. That turned a very happy childhood, when I didn't know any better, into a difficult time. As I grew older, I began to understand the impact my father's drinking was having on his life, my mom's life, and my own. Because of that, once I got to be independent, I became *very* independent. I was always out at friends' houses, never bringing my friends home. As soon as I could get out, I did. I just didn't want to bring anybody else into that environment."

With so many happy experiences linked to Colorado, Kristy immediately looked west after high school, enrolling in pre-med at the University of Colorado in Boulder. "I was very interested in medicine. I grew up watching the old TV program *Quincy*, and that's what I wanted to be—a forensic coroner.

"My first year and a half in college I had a 4.0 grade point average, carrying a really heavy load. Then I decided that I needed to have more fun in life. So, I turned to skiing, dropped out of school, and ended up getting married at a very early age. That took me in a very different direction for a while. I started working in retail to generate income. After two years, that marriage ended in divorce."

Gaining Business Experience

Some of the decisions Kristy made in this part of her life became significant learning experiences, and they empowered her perspectives about "taking accountability for one's actions and moving on." She learned for herself that it is how we handle the outcomes, the aftermath of our decisions, that truly defines us.

"After the divorce, I moved back to Pittsburgh," Kristy explains. "Luckily, the retail company I was working for thought well enough of me to offer me a position there." Kristy may have considered it "luck," but her drive, intelligence, and potential were apparent, and the company now saw her as a leader-in-the-making. "I went back to school part time while I was working. I knew I had kind of let myself down with my education, and I had better expectations of myself than I had lived up to at that time."

Before long, the company offered Kristy a management position in one of its Boston stores. She was flattered and excited but also a little apprehensive. "It was a new city and I only knew one person who lived there—the person who had offered me the job." Part of Kristy's concerns related to her management abilities. "At the time, I had some fear of failure. I felt fairly certain I could do the job, but I didn't know for sure. I hadn't had any management training or real experience. So, there were some doubts that I had to push back."

Kristy also had feelings of emotional jeopardy as she weighed the offer. "What if I don't like it in Boston? What if I just don't make it?" she queried. "I thought, 'If things don't work and I go back to Pittsburgh again, will people look at me and think that I am weak or indecisive, that I can't make up my mind?' Fear of failure was a big part of this decision—something I've had to overcome more than once in my life. I've always had it, but I've always forged forward anyway. I decided to look at Boston as another adventure, a chance to explore things, a chance to learn more about myself and about the world around me."

Upon arriving in Boston, her fears did not just disappear. At first, living in a new city with not many friends, she was frequently alone with her thoughts, and one major question overshadowed them all. "I kept wondering 'Am I ever going to find happiness, or am I just chasing a dream? Am I going to have to keep moving and bouncing around? Will I ever have some stability in my life?'"

Although she did not know it at the time, the answers to her inner questions were to be answered as she took Ownership, quieted her self-doubts as best she could, and forged ahead. Acting on hope rather than fear, Kristy prospered in her role as an assistant manager, her knowledge and skills growing parallel with her confidence. When a store manager position came open in one of the company's other Boston stores, Kristy applied.

"I was very excited about this opportunity," Kristy relates. "I actually competed against someone who had been in that market area for some time." As usual, some initial qualms sent a chill or two down Kristy's spine. "I had a flash of, 'Can I really do this? I've convinced myself and I'm about to convince everybody else that I can do this, but what happens when I actually step foot through the door of the new store. I am 24 years old. My raw energy and desire could easily be dismissed by this team of senior employees. Every one of them was older than I and had more seniority.'"

Kristy's Ownership thinking—acknowledging her self-doubts and fears, but not letting them stop her—served her well. "I went into the interview with the message of 'Here's what I know, here's what I'm going to do, here's my plan, and here's why I'm the best person for the job.'" The force of Kristy's commitment impressed the interviewers and she got the position.

Now she had to make good on her promises. Continuing to trust in herself, Kristy's drive and passion worked. Under her leadership the store grew and blossomed. The store's success earned her a laudable reputation for taking struggling operations and mending them quickly. "I became known as a turnaround manager—someone who could go in, assess what was going on, and fix something that was not working very well."

The management skills and confidence were not part of Kristy's repertoire when she first moved to Boston, packing a load of apprehensions with her. The seeds and potential had been there, of course, but they grew to fruition out of three Ownership elements: (1) *Believing* in herself despite her fears and self-doubts, (2) *Acting* on that belief by stepping into the unknown, and (3) *Working hard* to make her hopes, rather than her fears, come true.

"Hard work absolutely played a big part in my success. It truly was great business experience. I learned how to handle customers and do 15 things at once, how to juggle things and multi-task. Looking back, I can see that I knew the job from a technical standpoint better than anybody in the store. My biggest fear was that I didn't know a lot about leading people or managing. I just didn't have much experience. So, that piece made me a little nervous, and I fell and skinned my knee more than once by not dealing appropriately with some of my folks. If I had to do that part over again, I would be less dictatorial. Not that I was mean or nasty, I just hadn't learned the skills of enrolling people to collaborate and involve their ideas. That was part of my learning curve back then, and it's certainly a part of how I lead and motivate people now."

A New Career Direction

At a certain point, Kristy decided to take another risk and leave the retail business. Part of the risk was that she did not have a landing place actually specified when she left, but it did not take her long to secure a good management position with a large medical health insurance company. Experience in the insurance field enabled her to land a job in the auto claims division of one of the major insurance providers in America.

As before, Kristy moved rapidly up the ranks in that division, at times skipping some rungs on the ladder. Then, again willing to take some risk, Kristy eventually shifted into a whole new department and rose through the ranks once again, culminating in becoming the head of an entire newly formed department which she helped model and shape into the prototype for the rest of the company to follow. Sounds effortless and cozy, doesn't it?

Pressure Upon Pressure

The seeming ease with which Kristy Malone moved up the career ladder through this stage of her career belies her whole story. Each of these career moves required sacrifice and bigger leaps of faith for her and also for her husband, Keith; and there is more to her story than that.

"Keith and I have two beautiful children," Kristy says, "but we went through a lot from an infertility standpoint. It took lots of time, energy, and effort—and a ton of money—to get our children here.

"I lost my mom at the age of 36 due to poor health and my father was a raging alcoholic. At the exact same time, Keith and I were dealing with all the infertility issues and all of the trials and tribulations that went along with that. I think that was probably the toughest time of my life."

The illness and eventual passing away of Kristy's mother presented additional opportunities for growth. At first, her mother's health declined in gradual steps. She suffered a series of small strokes that were initially misdiagnosed as Bell's palsy. Being an only child placed an extra heavy responsibility on Kristy, especially when it came to dealing with her father. During this time of his wife's failing health, he would get drunk and call Kristy in the middle of the night, blaming her for not being there for him or her mother. In those tirades, her father played all the guilt and martyr cards conceivable. By morning, after he had sobered up, he retained no recollection of his accusations and the verbal abuse he had inflicted. (Her father has since gone through rehab and is sober).

Kristy and Keith did all they could. In the midst of the weekly series of fertility exams and treatments, wherein Kristy was admonished to live as calm and serene a life as possible, she was making the long multi-hour drives to her parents' home to be with them and look after her mother's care. "I wanted to make sure I was there for Mom and Dad and keep things on track. Mom would recover from one stroke and then have another. My father would be on the phone late at night, drunk, yelling at me, putting the blame on me. During the day, he wouldn't even realize what he had done or said. Meanwhile, my mom would continue to be the enabler. 'Don't be mad at your dad; he's under lots of pressure,' and all that.

"Mom's health just kept spiraling downward. At the same time, Keith and I were working through the fertility issues. At first, we were unsuccessful and tried different procedures. Eventually, we were referred to St. Barnabus, in New Jersey, one of the top three fertility clinics in the country. We would get up at 3 a.m. and drive three hours to New Jersey with our three Labrador retrievers in the van. We would bring their breakfast. When I would go in for my blood work, Keith would walk and feed the dogs. Then we'd get back in the van and drive home, and I would be back on the job at 10 a.m., conducting a meeting. We were doing that two and three times a week.

"One time, we were at St. Barnabus, and we decided to stay in New York City that night. Just as we got there, I got a call. Mom had

had another stroke. We checked out of the hotel and drove five hours to my parents' home. It was just non-stop craziness like that virtually all the time. On top of all of this, I am trying to maintain my position and professionalism and take care of all my people and responsibilities at work. Of course, I was trying to do my best to not let anyone pick up on the pressures and the problems I was dealing with at the time."

Darkness Before the Dawn

Not unexpectedly, the pressure and pace made it even more difficult for Kristy and Keith to achieve their goal of having a child. The couple's high hopes were repeatedly dashed, and they endured disappointment after disappointment. Multiple times, all the signs indicated that they might be pregnant, only to find out that they weren't. Then, after all their struggles, one summer they got the long awaited news.

"Finally, I got the positive news that I was pregnant. At the time Mom's health was really bad. She was in ICU and knew that I was pregnant. The doctors were monitoring me closely, and all the while, I was running back and forth from home to New Jersey and flying to my parents' home on the weekends to be with them. The load was almost overwhelming.

"Then we found out the pregnancy was not going well, but I did not let my mom know. Upon my doctors' recommendation, I went in for a procedure to terminate the pregnancy on Monday, and my mother died the following Sunday," Kristy states tearfully. "That was really a tough, tough time—probably the hardest week of my life."

As so often happens, the old proverb, "It's always darkest before the dawn," held true. What looked like the worst possible outcome turned out to be the answer to their heartfelt wishes and the doorway to the successful result Keith and Kristy sought.

"We had good news come out of that. From the procedure that resulted in the terminated pregnancy, several other fertilized eggs were recovered and frozen. A few months later, we went back and had the frozen eggs implanted, and that is how we got our first child— our miracle baby." A few years later, the successful procedure was repeated, and Keith and Kristy completed their family with the birth of another healthy baby.

"There truly was a blessing that came out of the bad news, and we made it through. And that's the Ownership Spirit. That's what gets you through. You say, 'Life sucks right now, but we're going to persevere, and we're going to do everything we can to make things work.' You have to look it as, 'Hey, this is what happens in life, and we're going to move on.'

More Courageous Decisions

To this portrait, another major facet needs to be added. Kristy Malone is a recovering alcoholic herself. "I grew up in a home where alcohol was present and plentiful. I started drinking at an early age, and I always thought that I was in control, but I later realized I was not. As I was going through my late teens and early 20s, I was always very functioning, but I drank a lot during those years. While I was going through my fertility treatments and when I got pregnant with my first child, I stopped drinking, and that continued during the time I was nursing. However, once I stopped nursing, I went back to drinking. It was then that I realized that I had an issue. I was thinking about it during the day. Keith became concerned with how I behaved in social situations. So, there were times that I began hiding it from him, and I knew that was a bad sign.

"I made the decision when our first child was nine months old. I knew I needed to give up alcohol for good. I was 38. I went through 11 weeks of outpatient counseling and have not had a drink since. I am so committed to this, knowing what I went through as a child and knowing the environment I want for my kids. Keith and I have worked so hard for the life we have; I have not had one ounce of desire to drink ever again. Period. And I know within myself, if I have one, that's it. That's just the way the disease is."

New Business

There are some things Kristy will no longer put at risk, like the home environment. Yet, when it comes to professional pursuits, Kristy's risk-leveraging, entrepreneurial spirit has moved her to take yet another step. She has left the comfortable confines of her corporate success and has started her own business.

"Keith and I had discussed this many times over the years, but the timing never seemed right. Then, one day an opportunity presented itself, and it seemed like the right time to take another big risk," Kristy explains.

For a couple heading full speed ahead into mid-life, raising two children, still making a mortgage payment, just coming into the years of greatest income need, this venture requires even greater faith and courage than anything Kristy has done before. "Financially, the risk is huge for us," Kristy confides. "We do not have the big financial cushion you'd like to have to pull something like this off. We don't have a lot of savings. We just did not have a big enough income, even with both of us working, to work through the infertility treatments and have money left over to put into a business. But, once we get our minds set on something there's no stopping."

When asked, "Is starting your own business the biggest risk you have ever taken in your life?" Kristy answers, "Probably. But, I feel good about it. I feel confident that we can make it work and be successful." There is no detectable tinge of arrogance or superficial bravado in her tone or attitude. Her expressions are just calm, firm expressions of faith and commitment. They convey a mature Tough-Minded Ownership born of experience and tempered in the fires of previous tests. Kristy is another living example of the truth, "Doing something hard gives you the power to do something even harder."

"I have my business license and I am underway. I am very, very excited because I am in a business that really helps people live better lives. I want to leave behind an important lesson to my children: 'Be considerate of other people—you have to live your life so you can do something good for others.' I feel that I am *showing them that* in what I do for a living. One wonderful thing about my business is that my children can be a part of it. I want them to see the importance of making a difference in people's lives one relationship at a time."

Kristy looks back with appreciation for how well some of her risk taking and fear fighting has paid off for her in the long run. "Things could have gone the other way and not worked out, I guess, but if you don't take a risk, you don't know what you've missed. I think you need to step a little bit beyond your risk tolerance once in awhile. If I had not taken the risk to move to Colorado on my own, I never would have experienced that marriage and divorce, and I have grown from that. If I hadn't taken the risk to move to Boston on my own, I never would have met Keith. Had I not taken the risk to leave retail, I never would have gotten on the career path I am now or be where I am now. Every day there's a fork in the road, and you have to make a decision. If you take the road that is always comfortable, and you know exactly what's going to happen, you're going to be at the end of that road someday and say, 'Man, I wish I would have done more with my life.'"

Chapter 18

Styles

Styles turned out to be the perfect name. Styles Scott Fitch had style, presence, character, and "esprit de vivre" in abundance, endearing himself to everyone who ever knew him or even briefly intersected his path. Adjectives used to describe him include "exuberant," "mischievously witty," "creative," "courageous," "extremely loving and kind," and "a bigger-than-life personality."

A good-natured dispute exists regarding how Styles' father, Scott, came up with the unique name for his son. Scott says the name struck him as he sat watching the credits roll in a movie theatre. He is not absolutely certain *which* movie, although he leans toward *Bill and Ted's Excellent Adventure*. His wife, Teri, Styles' mother, winces a bit at that possibility, questioning laughingly whether her husband's tastes in movies had ever sunk that low.

Whatever the source, the name stuck in Scott's mind and was given to Scott and Teri's firstborn child, and the name was both apt and prophetic.

Teri's pregnancy seemed normal, as did the ultrasounds administered along the way. Curled hands and turned-in feet appear to be normal fetal anatomy, but when Styles was born, it was discovered that three fingers on his left hand and four on the right would not open. Furthermore, his feet rotated inwardly in a clubfoot-like manner.

On an ultrasound, such deformities were not detectable, so the young couple had no warning or time to prepare. Their blessed event was still joyous; they just thought they had a few unexpected considerations to deal with. Scott simply says, "It was surprising news. It wasn't devastating, but it was something we had not anticipated."

As time went on, the surprises continued to mount for the Fitches, and the problems with Styles' hands and feet turned out to be minor compared to the discoveries yet to come.

Naturally, Scott and Teri immediately sought medical advice regarding what was thought to be isolated physical deformities. In the early examinations, anything beyond the obvious abnormalities went unseen. To correct the deformities and improve the function of his fingers and feet, Styles underwent a succession of surgeries on his fingers—one or two at a time, with varying degrees of success—and his feet were straightened.

As Styles continued to grow, however, it gradually became ever more evident that something more formidable underlay the deformity of his limbs. Parts of Styles' body began to grow "differently," principally his skull. The soft areas in his skull, the symphyses, began to harden prematurely, causing the plates to fuse far too early, impeding the natural growth of the brain. Cranial surgeries were performed to separate the plates so the brain would not be entrapped in an overly-constricted boney helmet.

Teri and Scott worked long hours, trying to find the root cause of Styles' many abnormalities. Searches, examinations, referrals, and consultation after consultation ensued. While Scott made the living, Teri, in particular, put in the time and patient effort to work through the tangled jungle of paperwork that goes along with our current medical and insurance systems. Finding the best doctors and specialists to deal with Styles' ever-menacing medical dilemmas was not easy, but getting the insurance companies to pay was even more difficult. Only people who have battled their way through such a morass of policies, stipulations and exceptions can appreciate the frustration and aggravation that goes along with that task.

Unintimidated by the height of the mountain they were climbing, Scott and Teri pressed forward, never relinquishing their hope of finding some answers. Their search took them to a number of clinics and hospitals in various states as they consulted with eminent physicians and geneticists. No one could ever quite render a definitive diagnosis. For a while, Styles' complex of symptoms was labeled Shprintzen-Goldberg syndrome, but that was dropped because most children with that syndrome are mentally deficient, and Styles was anything but that. He was super sharp with an acute sense of humor.

Later, the diagnosis was changed to Marfan-type syndrome, newly named Furlong syndrome, but that was not an accurate fit either. It seemed that Styles had bits and pieces of several of these extremely rare conditions. One geneticist said, "If there was a hallway filled with doors, and each door had a syndrome, Styles had a finger in this door and leg in that door and an arm in another." Because Styles' symptoms did not fit the pattern of any known syndrome, doctors had no basis for making predictions, much less a comprehensive treatment plan. Doing the best they could, the doctors tried to remedy each new problem as it occurred. Over time, Styles underwent in excess of 45 surgeries—many of them major, including 17 cranial operations and an ultra-risky open heart surgery.

Overcoming with Grace and Patience

The irregular growth of the bones of Styles' face and skull, in combination with the many surgeries, resulted in visible facial and cranial distortion. Nobody knew better than Styles that his appearance set him apart from other people, most poignantly from his peers. Nobody could have handled that situation with more grace and patience than he. Rude, hurtful comments from other children were frequent, especially from those who were meeting Styles for the first time, but he never returned rudeness for rudeness.

Even from adults, who should have had more sense, Styles suffered the indignity of inconsiderate comments. Demonstrating patience and composure beyond his years, Styles was able to set those insults aside. After one encounter with a tactless adult, Styles commented to his father, "Some people need a few lessons in how to be nice."

Styles' grandmother, Sheron Fitch, relates an illustration of Styles' ability to examine his emotional options and own his responses to insensitive people. One day Sheron and Styles were watching a movie that involved a man who had been so severely scratched in the face that another character winced and uttered, "Ewww, what happened to your face?" Styles looked up at Sheron and said, "Grandma, it's a *really* a good thing I'm a nice guy." She responded, "I agree. You really *are* a nice guy, and that *is* a good thing. But what made you say that?"

Styles answered, "Because that's what people say to me all the time— 'Ewww, what's wrong with your face.' If I wasn't a nice guy, I would just deck 'em."

Tests of Patience All Around

For Scott and Teri, each surgical procedure precipitated a skirmish with insurance companies over why the procedures were necessary. They patiently worked their way through the red tape and initial rejections. Scott gives Teri the credit for waging the battle against all the complexity. "Teri has been great at all this stuff. You don't plan on this kind of thing, and you don't have experience in it. Upon Teri fell most of the burden of arranging for insurance, often dealing with out-of-network providers. Most of Styles' doctors have been specialty doctors. Finding them, arranging for meetings, working all the facets, and overcoming all of the hurdles within the system has been an enormous task. Teri has championed Styles' cause tirelessly—all of which speaks highly of her character, strength, and love for Styles."

The same can be said of Scott. The couples' calm but resolute determination has been an inspiration to all familiar with the situation. One person close to the family said, "You just have to take your hats off to that couple. They never let it divide them and they never became angry or sharp with anyone they worked with. They were just amazing."

Through it all, Styles exemplified *Ownership Spirit* too. He never grew despondent or asked, "Why me?" He just went forward, squeezing as much out of life as he could. After each surgery, as soon as he had enough strength to get back into school and to play at full throttle, he would. "Styles was always just triumphant," Scott states. Throughout, he remained a strong, positive, good-natured boy; and he grew into his teens with many close friends. Everyone who knew Styles loved him.

More Complications

At age 12, on top of all the cranial complications and distortions, Styles began to have heart problems due to severe dilation of his heart tissue and the aorta, the major artery coming out of the heart. The doctors monitored the situation regularly. One time, after having some tests run, Teri took Styles back to school. Later, one of the doctors called, and in a concerned tone he asked Teri, "Where is he?"

"At school," she said.

"Go get him. Bring him home. Sit him on the couch."

The tests that day had revealed that Styles' heart muscle had stretched so thin that even a minor jolt could cause the heart wall to burst. It would be like getting shot through the heart; he would die within seconds.

Teri brought Styles home, and he missed the rest of the school year. Teri once again worked through the process of finding the right doctor and getting all the approvals so Styles could undergo the daunting heart operation he needed.

Describing the surgery, one surgeon pulled no punches. "Of all the surgeries that can be done," he said, "there are none more risky than this one." The doctors planned to replace a six-inch segment of Styles' aorta with Dacron tubing, hoping the heart tissue would be sturdy enough to hold the sutures. They also hoped the heart would resume pumping again once the aorta was replaced and that the brain would do its job of signaling the heart to beat normally once it restarted. Finally, they hoped the rest of Styles' frail systems would respond and go back to work after such extensive trauma.

The decision to go ahead was weighed carefully. Nearly 13 years of virtually relentless pressure—the work, fears, wonderings, coupled with hopes that waxed and then waned as each new problem arose—pressed down on Teri and Scott's shoulders as they approached this decision. Never, during all this time, was there an uttered complaint or a whine, and there wouldn't be this time either. Once again, Scott and Teri summoned their courage and exercised an unflinching degree of Tough-Minded Ownership, deciding to proceed with the surgery.

The heart surgery itself went as well as could be hoped. Getting in and out of Styles' fragile chest was another story. The bone in Styles' body was thin and friable. When the surgeons opened Styles' rib cage, it crumbled. Hence, once the delicate procedures on the heart and aorta were completed, the doctors still faced the arduous task of putting Styles' rib cage and sternum back together. It was tedious, tension-filled work. After several wearisome hours, the surgeons accomplished the near impossible, and Styles was wheeled out of the operating room, and he began yet another recovery.

All the surgeries—many of them protracted and extensive—had imposed a heavy tax on Styles' physical reserves. This time the impact was just too much for his body. Styles did well for a day or so. "Then," in Scott's words, "he just crashed."

"At first, he could not come off the respirator," Scott explains. "The doctors tried taking take him off, but his body just couldn't do it. He had to be reintubated. Eventually, he was able to come off the respirator with the help of a device that helped him breathe, but his body was succumbing. Styles' mind and spirit were not done; he was still ready to go through a wall. However, his body just couldn't do it anymore. During those long days in ICU, we just thought, 'How much longer can he keep going?' But, the thing with Styles is, he always did. He just always pulled it off and kept going."

As Styles began to rebound a bit from the heart surgery, he had to deal with more cranial problems. The repeated surgeries on his skull had left a small portion of sinus membrane trapped in one of Styles' eye sockets, which would fill and create mucous cysts behind his eye causing the eyeball to protrude. Cranial surgery was needed to drain the cysts and remove the sinus tissue. That surgery put Styles in the hospital for another three weeks and added further demands on his body. Losing 10 pounds off his already thin frame, Styles was put on a feeding tube for another month.

Then came another devastating blow. Two years after Styles' open heart surgery, a heart valve went bad. The relentlessly degrading quality of the heart tissue itself was now more than the doctors could deal with. The aortic valve had stretched way out of shape and size. "If 17 millimeters was normal for his size, Styles' had dilated to 56 millimeters," Teri said.

Once again, Styles, Scott, and Teri were back where they had been before. Styles' heart could tear or burst at any moment. Once again, Teri and Scott were faced with another life-and-death decision.

A panel of doctors—cardiologists and thoracic surgeons—studied the options and weighed the pros and cons. Their best judgment was that Styles would not survive another major heart surgery. Even if the valve replacement was successful, they feared they wouldn't be able to rebuild his fragile chest wall again. They also doubted whether he would be able to come off the respirator again. After painstaking deliberation, the doctors reluctantly concluded that all the realistic medical alternatives had been exhausted. Teri said, "This was a very difficult time. We thought a lot about how much pain he had been in for the past year or two. He lived in constant pain, but he never talked about it. He never complained. His tolerance for pain was much greater than most people's."

After much prayer and consideration, sensing the reality of the predicted and probable outcome, Teri and Scott made the soul-wrenching decision not to proceed with the surgery.

They informed all the adults in the family, their closest friends, and all of the parents of Styles' friends that they all needed to be prepared for what might happen. Styles' heart could rupture at any time, possibly even while playing at their homes. No one could say just when it might occur. The doctors could only say that they thought it was probable within the next three to nine months.

Styles did not return to school. He was home-schooled by two of his aunts and his mother. He did, with exuberance, resume his regular activity with his friends and cousins, although he would grow tired much more quickly. To most people's amazement, he refused to take his foot off the pedal of enjoying every moment he had. He never let his pain, appearance, or impairments diminish his spirited approach. One of his comments during this time, as he took a break from wrestling with one of his cousins was, "I'm not as sick as people think I am."

Two weeks later, on a cold winter day, Teri and Styles went to the hospital for some tests. When the tests were finished, they went to the car to head for home. Teri remembers that Styles commented on the door handles being frozen. Once inside the car, they waited for a few minutes while the engine warmed up a bit. Suddenly, it happened. Styles screamed, saying his chest hurt, and Teri knew what had happened. Still in the parking lot of the hospital, she quickly drove the short distance to the emergency room entrance and got help immediately. Styles was taken back inside the hospital. He was straightway attended to with earnest dispatch, but the end had come.

Scott received Teri's call and arrived at the hospital within minutes. "I was 10 or 15 minutes from the hospital when I got Teri's call.

I remember looking at the clock; it was 7:11 p.m. When I ran in, I saw him on the gurney, everything hooked up to him, everyone still around him. They were still trying to revive him. His eyes were open and his head was turned toward where Teri and I were standing. Looking at Styles, my first thought was, 'You can do this, son.' I thought he was going to turn and start talking to people. That was just the way he was; he was always triumphant. Then when he didn't move or speak, I realized that he was gone."

Teri added, "When it happened, how it happened, where we were—all of that seemed to be as it should have been. We knew we had done all we could do. We never had to doubt that there were other things that could have been done to help him. We knew that God had been merciful to Styles, and to us, as to when, where, and how Styles would exit this life."

"I just remember hanging onto Teri for a little bit," Scott recalled, "and then I went over to the doctors and nurses, asking them to stop, thanking them for their efforts. And that was it."

Chapter 19

Scott and Teri Fitch

When you let the mental pictures of the Styles Fitch story sink in, logic almost automatically assumes that Styles and his needs grew to become the all-consuming focus of the Fitches' lives. That assumption would be understandable but inaccurate.

As Teri and Scott became increasingly aware of the multiple facets of Styles' unique syndrome, they realized they were in for a long, laborious journey with no definite end in sight. Whether or not they would ever reach their goal of seeing Styles completely healthy and pain free, they did not know. What they did know for certain was that they were not about to let Styles' physical condition become the center of their world or even of his. Styles did not want that and neither did they. The Fitches were determined to carry on a life as close to normal as possible.

Fulfilling their vision of creating a full, well-rounded, happy home life required inordinate courage on at least two fronts. First, allowing Styles to dive into the full spectrum of childhood activity and boyhood experience required courageous and disciplined restraint on Scott and Teri's part. It would have been so easy for them to become fanatically over-protective and to coddle and pamper Styles, shielding him from anything that might lead to injury or further complication. His fragile skull and facial structure were simply not capable of withstanding any kind of forceful jolt or insult. A fall or collision that would mean nothing more than a bruise to the average boy, could have been far worse or even fatal to Styles. While they did not discount the potential danger, Scott and Teri made a concerted effort to parent a child, not a patient.

Like most responsible parents, Teri and Scott equipped their son with a bike helmet, which he only used for biking and boarding. Otherwise, they stepped back and let Styles play full-out in all the activities he wanted to pursue. That was exactly the way Styles wanted it. He lived his life with zest and energy, not holding back with any measure of fear or restraint on his own part. He ran, wrestled, skied, and crashed his bike and scooter just like any other kid his age. He played and competed against his peers with a contagious exuberance that radiated and engulfed others.

How many times Teri or Scott might have been tempted to tone down some of Styles' antics or activities, we have no way of knowing. We have to acknowledge the wisdom and courage it took for them to not let their apprehensions or fears siphon one ounce of joy out of their son's life.

Scott and Teri's commitment that Styles live a normal life also struck a healthy equilibrium when it came to roles and responsibilities around the house. Making no exceptions because of his conditions, Scott and Teri schooled and supported their son's development by teaching him discipline and the value of work. Styles was given his full share of the household chores, yard work, and family service projects and was expected to complete what he started. Thus, Styles became a responsible, respectful, well-adjusted boy—neither an indulged invalid nor a spoiled brat.

An Even Bigger Act of Courage

To realize their full vision of family life, Teri and Scott had to wrestle with a second heart-probing decision, one that required an even greater degree of courageous Ownership.

During their dating years, Scott and Teri had talked about having a family—a vision that always included more than one child. Once the extent of Styles' medical abnormalities became apparent, the question of having another child took on deep, character-testing dimensions. How do you make such a decision when the odds are unknowable? Were they out of their minds to even consider having another child? Was that being selfish and irresponsible? Such questions required much soul-searching and delving to the depths of faith, hope, love, and inner strength.

Scott and Teri consulted several doctors and held earnest discussions with the geneticists who were familiar with Styles' case as well as other rare syndromes. The question, "If we were to try again, what are the odds of having a healthy child?" weighed heavily on their minds. Since there never was a definitive diagnosis for Styles, no amount of hopeful reassurance or "best guesses" from qualified authorities could ever completely erase *all* the doubts. If they did decide to proceed with having another baby, there would always be the chance. As any responsible person would, Scott and Teri explored that question with great earnestness and respect. Perhaps only someone *actually in* that position can *fully* appreciate how heavy that question would weigh. Only they could fully understand the profound levels of courage required to say, "Yes; we will accept the risk and the responsibility and try again."

Faith and courage won. Sage was born four years after Styles, and Ally was born three years after Sage, two beautiful and perfectly healthy girls. These two sweet, loving daughters added immeasurable joy and strength to the Fitch family, and the five moved forward, blessing and balancing one another's lives.

Yet Another Trial

As you assimilate the Fitches' story and empathize with the huge load they were shouldering, the financial aspects of their situation may not burden your mind. For Scott and Teri, the financial challenges were immense and intense. The battles waged in persuading the insurance companies to honor their obligations was only part of the challenge. The costs for the kind of care Styles required were gargantuan, and much of that financial responsibility fell directly upon Scott and Teri.

Understandably, not much would have been more helpful and reassuring to the Fitches than to have a good stable job with significant income to bolster their spirits and help them meet their heavy financial obligations. That highly desirable resource would have been openly and gratefully welcomed. Yet even with Scott working a second job, such was not to be the case.

Scott has a special gift and love for teaching young people. With the bills piling up, Scott willingly made the sacrifice to leave teaching, where the salaries were far too meager to cover the endless stream of medical expenses. He went into industry, and for five years or so, he made much better money—not enough to clear their bills and debts completely, but enough to keep chipping away and make progress each month. The reality of the business world, however, is that markets are in perpetual flux and nothing remains constant except the lack of constancy. Without warning, as part of a company layoff, Scott lost his job. Besides their already more-than-substantial load of concerns, Scott and Teri now faced the added challenge of meeting all the medical obligations and making ends meet on an acutely constricted income. With the much-appreciated assistance of observant friends and family who helped out when and where they could, Teri and Scott persevered.

A few weeks of unemployment became months, and as the months added up, so did the financial pressure. Scott remained unemployed for nine months. It was during this time that the Fitches learned of the dilation of Styles' heart valve and the need for yet another open heart surgery with little chance for success.

How do you maintain your composure under the weight of such Himalayan-sized difficulties? What principles do you apply in order to march onward? To such questions, Teri says, "Sometimes you have to break it down to a day at a time. We tried to keep the big picture in focus. You can plan some things, but you can't plan everything. We realized there were many things that were out of our hands. You just can't let yourself stress out about what you can't control and what you can't know for sure."

To the same question, Scott responds, "For us to get worked up about something, we quickly found out just didn't work. I don't know that we actually thought about this; we just saw that getting upset or distraught about our situation was a waste of energy. It puts you in an emotional state that takes you down wrong paths.

"We never knew if Styles would get better. We never knew when his next surgery would be. We never knew what curves the road would take. So we just kept on. And then we kept on keeping on."

Handling "Why Me"

In the midst of such trying circumstances, one is not a coward or out of place in entertaining the question, "Why me?" or "Why us?" How long we dwell on that question and what results we produce depend on whether or not, at the Owner/Victim intersection, we choose to exercise the one grand key of Ownership.

Teri comments on her experience: "I was probably more the 'why me' person than Scott. He was more 'Why not me?' As for myself, it was frustrating to watch my child go through all that. I kept thinking, 'Why him? What did I do? Did I do something wrong?' I was working in a dentist's office when I was pregnant, and I wondered if I had been exposed to something crazy. There were some times when I wondered if I could have done something different so he wouldn't have had these problems.

"I visited 'why me' off and on, but I got over it. In over 45 surgeries, there were plenty of times to go there. I feel like we've been blessed in our marriage to share our burdens. When one of us was off, the other one was on. It was a good balance. We're not usually ever off at the same time.

"In anything that was hard, there was always a blessing in there somewhere, and I learned to look for it. If anyone ever wants to be humbled or be appreciative of anything they have, they should visit a children's hospital. Somebody always has a heavier bag to carry than you, and you can always look at what you have been given to carry and appreciate it. You sit in the waiting room and think, 'I'm glad I've got my bag and not theirs. I'll just take my bag and keep going.' I'm sure they look at us and think the same thing. Everybody's got their challenges, and Styles was in our family and it all worked. It wasn't too much to take."

"There were a handful of times when I'd be at work," Scott explains, "and I'd lock myself in my office. I had a window in my office door, so I'd shut the light off so people thought I was gone, and I'd just melt. It was never, 'Why me?' I just didn't understand why Styles would have to go through this. He'd get these little perforations or tears in his dura layer that were the size of a pin, and usually those types of small holes or tears heal by themselves, but his wouldn't. So we'd have to chase surgeries. Literally. Sometimes we'd have to go out of state to find the best place for some of his surgeries. Or, sometimes, things *would* heal. It's like Teri said, you can't control it, so you just keep doing the best you can.

"We've learned that things work out. They just work out, if you have the spirit of optimism. It's like when you were a little kid and you listen to the radio for one song when you had a favorite song. Sometimes, it would come on in 10 minutes and sometimes you'd wait all day and never hear it; and then when you heard it, you'd forget about waiting the day before to hear it. You're just happy you're hearing it. It's like that; you just keep going. Something will happen and things will work out."

Determining How You See and Are Seen

Other parts of living "as normal a life as possible" revolved around how they chose to view themselves and interact with others. The Fitches had observed that, in cases somewhat similar to theirs, some people had let *one* facet of their life—often the medical facet—dominate everything else. It was not *part* of that family's life; it became that family's *entire* life.

Scott and Teri did not want that to be so in their case. They felt that would not be in anyone's best interest, including Styles'. So amid all the pressures and trials of their medical saga, Scott and Teri made conscious choices to prevent Styles' medical realities from becoming Styles' persona, or theirs, or to push Sage's and Ally's needs and interests to the sidelines.

Scott put it this way: "We tried to not allow the medical issues to consume us or dominate any more than was absolutely necessary. Fortunately, Styles did his part on his own. We never had that conversation with him; he just did it himself. Teri would say, 'Styles, you need to go the hospital today.' Or, 'We're going to the doctor today.' It was not a big deal with him. It was okay. He never fought it, and Teri never complained that she had to do it or dreaded it. It was just one of the things to get done that day."

Even if the doctors had been able to come up with a name for Styles' syndrome, it wouldn't have made much difference. Scott and Teri chose not to define themselves or their family in terms of Styles' condition. They were committed and determined not to let the medical part of their life become their identity. "Every time we had conversations with people, it was not the topic of our conversation," Scott explains. "When people would ask, 'How are you doing?' we didn't 'go medical' on them. We just talked about our work, our church activity, or what Styles, Sage, and Ally were doing at school, church or whatever.

"How many keys are there on a piano? We all know people who play the same five notes, over and over again. Any time you have a conversation with them, you know you're going to hear one of those five keys. You can plan on it," Scott observed.

Teri adds, "We didn't want to be avoided and not invited to the neighborhood parties," as she laughs. "We'd answer people's questions, if they brought them up, but we didn't prolong the explanations or let it dissolve into a soap opera."

Scott continues, "There were times, obviously, when we would bring it up—times when we needed some help or needed to let somebody be aware of something that might impact them."

"Styles' medical needs changed our life—from where we lived to where we worked," Scott reflects. "It was a major part of our life for 14 years, but it didn't rule or ruin our life. In retrospect, it enriched us—it enriched our marriage and brought us closer. We grew not only as a couple, but as a family and as an extended family unit. It was a unifying thing.

"It changed where we lived; it changed how we did things; it changed our financial situation. It changed everything, but it did not become our life."

Then Scott summarizes it all with this powerful conclusion, "It was a consuming thing that didn't consume us."

Chapter 20

Steve Bodhaine

Steve Bodhaine is one of the brightest minds you are ever likely to meet. His current position, Group President of Yankelovich, directing the Segmentation Company, follows an impressive career path that includes international corporate experience and two successful entrepreneurial endeavors. Most importantly, he is an able and much-respected leader. People in his organization like him and look up to him.

Currently, he and his company are riding a promising wave of success and prosperity that would not be were it not for Steve's Ownership Spirit.

Yankelovich is not a household name to most consumers. You might not know them, but they know you—or, at least, they like to get to know you (and me) and understand our needs and points of view. That is their job; they are respected experts in consumer research. Through sophisticated methods, they are able to identify the needs and preferences of consumers in specific markets. Many of the biggest brand names—companies like PepsiCo, Unilever, and Wal-Mart—come to Yankelovich for data upon which to design their product strategies and marketing campaigns. Those large companies spend thousands of dollars in order to make millions of dollars, a fair investment that benefits us all. As consumers we get products that we need and want, and the companies make profits, providing jobs and adding strength to the economy.

At present, Steve has led Yankelovich to a strong position of influence in helping companies worldwide deal with the challenges of engaging employees and consumers in preventive health behavior. As we all well know, over the past couple of decades, the health care and pharmaceutical categories of our household budgets have soared, and the same holds true for most employers.

Working with several reputable organizations, including the Centers for Disease Control and Columbia University, Steve and his group are developing an employer-based health model that allows employers to introduce elements of individual accountability into the health care equation, benefiting both the employees and the companies they work for. Reduced illness and absenteeism, improved worker productivity, enhanced quality of life, and lower health care costs are among the attractive benefits stemming from this collaborative effort. With so much at stake, and because of the unique research elements that Steve's group adds to the mix, Yankelovich's current revenue stream is flowing very nicely and the future grows brighter by the day.

Getting to this promising position has not been a Sunday stroll by the lake. In fact, Steve has had to exercise his utmost leadership skills to navigate the choppy waters of corporate debate and strong differences of opinion over company vision, direction, and strategy. Put simply, Steve's group and their former parent company have not seen eye-to-eye on several key issues.

"Our company has always been very focused on segmentation research," Steve explains, "and our parent company at the time was trying to convert us into a big database operation." That may not strike you as significant, but this difference of opinion about the vision and direction of the company had far reaching implications. At stake was Yankelovich's hard won and much deserved reputation as a trusted leader in market research.

The Flash of Opportunity

Opportune moments occur without warning or fanfare. Astute leaders with their fingers on the wrist of economic trends often sense the pulse of a golden opportunity before they can fully quantify or "prove" it. At those strategic moments, they make courageous—often unpopular or unsupported—decisions and move vigorously ahead. Such a moment occurred during Steve's watch at the leadership helm of Yankelovich.

"I've always had a passion for health and health care," Steve says, "and a couple of years ago I was invited to a think tank session sponsored by Pfizer. The purpose of the meeting was to talk about the prevention of cardiovascular disease and to gain insight into how consumers in general thought about health issues.

"During the course of that session, there was a behavioral economist from Chicago who noted that if you could just get 5 or 10 percent of the U. S. population to lose 10 pounds, the reduction of health care costs in this country would be in the billions of dollars. The thought suddenly occurred to me, 'I don't need to get everybody in this country to a normal BMI (healthy weight). If I could just get 10 percent of them there, and then get maybe 2 percent more to follow the first 10 percent, the impact would be very significant," Steve recalls.

Suspecting the parent company might not be as excited about this idea as he was, Steve nonetheless decided to act on this flash of inspiration. He started devoting time, thought, and energy to fleshing out the ideas related to taking on this worthwhile issue. With so much at stake, and all the good that could come from it, Steve heightened his creative effort and began conquering the mountain a step at a time.

"I came back and conceived of a program of preventive health and wellness in America. The idea was to go out and identify that first 10 percent. 'Who were the people who were really in charge of their health? How do they think about it? What's their approach? What's their locus of control?'

"Following that line of questioning, we developed a model and an instrument to score that model to a database of 240 million U.S. adults. It became a very effective tool, and as a result of what we were finding, I started to speak to a lot of different leaders in food, retail, pharmaceutical, and insurance companies," Steve says. That research led companies, many of them with an international footprint, to ask questions about the broader, global picture. Steve says, "After I got done with the final road show, the word coming back was, 'Well, this is great for America, but what about the rest of the world?' So I got two large companies to put up some initial funding to handle the field costs, and we did a multinational health and wellness study that involved 22,000 respondents in 17 countries. Through this study, we were able to identify the fundamental mindset that drives or prevents people from engaging more completely in health or health behaviors."

Internal Struggles

Given the value of the results coming from Steve's model, you would think the board would be pleased and would get behind the full-scale development of the health care instrument. However, they were distracted by a desire to emphasize growth in another division of the company. Rather than supporting the new model, they started to impede it.

"Right now, I couldn't be more excited or pleased with where we are, but I'll tell you, about a year earlier I had pretty much had it," Steve explains, referring to this tumultuous time of disagreement between the board and the senior leaders of the Yankelovich team. "The board was still committed to converting us into a database operation, but even at that, they were not willing to invest new funds to fuel that effort. They were sucking all the profits out of our company and putting them elsewhere. I had people who were working like crazy and we could not hire new staff."

The discord in the senior ranks began to take on some rather unpleasant, even somewhat personal, tones. "We sat in some fairly mean-spirited meetings," Steve continues. "At one point, the board made some very threatening comments to one member of the team. That individual decided to leave the organization as a result of that board meeting."

In the midst of the tension, several key Yankelovich employees left the company. One was the team's chief marketing scientist—one of the top people in the country. Another was the person who had founded the custom research part of the company. Other bright, talented people—all solid producers—departed as well. "In a matter of months, I lost research consultants responsible for generating more than $9 million in revenue along with one of the top marketing scientists in the business," Steve states.

Standing at the crossroads of choice, Steve faced an Owner/Victim choice of significant proportions. Every facet of life would be affected—his career, his integrity to his beliefs, his income and financial future, his professional reputation and relationships, and the stability and security of his family. All of that hinged on this one decision.

After seeing some of his key people walk out the door, Steve was sorely tempted to go into the "all-or-nothing" mode of thinking—an indicator, as we have seen, of Victim-like overreaction. "Personally, I had gotten to the point where I was ready to take my health platform and go elsewhere too," he said. But recognizing the presence of the unproductive emotions associated with Victim thinking, Steve took a deep breath. Coaching himself to slow down a bit and think things through calmly and carefully, he gave himself time to entertain ideas outside his emotional states at the time.

"Not long after that," Steve explains, "I felt prompted to read something from a book I have. What I read talked about patience and humility. That helped me to recognize I was getting a little too wrapped up in personal emotions. My ego was getting in the way and I needed to own my attitude and tone down my pride. And I did.

"As I pondered the situation from a more dispassionate point of view, I reminded myself that I couldn't control the board or the decision to support the database platform. But I had a lot to say about what took place in my own part of the business. I wanted to make sure I was developing a business that was 'boutique' enough to compete with giants. I then began to focus on the three principles an organization needs in order to create a value-added proposition for its clients: (1) Functional Expertise, (2) Content Expertise, and (3) Relationships of Trust. As I analyzed our team's capabilities and commitment, I could see our segmentation expertise and health platform fit the criteria extremely well. I knew down deep that the Yankelovich team could stand on its own and succeed under any number of scenarios.

"About two weeks after that, I sat down with the CEO and said, 'Let me put three options on the table for you. Number one, sell me this division of the company; two, sell the company to a bigger firm; or three, opt into the health care strategy that we're doing and make it the main driving force behind the entire organization.'

"Frankly, I had gotten to the point that I was ready to risk my job and put some things in jeopardy for the sake of leading a vision I was truly passionate about. Nothing would be worse than to be in a job that was little more than drudgery," Steve states. "I didn't want to live that way, and I was not about to let someone else dictate my future. So I was willing to draw a line in the sand. I knew we needed to take action. It was in the best interest of all concerned, including the board, if they could see it. It was certainly in Yankelovich's best interest. I had hired many of the people still working there, and I felt a great loyalty to them to see that the company not only survived but continued to grow as a respected leader in market research. It was imperative to all of us that we have a vision that we could put our hearts and souls into. If the board was not going to move in that direction, then I was willing to take the risk of moving on."

Clear, calm thinking had led to insight and conviction. Conviction had led to passion and a courageous proposal. The ball was now in the board's court. Steve sat back, awaiting the board's decision. "I was not sure which way the board would go," Steve says, "but I knew I was in a calm, strong frame of mind when I made my proposal, and I was willing to let the chips fall where they may. So I sat tight and waited."

After due consideration, the board reached their decision. "They made the decision that maybe it was time for them to get out of this business," Steve says. "The board was composed of venture capitalists that had acquired Yankelovich nine or ten years earlier. It wasn't that they didn't like the business, it just was not scalable enough for them. It was never going to produce the market valuation fast enough to please a group of venture capitalists. Essentially, that is why they were trying to migrate out of research and get away from the core heartbeat of the company."

The board's decision to sell the company did not spell the end of the tension. The arduous process of orchestrating a sale was fraught with tenuous moments where various players involved in the sale could have pulled out and almost did a number of times. Once again, Steve's posture of patient, steady leadership helped hold things together. "We were engaged in a nine-month process, much longer than anybody had anticipated," Steve says. "During the sale process there were some tense moments—times when the board wanted to pull out of the deal. Had they done that, they would have forced our hand. There were three of us—the head of all the syndicated research, the executive vice president of sales, and myself—who would have reached the end of our enthusiasm to support the board," Steve says tactfully. "If the board wasn't going to be able to consummate the deal, the three of us would have had no other choice than to resign, and that would not have been good for Yankelovich or its respected 50-year history.

"The lengthy acquisition process was rough," Steve continues, "but we ended up being sold off to a larger, global company. That has put us in an extraordinary place with a company who loves what we do and who fully embraces the direction we are taking. I now have this whole health platform for innovation where I'm developing this employer health and wellness initiative that has enormous potential. As I look back, I can see how crucial it was for me to put my pride on hold. I can hardly begin to name all the benefits that have resulted because of that.

"The other thing that's interesting is that in the midst of this period of transition I developed a strategic plan to create a vertical health practice. Irrespective of what the board decided, I was determined to take this part of the company in that direction. Now, that is the core of our custom research and consulting offer. Rather than being frustrated by the other stuff that was going on, I was able to channel energy in a productive fashion that helped develop an important vital part of what we do today.

"Interestingly, this whole thing has given me a public voice in the larger health care debate. I speak all over the country now on health and wellness and how to engage consumers in health. That is something I did not foresee or expect to have come from this, and that has become an important part of that story too.

"I really believe in the Ownership message. I have seen it work too many times in my own life and in the situations I have witnessed along the path of my career. Ownership and leadership are not exactly synonymous," Steve says, "but they are closely linked.

"*The Ownership Spirit* message is really talking to business leaders, not the businesses. It reaches the business leader as a person. People really don't wear two different hats. Some people try to be one person one place and another person someplace else. The mental strength comes when people are true to themselves and that gives them the ability to pull through very, very difficult circumstances.

"Leadership is not a title; it's the heart and soul within. That's also where Ownership comes in. Leaders have to know their own thoughts and understand the mindset of the people they employ. So much of leadership is navigating through difficult times where tough-mindedness is what gets you through. There's a guy I used to work with who did some work with crisis management. The comment he was fond of making was that in the Chinese language there are two kanji or written characters that make up the symbol for crisis: One means dangerous and one means opportunity. His point was that every crisis represented a dangerous opportunity. I think this current chapter in my career illustrates that point. I also believe that, ironically, the more successful you become in life, the more likely you are to encounter crisis, because you have greater touch points in the market place. Those touch points open up many more opportunities, but you won't see them or take advantage of them unless you take Ownership of what you have been given first. One step leads to another as soon as you are ready for it."

Chapter 21

Tom Sullivan

At times in all of our lives, we make bad decisions. Some of us can veer off into some very rough roads. Such detours and dead ends can be brief, and some can be quite prolonged. The dependent variable as to how long and how rough those roads may be comes back to our willingness to recognize our Owner/Victim choices and to make the choice of Ownership.

People who adopt and cultivate an Ownership Spirit don't live perfect lives; they live *real* lives. They work past the denial and self-deception that typifies Victim living, and they rally enough self-honesty to look the "real me" square in the eye. Those moments, though rarely pleasant, offer significant opportunities for course corrections and *real* change.

It would be nice to say we can arrive at those honest assessments and unrationalized views all on our own. The truth is, however, few of us can do that. Generally, most of us have to be knocked to our knees by some happening or event that almost forces us to look at ourselves directly and honestly. Such moments of truth do not come along every day. When they do, the import of the Owner/Victim choice escalates dramatically. In those moments of crisis, the decision can go either way. Some will still turn away from reality and return to the comfort of displaced responsibility. Yet, others will summon the courage to stare the truth in the face and decide that, finally, the time has come to "get real." Those moments of elevated self-honesty often include admitting they cannot go it alone; outside help is needed. Far from signs of weakness, such admissions amount to pivotal turning-point moments, requiring both bravery and commitment.

Tom Sullivan has lived both sides of that Owner/Victim choice, and he doesn't mind admitting it. That is part of the real life he lives these days. His Ownership encompasses the consequences of his past decisions and fuels his daily, sometimes moment-by-moment, efforts to stay on the path of Ownership, battling the temptation to relapse into the destructive thought patterns that nearly destroyed all he holds dear.

Early Warnings

Tom describes his high school years as the time when he first started rebelling and running with a "wild crowd," and he got into drinking alcohol and the party scene. "There was minor experimentation with drugs," he says, "but not a lot. For a while I even left all of that—the partying and what not. I put that stuff behind me. Those thoughts came back periodically, some temptations, but I never went back to drinking or any drugs."

During this period of time, Tom met and married the love of his life—a woman who has been a rock of support in his life and who "has put up with a lot of my faults." As their children were born, the couple settled into a fairly happy, wholesome life. Tom was part owner in a construction company, and he and his wife enjoyed a good income. The Sullivan's were right in the middle of enjoying the good life, when Tom had an accident at work. "I dislocated my ankle and broke both of the bones in my lower leg. I stared at my left foot; it was turned 90 degrees to the outside and the bones were bulging out. I remember thinking, 'How am I going to be able to work and support my family? I'm in real trouble.' The ambulance was on its way. The pain was awful, and I thought my life was over as I knew it."

After the paramedics put Tom into the ambulance and made sure he was stabilized, they administered morphine. As the morphine entered Tom's body and began to do its work, he remembers thinking, "Everything is going to be all right now." That chemically induced wave of bliss, reassurance, and comfort that spread throughout his entire body was immediate and deeply familiar.

"All I could think about was how great I felt, almost like I was drunk. I felt the effect of something that was totally going to make everything better. I can really pinpoint the moment when something re-awakened within me. Something had been sleeping inside, waiting to be brought back. Whatever it was, it woke up. I don't mean to blame my addiction on the accident or the paramedics; I had a pre-existing problem and didn't know it. The reaction I had to the morphine was symptomatic of a deeper, underlying issue. I would not understand or accept this concept for a long time to come, well into the future. The drug was filling some kind of a void in my life I failed to fill with something good."

Deceptions

Tom underwent a total of five surgeries on his ankle after the accident. The medical procedures were all warranted, but they also provided avenues that Tom began to aggressively exploit.

"From day one, I was manipulating doctors to get more prescriptions for pain killers, and I quickly developed a severe addiction to them. My wife, who is a health professional, tried to watch and monitor the pills carefully. She was always worried about that, and I would always get real angry and tell her I needed them. I would just lie to her. I would tell her that it hurt a lot worse than it really did. I would hide the pills from her and get prescriptions without her knowing. So from early on, she kind of sensed that something was off with me."

As the tentacles of addiction wrapped ever tighter around him, Tom slid further and further away from *Owning* his reality. "When I was in the middle of my active addiction, the denial was really intense. In recent years, I have heard and seen this all-too-familiar denial from others who have gone through, or are in the middle of, active addiction of any kind. For myself, minimizing and shame became just as intense. I found that the quickest way to rid myself from all of these miserable feelings, temporality of course, was to lose myself in the drugs.

"I actually convinced myself that I was a better husband, a better father, a friendlier man, when I was medicated. When I made attempts to quit, I was more intolerant, on edge, and irritable. In the past, when I had a healthier way of life, these emotions would have been signs to tell me that something was not right. My denial had become so thick, that I would rather live with these ugly side effects, so that I could hold tight to my secret life of drugs. I knew that I needed to quit, but I was so afraid of the possible consequences of quitting and exposure. 'If I exposed what was really going on, what would people think? What if my ankle continues to hurt? What if, what if…' All those excuses were prominent in my mind. I was going to take my secrets and lies to the grave.

"I have since learned that, eventually, the pain of the problem will become worse than the pain of the solution. I began to be careless, forgetting what lies I had told, and where I had hid pills. My short-term memory was failing me; I was turning into a liability. Pills were the first thing on my mind when I woke up in the morning and the last thing I thought of when I went to sleep at night. My priorities were completely out of whack.

"My marriage was crumbling. I prided myself on not letting anything bother me. My wife was left to deal with the stresses of life, bills, raising the children, and so forth. In the meantime, I was escaping through medication. At that time, in my mind, I was totally in control, very happy, and managing my life just fine. In reality, I was dropping out of everything. Without fully realizing it, I was on the verge of losing everything important in my life."

It's worth noting an important part of Tom's account. Tom has been able to spring his own traps, to move from Victim to Owner, by learning to think about his thinking. Snares that he unknowingly set for himself in the past are now more evident to him, and he knows what to do with them. That is an indispensable first step, but it's only the first step. He then has to practice acting on that awareness again and again. Tom is an addict, now a recovering one. He has to fight the battle many times every day. He has to constantly remind himself to stay alert and watch for the rationalizations. Then, once he sees them, he has to replace them with higher thoughts and then act upon those.

"Knowing what to look for is a wonderful thing. Through this ordeal, I obtained tools that allow me to recognize and change old behaviors. When I was in my active addiction, I used to con myself into thinking I needed to calm my nerves before I could deal with anything. My first priority was always to feel good first. Now, I realize where that kind of thinking takes me, and I have learned to catch that thought and say, 'Stress is not a bad thing. I can face it.' I have learned

I can actually turn stress into a motivator to help me move forward and solve my problems. So, absolutely, it all comes down to learning to think about, and take charge of, my thoughts and not let them rule over me."

As Tom's addiction progressed, his relationship with his wife deteriorated. She couldn't shake her suspicions that something was not right, and the couple began to be short and critical of each other. At the time, both of them thought the problem was with the other person. "I convinced myself, and a lot of the people around me, that *she* was the problem. I could still convince myself that I did not have a problem—my problem is my wife or the pain in my ankle, that's why I am irritable. My wife doesn't understand me. Why can't she just get off my back?"

Fortunately for Tom, a moment of truth arrived in time.

Tom's little daughter was crawling around on the floor one day and happened upon one of the stashes of pills Tom had hidden. She was just about to eat what could easily have been a lethal dose of a potent pain medication. Tom chokes up as he explains, "It was a 10 milligram Percocet and it could have killed her." At that instant, Tom's wife happened to notice what her daughter was doing. Just before the little girl swallowed it, she dashed over and snatched the pill out of her little girl's mouth. She didn't immediately know exactly what pill it was, but with her medical background, she knew how to find out. She called poison control and they identified what it was.

Tom's wife had the confirmation she needed and a no-holds-barred confrontation with Tom took place. The time had come. Tom had a choice to make—to face reality and do something about it or else refuse to take responsibility and forfeit everything of value in his life as a consequence.

He made the choice. No more deception and denial. "Thank goodness my wife was strong enough to lay that on me. She was going to go and take the kids with her, if I didn't decide to get some help." Tom finally realized how blatant and dangerous all his self-deception had become. "When I could see that my denial had almost killed my daughter, I realized I had not been living in reality. I needed to face the truth, get help, and shape up. The pain of the problem had now surpassed the pain of being exposed."

The Beginning of a Lifelong Journey

Tom entered rehab. He says it was the hardest thing he has ever done. At first, he didn't know whether he really wanted to give up the pills. "I had a love-hate relationship with my addiction. I knew I couldn't have the drugs anymore. I hated what was happening in my life, yet I wasn't sure I could live without them. I couldn't see myself *with* the drugs, and I couldn't see my life without them either. I kept wondering, 'How can I ever live without this stuff?' I would negotiate with myself, making promises that I knew I would break. 'Maybe I can just wean myself off of this stuff… Maybe I can just take less and still function. I don't need rehab. I am not a druggy like all these other people here.'"

By design, in formal inpatient rehab programs, you simply cannot get your hands on the drugs even if you want to return to your addiction. Over time, Tom was able to get enough time and distance between himself and the drugs that he could actually start dealing with his addict thinking. He began seeing different ways to look at himself and the options he had. As the separation lengthened, Tom was able to learn to become more analytical and capable of examining his inner world.

"Until I was in treatment, I never realized there was an underlying issue there—a reason why the drugs worked for me and gave me such a sense of security. There was a void the drugs filled and it was my job to find out what that void was. My way of thinking in itself was extremely unhealthy. I thought the world owed me, that I was entitled to everything. I also thought when I was on drugs I was a better person because I was in a better mood.

"Once my body was detoxed, I learned more about the chemistry of the drugs. I learned what they were doing to my body and how I let my spirituality suffer in the process. I then began to honestly feel good about myself for the first time in a long time. I began to see that I could feel good about myself *without* the drugs, better in fact than with them. Being totally honest about everything felt good, hard but good. This kind of high felt better than what I had felt with the drugs. What felt best of all was being totally honest with my wife. We had to work through some serious issues, but there was a glimpse of hope—the thought, 'Now that I give up and know that I can't do this on my own, I am going to make it! I'm going to make it one day at a time."

Real Life Continues

Tom has been out of rehab for a couple of years now. He and his wife enjoy a good marriage and they are committed to keep working to make it better. Both of them know that the journey never really ends. They continually have to dedicate time and energy to keep building their relationship. The same is true with Tom's relationships with his business partners. His past actions have done damage to the trust and confidence his partners once had in him. Day by day, he rebuilds the trust. There are no quick fixes here either.

Not unexpectedly, Tom has to apply the same determined effort when it comes to managing his thoughts and take Ownership for everything he allows his mind to dwell on. He knows he cannot afford to loiter in self-pity. Neither can he allow himself to indulge in pride. He has to keep alert and aware whenever he starts to revisit all of those old self-destructive patterns.

"What I've developed, and hopefully hung on to since entering into recovery, is to recognize the red flags. It's not like I actually want to go back and pick up the drug again; but, if I start to notice that I'm resenting people and not forgiving them, I know that's my addict (that's what I've labeled him) just trying to wake up again. Every once in awhile, I do have those thoughts. The thought will come, 'It's getting tough right now, and there's one thing I can do to block it all out and feel good in the situation, and that is by popping a pill.' When I have that thought, I get scared to death. I get scared that I even entertained that thought. It's then that I know I have to play it out and go work on myself right then and there. I know I need to go talk to somebody. I need to go say 'sorry' to somebody that I may have offended, or find out what I let get under my skin. Either way, I know I need to deal with the immediate stress in my life or I'll take a turn for the worse. Whereas before I'd think that things would just work themselves out or 'I'll fix this later,' now I know that I have to do something right at the time. I can't just put things off and hope they will go away by themselves. I have to deal with them on a day-to-day basis. I have learned this about myself. I know where procrastination, denial, and self-pity will inevitably lead me.

"In the past, I let stressful moments overwhelm me; maybe I still do to some extent, but I know now it is okay to have stress and high emotions. I also know I can deal with them head on, and I don't need drugs or anything else to mask and numb my emotions. Stress can be, and has been, a motivator for me to rise above, own what is mine, and do what I can when I can. I can place in God's hands what is His to control. This kind of thinking is what has changed my life. By transforming my thinking, I have been able to transform everything else in my life."

Chapter 22

Joan Gustafson

Fourteen-year-old Joan Gustafson had an idol. She had respected and looked up to her uncle, Ralph, for as long as she could remember. One day, while riding in a car to Ralph's office, her mind went back to the time when Ralph was in the Marine Corps. He had written such interesting and wonderful letters home to the family. In them, he had gone out of his way to make Joan feel special.

"Since I wasn't old enough to read his letters at the time, he would take the time to interpret the letters for me by drawing some pictures," Joan said. "I was impressed with Uncle Ralph's letters and became even more impressed when he returned home."

Part of the admiration came from Ralph's courage to break new ground for the family. He was the first person in the clan to earn a college degree, and that degree in mathematics led him to entering a new, groundbreaking field: computer science. To Joan, as to many people who witnessed the unfolding of this new technological age, computers seemed almost mystical in their powers. Anyone who could become a respected computer systems engineer just had to be unique and gifted.

To Joan's utter delight, this day's visit went beyond a typical trip to Ralph's home. Uncle Ralph had actually invited her to spend a day with him *at work*. Each time Joan thought about actually seeing a real computer and spending time with her hero—someone who knew how to program and use one of those marvelous machines—she could hardly contain her excitement.

Sometimes expectations exceed reality but, in this case, they did not. Joan was wowed several times during the day. One of those "wow moments" still stands out in her memory—the moment she walked into a large room, the size of a gymnasium, sufficiently spacious to contain one, single computer. Back in the days of transistors and vacuum tubes, well before the discovery of microchips, computers were gigantic, room-filling monstrosities. Still, though those mammoth instruments had hardly a fraction of one percent of the power of the common laptop today, they were most impressive, and for Joan that singular experience surpassed her expectations.

Amid all her dream-come-true excitement, however, was one disappointment that Joan hadn't expected. This was in the day when the computer field was dominated by males, so all of the computer systems specialists working with Ralph were men. "That disappointed me a little. Nevertheless, I was so fascinated by this computer and all the amazing things that it could do that I made a career decision that day. I was determined to follow in my Uncle Ralph's footsteps and work with computers," Joan said.

If you are picturing Joan's youthful energy and openness, how enthralled she was with the setting, and how excited she was with her decision, you can envision the exuberance with which she shared her decision with her uncle. You can also picture how crestfallen she must have been when his response was far less than enthusiastic.

"When I told Ralph of my decision, I thought he would be excited; however, he looked at me for a moment before saying, 'Well, I suppose a woman could do that; however, you need to know that she would never make as much money as a man.' I really didn't expect (or care at that point) to make as much money as a man. I just wanted to have a career as exciting as that of my uncle."

Humble Beginnings

To understand why an exciting career in computer science was a major stretch for Joan, you need to know her background. Joan's parents were married while still in high school. Joan was their first child, born when her father was 18. Within another year, he was supporting a family of four. The family home in Minnesota consisted of four small rooms—a kitchen, a living room, and two bedrooms—but no bathroom or running water.

"Some of my earliest memories were of my dad shoveling snow to make a path to the well, where my mother would pump water for our daily needs. She would heat some of the water on the stove and then pour it into a metal tub for bathing."

Joan's parents were kind, loving, hard-working people. She views them as her life's greatest role models and appreciates their example and family values they taught her. Though Joan shouldered a lot of responsibility around the house, she enjoyed those years, both at home and at school.

Joan hung on to the aspiration she had made at age 14. As she neared graduation from high school, she still dreamed of becoming a computer engineer. However, at this point in her life, she had not made the critical connection between one's decisions and achieving one's desired destinations.

"I didn't do the things I needed to do in order to reach those goals. One of my high school graduation gifts was an engagement ring. Since I had been dating this boy for about five months and didn't want to hurt his feelings, I agreed to marry him. Shortly after we were married, I learned that my husband was deeply in debt. Because all of his income was needed to pay his past expenses, I had to work full time to support the two of us and could not afford to go to college. Knowing that most computer programming and systems analysis jobs required a college degree, I gave up on my goals."

The marriage ended in divorce.

In her 20s, as the single mother of two children, and their sole support, Joan worked for the state of Minnesota at a fairly low-paying job. Then, at age 27, she obtained an entry level position with 3M. Her future weighed heavily on her mind during those months, and she fretted and worried over her difficult situation and the needs of her children.

"I began worrying about my life, the choices I had made, and my future. As I worried, I became physically ill with various ailments including a serious heart condition and spent most of my 20s in and out of hospitals. Finally when I was 29 years old, my doctor said, 'Joan, there's no way that you'll ever be able to work again. Your heart has gotten worse and will not sustain it. You need to quit your job, stay home, and take care of yourself, or else undergo open heart surgery.' So I quit work, stayed home, and worried even more."

Clearly, one of Joan's concerns was whether or not she would live long enough to raise her children. With so much time on her hands, Joan began to read. Some way or another, a book by William James, father of modern psychology, came into her possession. That book changed her life. One statement in particular struck her: "The greatest discovery of my generation is that human beings can alter their lives by altering their attitudes of mind." She recalls reading that statement to herself several times, and she kept coming back to it. The more that concept pervaded her mind, the more she realized that the quality of her life was largely up to her. If she were to make anything of herself, she would have to take Ownership of her outcomes, her goals, and the course of her life. Most importantly, she came to realize that in order to do all this, she would have to take charge of her mindset.

"As I went over that thought in my mind, I realized I had the power within me to control my life. I made myself a promise: Not only would I alter my attitude, but I would also develop a plan to reach my goals. At that time, I made a firm commitment to get better and make something of my life."

Not surprisingly, as rays of hope and more powerful thoughts dominated her mind, Joan's health took a turn for the better and she began to improve. "A few months later, I went to my doctor for an examination and was shocked. 'I am amazed!' he said. 'I've never seen this happen before. You are well enough to go back to work part time.'"

Joan not only went back to work full time at 3M, she started taking classes at night at a nearby college. Step by step, her outlook and confidence grew as she crept gradually closer toward earning a degree. The more her actions aligned with her self-selected goals, the better she felt. The day she graduated from college with her bachelor's degree was a happy and fulfilling day.

A big part of the joy stemmed from the steady improvement in her self-esteem. Low self-esteem had been the hidden plague of her existence. While she could not recall any devastating experiences that negatively affected her self-perception, it had just been there, dogging her every footstep all those years.

"It had always been there. For as far back as I can remember, I always looked at everybody else as being better than I. I don't know why that was or where it came from. I think my low self-esteem led to a lot of the poor decisions I made back then. It was a big part of my decision to marry my first husband. Neither of us was ready for marriage at such a young age. My self-esteem was so low at the time that I was afraid I wasn't going to be good enough for anybody, and this was the only person that would ever ask me to marry him."

As Joan re-immersed herself in her work at 3M, she made the decision to put even more effort into overcoming her old nemesis. She had recognized that the more she fed her mind uplifting subject matter and the more she acted on goals and milestones, the better she felt about herself. Seeing more clearly how to win the internal war, Joan made an all-out attack on her fears by joining Toastmasters International. Having to stand up and speak in front of people triggered her greatest inner doubts and insecurities. However, by facing her fears deliberately, Joan gained confidence and poise in making effective presentations. This helped her career immensely.

Operating from this stronger platform, Joan began to aspire to management positions and saw that having an MBA was essential and indispensable. When she went back to college, her children were in school. Two nights a week, Joan went to class while the children spent the evenings with Joan's parents. The other nights of the week, the family of three studied together.

Joan says, "I focused on three areas: my children, my work, and my education, and I sacrificed everything else. It seems trivial now, but I gave up watching television. (Still today, I don't watch much.) I curtailed my social life and did not go out with my friends very often." Her behaviors were clearly being driven by her goals.

On the day of her graduation with an MBA degree, Joan looked back over her life with deep gratitude and happiness. She had come such a long, long way from her beginnings. She had learned from her mistakes and taken charge of her journey upward. She had reached her goal of becoming a computer programmer and gone beyond it to become a senior systems analyst. She had earned a bachelor's degree and now a master's degree. She was ascending rapidly in a Fortune 500 company, and she had a happy home life, spending time and staying close to her beloved children. Joan was reaping the just rewards flowing from her application of the most fundamental Ownership concept of all. She had altered her destiny by owning, and altering, her thoughts.

Joan's story would warm Horatio Alger's heart. Hers is truly a rags-to-riches story. During the ensuing years, Joan found "the love of her life" and remarried. She plied her talents in the marketing department at 3M. Her commitment and dedication propelled her upward, and Joan held one responsible position after another. Eventually, her career blossomed beyond her wildest dreams, even taking on international elements. One of her cherished highlights was her selection to lead 3M's marketing and sales productivity and quality effort in Europe for two years. Living in Paris and managing offices in both France and Belgium, she and her husband enjoyed the charms of this high-status, overseas assignment to the fullest. By the time she retired, Joan had risen to hold a position in the top one-half of one percent of the more than 75,000 employees working at 3M.

After retiring from 3M, Joan set her sights on another career. The young woman who suffered so severely from low self-esteem is now a successful professional speaker, business consultant, and author.

"Thus far in my career, I have spoken to almost 4,000 audiences in 10 countries. I have written four books on leadership and success, and I have co-authored five others. In addition to being successful in my career, I'm fortunate to enjoy success in all facets of my life. Seventeen years ago, I met the love of my life, and we have been married for almost 15 years. My husband, Cliff, is the most understanding, supportive, and compatible individual I could have ever dreamed of finding. I have two wonderful children, who are now adults. I did live long enough to see them grow up. My daughter has provided me with four of the most beautiful grandchildren you would ever want to see. I also have close relationships with my parents, my brothers and sisters, and many friends. Reading that quote by William James started me on a path to success *by choice,* and I am extremely grateful that I found that quote so many years ago."

Chapter 23

Becky Douglas

Sometimes you just have to wonder. Sometimes so many disparate pieces, from such diverse origins and disconnected places, come together and coalesce in such amazingly coincidental ways, at such strangely opportune moments, it's hard for even the most jaundiced of us to believe it was all just purely random chance.

How could an all-American family's worst nightmare, an ideal teen's horrific suffering, a charity's bleak plight, many orphans' prayers, callous greed, and a leprosy colony's need to give independence to its members become woven into such an improbably beautiful tapestry? How could all these ingredients blend into a conduit that would literally change the lives of thousands of people on at least two continents? How could all of this be mere happenstantial coincidence? Sometimes you just have to wonder.

How could a mother and housewife, with no formal training, nor business or organizational leadership experience, nor the slightest inclination to start a global movement wind up doing just that? How could a father and husband, who makes a good living but who is far from abundantly wealthy, provide the financial resources to launch that movement and propel it forward? Why would people with no previous involvement in any type of humanitarian effort, and with no intention of disrupting their comfortable lifestyles, be drawn into an all-out heart, soul, and wallet effort to aid a fledgling non-profit venture? Sometimes you just have to wonder.

The way this incredible example of Ownership began was not wonderful. Beautiful, talented, 17-year-old, Amber Douglas was happy, active, and seemingly thrilled with every facet of life. She was faithful in her church activity, conscientious in her studies, involved in numerous talent-expressing activities, and successful in her school studies. She loved drama and acted in many school plays and community theatre performances, often in the lead role.

"She was active in many things," her mother, Becky, relates.

Yet, behind that cheerful facade lurked a sinister foe, a nightmarish opponent bent on desecrating and destroying the perfect life of this vibrant young woman. The first sign of this hidden trouble came in the form of strange, distorted stories Amber told to people outside the family circle, which filtered back to her family. Over time, the stories became more and more bizarre, even grotesque. She told people she had a twin who had died, that her mother had sewn her up in a goat stomach, and that her parents had hung her in the closet and burned her with cigarette butts.

A Diabolical Foe

Neither Becky, nor her husband, John, were naive to the enormous pressures and challenges facing young people as they grow into maturity these days. Together, they were the parents of nine thriving children. John, a successful lawyer and leader in his community and church, had worked with and counseled young people for years. Becky, a petite blonde, who played the violin and had won several beauty pageants, had also taught and worked with teens in various contexts over the years. The Douglases had seen drug abuse, rebellion, depression, and eating disorders. They had reached out and pulled more than one teenager to safety.

Despite their experience, Becky and John were completely caught off guard, taken by surprise and blind-sided by Amber's unfathomable behavior.

"I'd never seen anything like this. It just came out of nowhere, it seems like," Becky says, adding that they soon realized, "It was more serious than we knew how to deal with."

The Douglases took Amber to see a psychiatrist. Three days after that first appointment, Becky discovered something far more disturbing than the strangest of Amber's bizarre stories.

"I remember it as vividly as if it was yesterday. It was summer in Atlanta, so it was hot and Amber was in long sleeves," her mother recalls.

When questioned, Amber said she'd scratched her arms while moving furniture. Becky asked to see her arms and Amber rolled up her sleeves, revealing the frightening truth.

"She had slashed herself about six times," Becky says. "This was long before all the publicity about cutting. I had never in my life heard of such a thing and I was blown away."

Becky immediately called the counselor, but before she got off the phone, Amber had run away. That afternoon, the Douglases were introduced to the horror that would stalk and haunt them for the better part of the decade to come. Amber tried what would be the first in a long series of suicide attempts. She was admitted to the hospital, tests were run, and the diagnosis came back: Amber was bipolar. Severely.

Over the next seven years, Amber was in and out of psychiatric hospitals more than 15 times, and she attempted suicide more than 30 times. All the while the Douglases were doing everything they could to save her from herself and her disease.

Blindness in the System

As sophisticated as we think we are, our society nurtures a medieval mentality when it comes to mental illnesses. This lack of understanding pervades the minds of those of us who have never dealt with such heart-wrenching challenges. The ignorance is also institutional. Most medical insurance companies turn their backs on families like the Douglases. Benefits are denied out-of-hand or are so constricted and limited that they are an affront to the sufferers and a disgrace to humanity.

Like so many other families dealing with severe mental illness, once the insurance's limited medical benefits had been exhausted, the Douglases had to bear the financial burden almost completely on their own shoulders.

"We spent hundreds of thousands of dollars trying to get her healed," Becky says, adding that they also went to nearly that many doctor appointments and voiced nearly that many prayers.

"We tried everything we could think of, but she just kept getting worse and worse and worse."

Doctors warned the Douglases, predicting that Amber would eventually succeed in taking her life. They said Amber was virtually incurable.

At first, Becky and John refused to believe what the doctors were telling them, despite sensing that such discouraging news was not without reasons. Medical tests showed Amber's brain chemistry was appallingly out of whack. For one thing, her brain produced absolutely no dopamine, the neurotransmitter so closely linked with feelings of well-being. Not only was she severely bipolar but her blood-brain barrier was nearly impenetrable, meaning medication that could usually help was largely ineffective, unable to get to her brain.

The disease showed no mercy; Amber grew sicker and sicker right before John and Becky's eyes.

Such a soul-staggering situation triggers merciless mind-games in the heads of those standing helplessly by the side of their loved one.

"I was literally living through hell," Becky says. "The first thing you think when you have a child who is trying to kill herself is, 'Oh, my gosh, I must be terrible. How could I have missed all this? How could I have a child suffering so much and not even know?' Then, 'What have I done that's caused her to be this way?'"

Amber's struggle affected the entire family.

"We have eight other children, and everyone was suffering," Becky says. "They'd come home, and she'd be in a pool of blood from slashing herself. I can't even tell you the number of times we had to call ambulances and have her taken to the hospital to have her stomach pumped over and over again. Every one of our children, in their own way, was trying to deal with a sister who was constantly trying to kill herself."

The pressure on two loving parents seemed relentless. They felt themselves stretched to the limit, trying to give Amber all she needed, while trying to help and nurture her siblings through these traumatic times. Because the family was close, every child felt the impact. One of Amber's brothers shut down, quit participating in class, and sat like a zombie in school, refusing to even take his coat off.

The Darkness and the Light

"It was a time when it was easy to feel abandoned by God," Becky continues. "It was very hard for me to imagine why. We did everything we could. We felt we had given everything; we offered everything on the altar to help Amber become healthy, and we lost. We lost.

"It was a hard battle. It was a battle we kept insisting we were going to win," Becky says, "but we didn't."

Amber died almost eight years after Becky first discovered the slashings on her daughter's arms. Within hours, amazing things ensued.

"Literally, the minute the policeman told us that she was dead, this incredible feeling came over us, a feeling of peace and a feeling of, 'This is okay.'"

That quiet reassurance served to console the Douglases in the days and weeks ahead, when doubt, discouragement, and grief exerted their dark influence.

"There were some really hard moments," Becky says. "Yet, there was a light and darkness to these feelings."

The Douglases worked hard at focusing on the light, and they began sharing that light with others. As Becky was cleaning out Amber's room, she found out that Amber had been sending money to the Belmont Mercy Home, an orphanage serving needy and leprosy-affected children in India. That discovery sparked an idea in Becky's mind. In lieu of flowers for the funeral, the Douglases asked Amber's friends and neighbors to donate money to the orphanage.

Although it just seemed like the "right thing to do" at the time, no one in the Douglas family could have dreamed how right it would turn out to be and what that first donation would ignite.

The first small flicker occurred when the orphanage communicated back to Becky, asking her to join their board. Within a year, Becky Douglas made her first trip to India to visit the orphanage.

Face to Face with India

There are at least two ways to visit India. There is the insolated, touristy way, where you stay in five-star hotels, visit the ritzy tourist sites, dine in sanitary restaurants, and only occasionally, almost by accident, get a glimpse of the fabled poverty of India's population. Then, there is the raw, unedited way—where you go for the specific reason of witnessing and confronting the stark realities of the impoverished masses in "high-def." This latter way was Becky's introduction to India and to a new perspective for her life, though she did not know it at the time.

Her first hours were unnerving and unsettling. She was not escorted to the posh refuges. Instead, she was thrust right into the middle of the orphanage's desperate reality. In the leprosy colonies, Becky encountered horribly disfigured, diseased, and dying people—sights far beyond her capacity to absorb. Becky hardly slept a wink that first night. Images of these pathetic people—with rotting flesh, missing fingers, blind from the disease that had earned them the label, "untouchable"—plagued her mind. It was not the ghastly appearance of these leprous human beings that distressed her nearly as much as her inability to *treat* them as human beings. Her revulsion had overridden her sympathy, and that reaction bothered her deeply. Becky says she remembers praying that night, "'I'm just a housewife. Tell me what I should do.' The thought came to me: 'You can at least look at them. You can at least acknowledge that they're suffering.' And, the next day, I did."

As Becky opened herself up to the people, she came to learn some rather interesting things—things that seemed to be a step or two beyond mere coincidence.

From the caretaker at the orphanage, Becky learned that at almost the very hour of Amber's death, the Belmont Mercy Home was facing a daunting, seemingly irresolvable crisis. The little orphanage had been doing fine until a day or two before Amber died, when the landlord found out that the orphanage was being funded from sources in America. Deciding that this was his ticket to riches, this greedy landlord promptly informed the caretaker that he would turn off the water and shut off the electricity unless he was paid a large sum of money. His extortion request was rejected. However, the handwriting was on the wall. The people in America who funded the orphanage ordered the caretaker to vacate the building.

The caretaker told the Douglases, "The day before Amber died, we took those children out of the orphanage. We had no place to go but our own small house. We did not have enough room in the house for all of the children. Some of them had to sleep in the dirt around our house."

Becky says, "When Amber died, thousands of dollars came in to help them. God knew that this would be this little home's—these children's—great hour of need." For Becky, it was "like a love pat from heaven" to feel that "God was in on all of this. In a way I couldn't fathom, He allowed Amber to come home at a time He could make some good out of it." That good has since multiplied many times over.

The Scope of Needs

The first trip to India was truly life altering for Becky. She and John were awakened to the two-fold plight of leprosy-affected families. Obvious are the needs of those who actually have the disease. There are also the desperate needs of those who are highly susceptible to the disease but who have not yet developed symptoms—the babies and young children of those affected. Though it is one of the oldest diseases afflicting mankind, the exact cause of leprosy is still not certain. Many factors are involved—genetics, weak links in the immune system (which can also have familial tendencies), and malnutrition all play a role. For those with these predisposing factors, prolonged exposure to the bacterium seems to be a deciding link.

For this reason, some feel it is vital that children of leprosy victims be separated from their parents and removed from the colonies. It's not hard to grasp what a heart-rending decision this is for loving parents afflicted with this cruel disease. Understandably, many parents in the colonies choose to keep their families intact. Others want to have their children placed in a situation that will provide them more opportunity and safety. The desires of this latter group of families has led to the establishment of boarding schools. Though sounding well-intentioned, some of those schools fall deplorably short of offering the children a safe, supportive environment.

"Our decision to provide boarding schools for the children relates to our commitment to help break the destructive cycles, both of leprosy and of begging," Becky explains.

The dire needs of these families struck deep chords within the Douglases and they threw their energies into working both sides of this pathetic equation. At first the sheer scale of the needs seemed too overwhelming for them to tackle alone. "We worked with various charities for about a year, and they were really doing fine, but there were just so many people we saw in the streets in India that it drove us crazy," Becky relates.

Equal to the disturbing images of leprous people that had haunted Becky her first night in India, was the realization that some of the charities the Douglases sponsored were pocketing the money and were actually starving the children—or beating them. As a result, the Douglases, and four of their friends decided to take Ownership of the situation and do something. Surrounding John and Becky's kitchen table, this small group of owners conceived the idea of starting their own charity, now called Rising Star Outreach.

"We opened our first little children's home with 30 kids, and we were terrified that we were going to fall flat on our faces," Becky says. "That was three years ago. Today, we have homes for 200 children and are building as fast as we can and will soon have homes for nearly 400. The school also draws from the surrounding villages. This is on purpose. We mix the village children fifty-fifty with the leprosy-affected children to help eliminate the stigma faced by the leprosy-affected ones. So far, this approach is proving to be effective.

"The school will eventually serve nearly 800 children," Becky continues. "In addition, we provide funding for more than 200 leprosy-affected children to attend nearby government schools, whose families want the children to remain with them. So, all together, we will be helping nearly 1,000 children."

In addition to establishing homes and providing educational opportunities for the children whose parents have leprosy, the fledgling organization knew something needed to be done to help the many thousands of leprosy victims who, traditionally, have survived through the only means available to them—begging.

"It didn't take us long to figure out that if we fed them today, we had to feed them tomorrow. There were just too many of them and we could only help just a very few. We kind of learned from stumbling our way along that what we were doing really wasn't working very well. The longer we're in India, the more we're learning."

Providing Victims Means of Ownership

One of the brilliant revelations that came to the Douglases has yet to dawn on many governments and well-meaning charities. Ownership is not only a principle, it is a great human *need*. Human beings *need* the dignity and self-esteem that flow from individual independence, industry, and self-reliance. The Douglases saw that handing out hand-outs, no matter how well intentioned, is not enough. The members of the colonies needed more than fish or even the instruction on how to fish. They also needed a few fishhooks.

"As long as you give things, you make them beggars to you," observes Becky. "You do it because you get a rush, and you feel magnanimous, but you haven't helped the human being.

"If I gave $20 to a woman on the street who was begging at my car, that money would be used for food, probably for some drink. Within a few weeks, or months at the most, that money would be gone. However, when you give a woman $20 to create a little business, you change her life. Her life is different. It's not the amount; it's how it's given. It can be given in such a way that the person remains a beggar, or it can be given in such a way that it empowers the individual and their life is never the same. They aren't dependent on you anymore."

For this reason, Rising Star Outreach works with those in the leprosy colonies to gain independence by helping them create small businesses, allowing them to become self-sufficient. They do this through a partnership with Padma Venkataraman, daughter of India's former president and a well-known activist for the poor. Amazingly small microloans of between $10 and $200 (US) provide sufficient capital to get people started on economic enterprises of their own.

"Three years ago, we were taking rice and beans to two colonies once a month. Now, we work with 45 colonies. We have 4,000 loans out. Through our micro-lending efforts, whole families are being blessed. At this point, the numbers of individual lives affected is somewhere between 10,000 and 20,000. Not all are leprosy-affected; a lot of them were tsunami-affected," Becky explains.

Ownership turns attention outwardly, leading us to consider the needs and interests of others, as well as our own. Victim thinking turns attention inwardly, leading us to disregard the needs and interests of others and focus only on our own. One act of Ownership generally begets another, and the converse is equally true. One act of Victimhood generally begets another. Like seeds, each reproduces after its kind.

"What we've been able to do in three years is way beyond what we imagined we'd be doing, and it's way beyond what we're smart enough to be doing. We're not smart enough to have done this ourselves … this organization has grown and grown and it keeps on growing."

Amazing stories abound on both side of the equation. Stories of what some of the colonists have done with their opportunities are extremely heartwarming. Equally intriguing are the stories of people who have been drawn to the "supply side" of Rising Star.

Becky does a lot of public speaking. She relates, "This particular man came up after one of my sessions. 'I want to be on your board of directors,' he said. Now, I'm always looking for more people to join my board of directors, but I do make sure they know what they're getting into. They don't get paid. My average board member spent $35,000 this year, out of pocket, to cover expenses. This man gulped, and he said, 'Well, whatever. Let me tell you what just happened to me. I'm a developer in Idaho and I came down here to this conference, but I'm overseeing a big project and I really needed to get back to Idaho today. So I was on I-15, speeding toward home when I got this message from the Spirit: 'Turn around and go back.' I've learned to listen, to recognize that voice and to respond to it. So, kind of grumbling, I turned around and came back, and I was directed to your class. So, whatever it is you're doing, I have to be a part of this.' That man is now a Rising Star Outreach board member.

"To me, that was a miracle," Becky states. "It's not that I was smart enough to figure out how to make that happen or know what to say that might touch that man. It was just something God did. Things like that seem to happen every day."

Tough-Minded Ownership in Action

Becky Douglas expresses strong perspectives of how human efforts coupled with strong states of mind produce remarkable results. "That's just how God works," she declares. "He just says, 'You do what I need you to do for my children, and I'll make it happen for you. You just show that you're willing, and I'll enable you to do what I need you to do. I'll bring the world to you.' It's pretty cool," she adds. "And, I really believe that it works for anyone who will trust and move forward.

"There are all kinds of stories of people who had leprosy and, for all practical purposes, their lives were over. Then they took positive steps and now feel like real human beings again," she continues. One man, who lost both of his arms to leprosy, created a new life for himself with the aid of a microloan. Starting with one teapot and two cups, he turned those resources into a successful business. His main customer is a shop where the owner used to drive him away from the front door. Another man was able to buy two tools with a microloan of less than $20 and start a carpentry business. Others garden, raise livestock, or provide services that allow them to rise out of poverty and live in dignity.

"My story is not the only story out there," Becky says. "There are tons of people who have faced a great tragedy in their lives and have turned it into a blessing, God can take even the most horrible thing and use it in phenomenal ways," she observes.

As an example, she points out children at Rising Star Outreach schools are able to attend *because* they are leprosy-affected, and they are actually enjoying benefits that non-leprosy-affected families envy. Becky explains, "We're teaching computers and English and all the things that give these children a chance to rise above poverty. My executive director said to me, 'Don't you think it's interesting that what was once these people's greatest trial in life, being from a leprosy family, now has become their greatest advantage? Now they're going to rise above all these other thousands of people in these villages and have opportunities the others can only dream about *because* they came from a leprosy-affected family.'"

As the resources of Rising Star Outreach permit and space is available, children from non-leprosy-affected families in the surrounding area are brought into the school as well.* The Douglases do all they can, but none of it is easy. Each day is a battle, and that battle is part of a war.

---

*For more information, including ways you can help Rising Star Outreach, please visit www.RisingStarOutreach.org.

Lest any of us should get the mistaken idea that Ownership is a button you push one time and everything works out happily ever after, Becky Douglas will tell you that Ownership is something you must rekindle every day and hang on to, so you can find ways to keep going, no matter how tough it gets.

"I can tell you thousands of stories about why I should have given up in India," she states candidly. "There's not a day that goes by when I don't think, 'That does it; I've had it. I'm not doing it anymore. India can just go to hell.' But, you just can't give up. When you set a course, you just trust in God and keep going, no matter what happens.

"I've had my life threatened in India. People have threatened to kill my children in India. People we trusted have stolen thousands of dollars from us, and my husband has had to put money back into the pot so we could keep going. It's not all the sweet things and heart-warming successes that I put into my 45-minute presentations," Becky admits.

"Right now, our backs are up against the wall. We either get a special license from the government in the next two months, or we shut down. It's not looking great," she observes. "It seems like we go constantly from one crisis to another. There have been a million times when I felt like quitting. I've lost one of my best friends in the whole world over India."

That Choice Again

In times of tragedy and adversity our sensitivities are heightened and our perspectives are sharpened. How we choose to experience those tragedies and adversities, and what we choose to do with our heightened sensitivity and sharpened perspectives, comes down again to another Owner/Victim choice, one with expansively far-reaching consequences.

"For me, losing Amber is what it took. It took going through that experience for me to see the suffering that was out there in the world," Becky says. "I'm not sure if I'd been to India before Amber died, if I would have reacted in any other way other than repulsion, but once you've been hurt, you think, 'I know what it's like to hurt; I can't let this go.'"

The Douglases are Ownership personified and magnified. They could have taken the loss of their daughter and turned inward. Instead, they converted their grief into empathy, and acting upon that empathy, they have witnessed and been the catalyst in miracle after miracle after miracle.

So, how could an all-American family's worst nightmare, an ideal teen's horrific suffering, a charity's bleak plight, many orphans' prayers, and a leprosy colony's need to give independence to its members, become woven into such an improbably beautiful tapestry? How could all those ingredients blend into a conduit of good that would literally change the lives of thousands of people on at least two continents? Sometimes you just have to wonder. Sometimes you just have to sit back *in* wonder—complete, awe-filled wonder.

Chapter 24

Carrie Nielsen

Growing up on a farm in a large family builds work ethic, and Carrie Nielsen grew up on a farm in a large family. The fourth of seven children, she says, "I was right in the middle of the litter, and I learned to be a hard worker from my dad."

Being "in the middle" was not only her familial birth position but it was also the way her life started, symbolic of what lay ahead. Carrie apparently was ready and eager to take on the tests right from the outset. As her mother began to experience the first steady contractions signaling the onset of labor, Carrie's father rushed to the fields to change the dams that had been set to allow water to pour into the farm's irrigation system and onto the furrowed land. The water had been on through the night and the ground was already well irrigated. Another five or six hours would have been too much; the farm would have been utterly flooded.

After hurriedly resetting the dams and siphoning tubes, her father headed back to the house to drive his very pregnant wife to the hospital, some 20 miles from the farm. In his hurry, he somehow managed to get his old truck stuck in the newly irrigated field, and he burned several precious minutes trying to extract the truck from the mire. Unable to free the truck, he abandoned it and ran home on foot. By then, full-scale labor was underway and Carrie's mother was frantic, knowing the birth was imminent.

Carrie's father managed to get his wife into the family car. Then, despite the emergency, Carrie's father, ever the conscientious, law-abiding citizen, dutifully stopped at each red light on the way to the hospital. When they finally arrived, the father quickly got the attention of a couple of nurses, and they got Carrie's mother onto a stretcher, and rushed her toward the delivery room. He parked the car a couple of spaces from the hospital's front door and ran inside. As he stepped through the door, he could hear a baby crying, and one of the nurses said, "Congratulations, sir, you have a daughter."

So that was how Carrie arrived. Born in the middle of the hospital, halfway from the front door to the delivery room, being "in the middle" has not changed over the years. She finds herself there now.

Typical of the era in which she grew up, the "men folk" worked in the fields and the "women folk" did the household chores. Carrie did her share and then some. Her mother, undiagnosed with a bipolar condition for years, was often unable to perform and do her part, especially when she was in one of the down phases. So Carrie and her older sister would pick up the slack.

Overall, Carrie describes her childhood and youth as happy. In high school, she was a straight-A student at a small public high school and participated in several extracurricular activities, like pep club. At graduation, she was awarded college scholarships based on two significant qualifications. One, her academic record. Two, her disability: She is blind in one eye.

Carrie was born with a condition called amblyopia, where the brain does not interpret signals coming from the amblyopic eye, resulting in blindness. Often, this condition affects both eyes, but Carrie says, "I see fairly well out of my right eye, except my depth perception is poor. I don't like to drive at night, and when I am going down narrow streets, I have a hard time judging how close I am to things. When I was growing up, my dad helped me with that. As I drove, he would let me know how close I was to things, and so I learned to get a feel for that and got along fairly well."

The scholarships were a godsend. Had it not been for the financial assistance, Carrie would likely not have been able to graduate from college, obtain a teaching certification, and prepare herself to be self-sustaining in the years ahead. She was grateful for the opportunity to become independent, and she applied her work ethic vigorously to her education, graduating from college in just over three years at age 21.

"Because I was dependent on the scholarships and the little work I could do on my own, my philosophy was 'get in and get out.' Even with the scholarships, I was just barely getting by and surviving, and I wanted to get beyond that point. I wanted to be self-sufficient."

Carrie accepted a teaching position in a newly opened elementary school and enjoyed teaching fourth grade, mentored by two kindly veteran teachers. After teaching for three years, Carrie met a man with a similar background. He, too, had grown up on a farm and continued to make his living working with his father and brothers on a family operation where they shared expenses and income. He was attentive while dating, and Carrie accepted his marriage proposal and moved to a new state, into a singlewide trailer that the groom's family provided for the new couple's home.

The adjustment period did not go well. Carrie wanted to establish her teaching credentials in her new state and teach part time. Her husband wanted her to stay at home. After taking a position as a substitute teacher, Carrie contracted mononucleosis, which eventuated into hepatitis. During her illness, more tension developed between her and her husband as she became pregnant and bore their first child.

More misunderstanding and even greater distance developed when the couple's second child, Cindy, was born. Shortly after her birth, it became apparent that Cindy had serious problems. Sickly and developmentally delayed, she did not progress. She could not hold up her head as an infant, and Carrie says, "It took her forever to crawl."

Cindy was eventually diagnosed with Megalocornea—mental retardation syndrome, otherwise known as Neuhauser syndrome. The medical help Cindy needed was both far away and expensive. As the medical bills mounted, so did the family turmoil, involving discontent from the extended family. Carrie and her husband were living entirely on his farming income, which was established by his parents. They were given what her in-laws thought was enough to live on without consideration of the added medical expenses.

Carrie was once more in the middle. Caught between the bills and the allotted income, she decided to go back to teaching to help meet the expenses. "I guess you could say my Ownership Spirit was too strong to not do everything I could in this situation. I just did not feel right about going on welfare when I had a teaching degree," she said. That was only part of the crunch. The doctors had determined that Cindy's problems were genetic in origin, and they advised Carrie and her husband against having more children. Carrie's husband earnestly wanted a son, and for him adoption was not an acceptable option. Stating he "could never love another man's child," he was adamant that they try again.

Looking back, she said, "I probably should have left right then. But, I felt vulnerable and scared, and I didn't know what to do. After four years, I finally gave in. 'Okay I'll have one more child,' she said, 'Let's just hope and pray that he is a normal, healthy boy.'"

About a year later, the couple's worst fears were realized. Carrie gave birth to a son with another genetic syndrome, commonly known as Down syndrome. They named him Michael.

The couple now faced a second heavy responsibility, one that Carrie accepted and intended to shoulder as honorably as possible. As she sought to provide the best support and care possible for her two youngest children, her in-laws continually questioned the need for all the testing and evaluation which was viewed as fruitless and a waste of time and money. The chasm that developed between her and her spouse widened under the constant in-law scrutiny and disapproval.

For Carrie, it became unbearable when the doctors informed the family that Michael needed open heart surgery to correct a hole in the ventricular wall of the heart. Response from her husband's side of the family was prompt: "Children with Down syndrome don't have a full life expectancy. The boy would never be normal and may not live all that long anyway. Why waste money and prolong the inevitable?"

"I was just beside myself," Carrie said. "I couldn't understand that thinking."

This was the final straw as far as Carrie was concerned. Taking Ownership of the future and summoning a good deal of courage, she filed for divorce and moved herself and her three children to a new state. There she obtained a teaching position, which she still holds today. She has supported herself and her family on her teacher's income. The children have grown up. Michael is almost out of his teens and still lives at home with Carrie. Her oldest daughter is married, and Cindy lives a fairly independent life on her own. She has a job and lives in a group home with other young adults who have similar disabilities. Carrie is close to all of her children. Her daughters live nearby and she sees them regularly and speaks with them daily on the phone.

Carrie does not have a man in her life right now. She has lived all these years with that vacancy in her heart but not by preference. She is attractive and personable, and there are men who have initially shown interest. "But when they find out that I have two special needs children," she says, "they think there is something wrong with me, and they draw away."

Just about everywhere Carrie goes, Michael goes too. "I have never tried to hide my children. They are the loves of my life. I have seen people who are uncomfortable around them, and I am not trying to impose on them or make them feel uncomfortable. But that is not going to stop me from being who I am or my children from being who they are. I want my children to know other people and learn to respect other people."

Her life has not been easy in the past, and it is still not. She has a busy life—a very full load of responsibilities. She arises early to get Michael to his special needs school then gets to her school and puts in a full day of teaching there. Picking up Michael immediately after school, she heads home to prepare supper, help him with his home-work, correct papers, and prepare for the next day of school work. She does all of this with little complaint or self-pity. Added to this sched-ule lately, she now fits in frequent visits to her father's care facility, where she shoulders more than her share of the load for his care and disposition.

Carrie's brothers and sisters are loving and supportive, but with the exception of one brother, they all live out of state. While they do what they can, most of the "heavy lifting" falls on Carrie's shoulders, who lives the closest. Her brother who lives about an hour away is a physician; he does all his schedule allows and takes over most of the medical decisions for his father's care. That leaves Carrie to be her father's mainstay and principal source of cheer and support. "I really don't mind being in the middle on this one," she says, "My father has been my best friend throughout my life. He has always been there for me—loving me and supporting me. This is my chance to show my thanks."

Carrie says, "Life is not easy. Expect the unexpected; and when it takes unexpected twists, do the best you can. I don't see myself as anything other than ordinary. I have just been handed a plate full of situations, and I have just tried to deal with it. I think the majority of other people given my same situations, would do the same things I am doing.

"I have seen exceptions. I have seen a few women in a situation somewhat similar to mine abandon their children. At one time, it bothered me. I'd see young women sleeping around and getting pregnant and they were having normal, healthy babies. I would think, 'How is this fair?' I have come to a conclusion. I know I am not perfect. I know I make mistakes, but I think I am more capable of providing for my children—especially the two that have special needs—a more normal, productive and satisfying life than some of those other women who may not have some of the standards, values, and support of extended family I have.

"I also need to say that I have not done it all on my own. My father has been a wonderful support—always there to love and do whatever he could to help. Prayer has always helped me make it through the challenges. Whenever I really needed something, help seemed to show up at the right time. Many times God has answered my prayers through other people."

From her experiences, Carrie has learned not to complain too much or be overly fearful. "Things always have a way of working out. It's much better to put a smile on your face and move ahead.

"There are challenges other people get that I wouldn't want to deal with. When the feeling comes over me to feel sorry for myself, I know it's time to get over to the children's hospital. I used to take Michael there for tests once in a while. You see *severe* cases there. It has taken a lot of therapy and a lot of patience, but both of my special needs children are functional. They can communicate. Both of them are ambulatory and they both have fun personalities. Other people don't have any of that.

"We've all heard we won't be given more challenges than we can handle, but there have been times when I've said, 'Oh, come on! I'm way past that point.' Yet no matter what happens, I keep making it through. And, I can truthfully say that the situations with my children have led me to be a better human being, less selfish, more sensitive to other people's feelings, and more sensitive to their circumstances. I just think it's made me a better person, but it hasn't been easy."

Chapter 25

Jeff and Katy Johnson

Jeff and Katy Johnson thought they had life down pat. On every front, from their financial life to their home life, the Johnsons were winning the battle. They had even prided themselves on being able to quickly quell and quiet any skirmishes that had the audacity of flaring up to threaten their near-perfect journey through life.

Their highest priority was clearly their family. Rearing their much-loved offspring never took a backseat to any other consideration. It was God and family first in each and every case. Anyone and everyone who knew the Johnsons would, without hesitation, have labeled them as "the model family," "what we'd like our family to be like," or "the Cleavers of the 21st century." They were on Emotional Easy Street, their family life cruising along on automatic pilot.

Jeff and Katy met in high school. Having lived in the same town all their lives, their backgrounds were nearly identical. Both had been raised in strong, Christian, God-fearing homes, where church attendance was the norm and where prayer and scripture reading were common practices. Their experience had taught them that "family problems" consisted of nothing more than nursing minor illnesses, arranging schedules, and planning menus that would satisfy Uncle Harry's sweet tooth without upsetting Aunt Bertha's diabetes. Most of all, they were accustomed to families in which children grew up adopting and replicating the beliefs and patterns of their parents, just as they had done.

Katy and Jeff established the same practices and traditions in their home right from the day they were married. In time, their family grew to five happy, healthy children, and their life plan seemed to be working perfectly.

"We figured we had everything down," says Jeff. "We were very in sync as far as how to raise the children. We both had strong, similar opinions. We disciplined the same way and were pretty much united on everything all the way through."

Under Jeff and Katy's loving leadership and tireless support, the Johnson children prospered. They developed strong social, academic, musical, athletic and leadership skills. Jeff and Katy devoted their time and energy to their children's endeavors. When Jeff wasn't coaching the ball teams his kids played on, he was one of the avid spectators, cheering them on to do their best. He was the Scoutmaster taking them on camping trips, the youth leader taking them on special activities. He was totally involved in their hobbies and interests. Katy was the same way, the typical soccer mom, running the children to all the sports practices, games, and events; chauffeuring them to all the music and dance lessons, and coordinating all the homework, school projects, and science fairs.

"We've been to hundreds of games and concerts," Jeff says. "We've had a fantastic family life with our kids. It's just been amazing," he continues. "Both of us were convinced that the way we had raised them was right on target, and everything was done exactly the way it was supposed to have been done. We were convinced of that—in every way."

Katy laughs, "We were probably arrogant parents."

"We were. There is no question about it," Jeff admits. "We were pretty proud of the way everything was going. When we saw people who had struggles with their children, we knew why. They had dropped the ball somewhere and not done what Katy and I had done."

Katy and Jeff had every reason to be proud. Their children's accolades just kept piling up. The Johnson children garnered awards and recognition in everything they did. At the top of their classes in every category, they either won full-ride scholarships for academics, or leadership, or athletics. They were socially confident and popular, elected to student body offices in both high school and college. Perfection personified.

"We were positive we had it all figured out," Katy says.

Positive that is, until they got slapped in the face with the cold hand of adversity.

"We got hit by a train," Katy says.

"We got hit by a *couple* of trains," Jeff adds.

Those trains came forcefully and fast, hitting them in a series of bone-jolting, foundation-shaking, dream-shattering revelations crammed into an uncomfortably tight sequence of events.

"We both had lived our lives with the belief that as long as you do everything you're supposed to, everything would go pretty smooth," Katy says.

Yet, without any polite warning, they were suddenly confronted with the fact that one of their sons was into drugs. He was the one they had thought was the easiest to raise, a boy they felt was cruising right down the outlined track.

There had been no telltale signs, no change in behavior, no disrespect, no failing grades, nothing.

"We had no idea," Katy says. "He was a good actor."

With the wind momentarily knocked out of them by such devastating news, Jeff and Katy quickly turned to their patented, "we can fix this in no time" position. Yet, before long, they were brought to realize there weren't going to be any quick fixes. Their initial efforts to get their son back on track proved futile. As their son opened up to them more and more, they learned how deep seated his divergence from the family path really was. It was more than drugs. Fundamentally, he flatly did not believe what his parents believed or had taught him. He held diametrically different views about drugs, morals, religion, and premarital sex. In one of those discussions, their son informed Katy and Jeff that he would be leaving on a trip with his girlfriend and her family. He also made it clear that he hadn't been, and was not planning on, living by the family's moral code.

"We were taken aback, and we kind of put our feet down and drew a line in the sand. But he went anyway," Jeff says. "That was really kind of a turning point."

Amid dealing with all the turmoil, emotions, and second-guessing associated with train number one, almost simultaneously along came train number two.

The Johnsons' college-age daughter, an excellent student, a student body officer, a young woman "thriving at college and loving it," had moved across the country to California to complete an internship. Her conscientious conduct, ever level-headed and responsible, suggested she was ready for life totally on her own, and Jeff and Katy had nary a qualm about her decision-making. Then the second train hit, and it rocked Jeff and Katy's world.

"We were being completely misled, being fed a story that was false on all fronts," Jeff says. A friend of their daughter's exposed the lie. The truth was that this much-trusted daughter also was into drugs and was making other unwise, short-sighted, self-harming, even markedly self-destructive choices.

Still reeling from the jolting revelations from their son, Katy and Jeff were now faced with similar, but even larger, issues with one of their daughters. A bit battered, but still battling, the Johnsons reached out to their daughter. Without telling her she was coming, Katy flew out to see her daughter.

"She couldn't believe that I was there and that I could see what was going on in her life," Katy says, "but she was relieved to finally have us know. It had been 18 months or so that she had been living this lie."

Their daughter was not ready to change her ways, but she was relieved and thankful to accept some parental assistance. Katy didn't issue any ultimatums or insist that her daughter come home. Instead, she helped her daughter find an apartment and moved her out of the unsavory and dangerous situation in which she was living.

By the time Katy returned home, things had deteriorated even more with their troubled son. Jeff and Katy held clear standards about what was and what wasn't acceptable conduct under the roof of their home. When their son blatantly refused to abide by those standards, no pleasant alternatives remained.

Jeff explains, "We reached a point where we couldn't allow him to stay."

"Jeff took him to a hotel and came home. It was probably the hardest night of our lives," Katy solemnly states.

"That's probably one of the most unnatural things a parent can ever do: kick a kid out of the house. It goes completely against the laws of nature and parental love—to ban your kids from your house," Jeff says.

Within 10 days, their son was back home, but two weeks later he left again, this time to take a job in another state. Two weeks after that, he called his parents with the news: His girlfriend was pregnant.

"It was akin to having a death in the family," Jeff says. "The reason it was that traumatic is because, as parents, from the time even before we were married, our whole goal was to raise a family according to the high standards we had grown up with. All those dreams, all you had carved out for them, goes away when something like this happens, and you know it will never be the same."

The painful pressure did not relent at this point; it accelerated. Just a few weeks later, Katy and Jeff learned their daughter had slid deeper into the drug scene, had gotten into heavy cocaine use, and her life was hanging in the balance. Their oldest son drove to his sister's apartment, packed up her belongings, and drove her across country and delivered her home to her parents.

"She went into a rehab center right away," Katy explains. From that point it was, "two steps forward and one back for another year" as her destructive behavior continued. "We went through it all with her, doing everything we could think of to help and support her. But, there's only so much you can do."

While all of this was happening, Jeff's business was also about to be slammed by yet another train, just at the time that financial resources were so acutely needed. One of Jeff's main suppliers went bankrupt and, as a result, Jeff's entire inventory was frozen. On top of that, a lawsuit, which had nothing directly to do with Jeff's business, crippled sales for an extended period of time.

With financial troubles accentuating the pathos of their situation, and at times wondering what was coming next, Katy and Jeff did their best to focus on what mattered most—what they could do for their children.

"We were always talking about it and about what we were going to do," Jeff recalls. "As you rack your brain for answers, it's easy to wind up with a hopeless feeling, because there are no answers. No quick ways to fix it," Jeff says. "We couldn't have a meal together without obsessing."

They talked about finances, about why Katy's daily workouts with her daughter didn't seem to make a difference, and how they were going to handle a wedding between their son and his obviously pregnant fiancée.

"We really did get sad," Katy says, remembering that there was a time when she asked Jeff, "Are we ever going to be happy again?" After a pause, Jeff said, "I don't know."

At one of Katy's low points, a friend told her, "I hate to tell you this: You're going to go to a dark place. But you get to decide when you're going to come out."

"I did," Katy says. "I went to a dark place where I was depressed. I was sad, and I felt hopeless. I think that's a dark place."

At that point, Jeff and Katy made a choice.

"We figured it had been about 18 months. We decided that was long enough. We made the conscious choice to be happy again," Jeff says. "It finally became clear to us we didn't have control over our children's choices. We had to let go. Ultimately, it was all in the Savior's hands and we turned it over. We didn't have to fix anything. All we had to do was love our kids and include them."

By choosing to let go of the sadness and the obsession with trying to get back on the perfect road they had once envisioned, the Johnsons learned some powerful lessons.

"If I was to help or counsel other parents, I'd say, you have got to allow your kids to be who they are. You have to let them make their choices and not take it personal if they make choices that will cause them pain and more problems in the future. They have to learn. That's the toughest part of being a parent," observes Jeff.

Jeff and Katy have learned to be at peace with the truth that, "The road is very different from the map."

"We're realizing that just because it's not exactly the way it should be, it's still going to be okay," Katy says.

Jeff continues, "The whole thing has taught us so much. When we came out of our funk, we realized, 'You know, we're probably not through.' There could be something around the corner that could shake us up again. If it does, we will take it. The one thing we've learned, above all, is that we can be shaken pretty hard and our faith will see us through."

Today, Jeff and Katy look at the road ahead very differently.

"There is a certain level of confidence you gain; I'm not as afraid of adversity as I once was. I could lose it all and still say, 'You know what, there's still time.' We could have another one of our kids go through some extreme challenges and we know it wouldn't crush us. The Lord can help us work it out. There's a level of hope and confidence that goes along with severe trials that, I think, for us, is empowering," Jeff says, and he adds, "We have more character in our lives. More depth, more substance."

Katy, too, has come to recognize the gifts that "Ownership amid adversity" leaves behind. "I am so much less judgmental of others now because no one knows the circumstances behind someone else's actions or inactions. I also think I have a lot more empathy for what they're going through in their lives. I'm a different person now. Looking back, I wonder, 'Why did we get so sad? Why did we take it so personally? Why did we feel such despair?'

"I never thought I'd ever admit this. But if five years ago I'd had a crystal ball and I'd known what we were going to be going through, and could see then what the outcome was going to be, I wouldn't hesitate. I'd choose me now over how I was before," Katy says. "I am just so grateful."

Chapter 26

Edie and The Amish

Heroic examples of Ownership in Action are always preceded by heroic decisions, made by people who hardly ever think of themselves as being extraordinary or heroic. Yet, heroic and exemplary they are. Having endured cruel treatment and heinous abuse, they could have almost reflexively chosen to foment anger and bitterness, inciting themselves to hold onto and perpetuate their animosity whenever they felt it weaken or wane. But, instead, they used the One Grand Key of Ownership to ignore their initial impulse to hate and chose to completely and unreservedly forgive.

Some of them made that choice immediately and some made it later. At whatever point the choice was made, they accrued a priceless result—they transcended the circumstances and gained freedom and peace.

Edith Eva Eger

Dr. Edith Eva Eger is a Ph.D. If anyone ever deserved that credential, she certainly did. Not only has she graduated from an accredited institution of higher learning, but she has graduated "summa cum laude" from the University of Life.

"Edie," as she is known to her friends, grew up in Kassa, Hungary. Beginning at age four, she devoted herself to gymnastics and the art of ballet. Even though ominous developments unfolded across Europe during her childhood, she had no idea how directly they would impact her life. The omens turned into gruesome reality at age 16. In May 1944,

Edie was "arrested" along with her family and deported to the ill-famed Nazi concentration camp, Auschwitz. There she was separated from her mother by none other than the notorious "Angel of Death" himself, Dr. Josef Mengele. "He pointed my mom to the left, and I followed my mom. He looked me in the eye and said, 'You're going to see your mother very soon; she is just going to take a shower.' Then he promptly threw me to the other side, which meant life."

Edie never saw her mother again. Her mother, along with most of her family members, were put to death in Auschwitz, but Mengele decided to keep Edie alive for a while because she was an accomplished ballerina. Part of her ordeal in Auschwitz involved ballet "performances" for this sadistic SS physician and his cronies. To that was added all the brutality, inhumanity, and horrors of the Holocaust, which Edie, along with thousands of others, endured.

As the Nazi grip on Europe crumbled in the winter of 1944–45, the Nazis mounted a vain attempt to hide their atrocities. They forced their sick and starving prisoners to slog through the snow to concentration camps located farther from the front, inside Germany. Edie was one of those prisoners who was forced to march through the winter, finally arriving at another death camp in Gunzkirchen, Germany. By the end of the infamous Death March, she was an emaciated, walking skeleton, clinging to life.

Edie's physical survival itself was something of a miracle. When the American forces reached Gunzkirchen, she was found unconscious, with a broken back, carelessly discarded among a pile of corpses—alive, but barely so. Appearing lifeless herself, she lay within the grisly heap of dead bodies, weighing a scant and ghastly 40 pounds. Only a reflexive twitch of her hand, noticed by one of the GIs, prevented her from being buried alive, along with this group of desecrated corpses.

Over a period of weeks, Edie recovered physically. She regained her strength and returned to a healthy body weight. Her emotional recovery took more time. That journey required her to enter some deep valleys of introspective Ownership in order to climb to the pinnacles of personal liberation and the freedom she enjoys today. Her experience holds lessons for us all.

For many years, Edie suppressed her hatred for the Nazis and her guilt about living while so many others had died. "I was a guilty survivor for 40 years. I didn't tell my story until I returned to Auschwitz and I forgave myself for surviving. I suffered a tremendous amount of survivor's guilt and survivor's shame. For most of my life, if you had asked me about the Holocaust, I would have said, 'What Holocaust?' It was like it happened to someone else. I ran from my past for many, many, many years."

Something inside must have been leading Edie forward toward health and healing. As she thought about what to do with her life, she made the decision to pursue a career in clinical psychology and counseling. Earning her doctorate in psychology from the University of Texas, she has become one of the most respected and effective counselors in the United States.

"My husband became a CPA, and I became a shrink. Instead of a shrink, I call myself a stretch," Edie says with an impish tone in her voice. "I stretch people's possibilities. I like to be a stretch and help people reach for more freedom and happiness in their lives." And, truly she does. Both through her speaking engagements and her work as a therapist, Edie has touched the lives of thousands of people.

"What makes me effective I did not learn in my psychology program. Everything I know I learned from Auschwitz," Edie explains. "I can't erase the experience, but I can integrate it and come to terms with it."

"Coming to terms" and "integrating life's experiences" into healthy, personally empowering energy has a lot to do with shifting perspective from victim to owner. "I'd like to tell you about my journey from victimization," Edie says to her audiences, "and how I was able to recognize that victims do not heal. Yesterday, I may have been a victim, but today I am more than a survivor. I can thrive! I can truly celebrate life! I am *for* something rather than *against*.

"The 'Ps'—paranoia and paralysis—are dangerous. Begin moving from the 'Ps' to the 'As.' Give yourself the kind of attention, the affection, the approval that you need. The healing journey is not going to ever truly take place without the choice to open up inside. There is no healing without feeling. In our society, we do everything to avoid feeling the feelings."

Edie goes even deeper, pointing out that one of the pitfalls of playing the victim is the penchant for self-justification. "We may get addicted to being right. Then, when I'm right, of course, you're wrong. When I'm good, you're bad," she continues. That train of thought leads to grudge-building and more enmity, "I'll be angry long enough for you to apologize for what you did to me," she reasons.

Edie could have remained a closet victim for her entire life, but it is never too late to make a major breakthrough. No matter how far down the road we may have walked, we can always turn around, and put ourselves on a higher plane and live a better life.

"I lost my family in Auschwitz, and I never went to a funeral," she states, as she tries to help people see that closure is an internal choice, not an outward event. It's a decision we make so we can free ourselves from the pain of the past and move on. Edie urges her listeners to forgive those who have wronged them, no matter how unjustifiable those wrongs may be. She points out that forgiveness is the most self-loving, self-healing thing we can do for ourselves. "I emphasize closure and conflict resolution from the inside," she says. "Make peace with the past. Release the feelings. Learn to live again. Today."

The power of Edie's teachings comes from the certainty of personal experience. By looking within and taking responsibility for her thoughts about the Holocaust, she came to realize her freedom depended upon overcoming her perspectives about the past. Then, she took it one triumphant step further. She made the choice to forgive some people who did not deserve to be forgiven. She realized that in the final analysis it was not about *them*; it was about her. *She* was the one hanging onto the poisons of the past, the one suffering the consequences of her pent up emotions. She didn't have to wait until they "got what was coming to them" or until they came and threw themselves at her feet begging forgiveness. She realized *she alone* was the one who held the key to her emotional freedom, and the day and hour had come for her to turn that key and liberate herself.

"To overcome my experience in Auschwitz, I had to learn to become compassionate and forgiving. You must be strong to forgive. Forgiveness is not condoning or excusing. Forgiveness has nothing to do with justice. Forgiving is a personal act of liberation to free yourself from being controlled by your past.

"I lost my family in Auschwitz. It was very traumatic. But I have integrated the experience, and I'm the person I am today because of it."

In the end, it does not matter all that much *how long* it takes for us to arrive at these inner states of strength and peace born of Ownership. Like a mother in childbirth, whether her labor is long or relatively brief, the pain is largely forgotten when the baby issues forth and a new life enters the world. The joy and rejoicing in this new life swallows up the travail that precedes it.

Similarly, Edie's painful journey has cultivated deep understanding and profound empathy. From that depth springs a fountain of insight for those she speaks to and counsels. While her breakthrough took some time, it gave her added compassionate patience with those who seek her help. No matter what any client may have to share about abuse and mistreatment, due to her own odyssey, Edie can truthfully say, "I understand." When someone talks about how hard it is to face the past and deal with it, Edie can say, "I get it." When a client says, "I'm not sure I even *want* to forgive," Edie can say, "I know what you mean. It is not easy, but I have done it. Trust me, it's worth it."

The Example of the Amish

To the sterling example of Edith Eger, I add another, hoping that it will not be viewed as "better than" or "superior to" the one just recounted. I simply submit it as a second witness, another beacon casting light on the incomparable value and power of owning our thoughts and interpretations of the past, which is the key to emotional serenity. Ownership begets new perspectives, and new perspectives beget new actions (such as forgiveness). New actions such as forgiveness beget peace. Victim thinking foments and perpetuates grudges, and grudges prolong anguish and animosity, and anguish and animosity poison our bodies and our lives—unnecessarily. We are capable of either hatred or forgiveness. Only we can decide the "if" and the "when" for both sides of the coin. We decide if our hatred will be "immediate, right now, and forever" or "never in a million years." Just as surely, we decide if our forgiveness will be "never in a million years" or "immediate, right now, and everlasting."

I still remember the stomach-churning, sickening feeling that came over me as I heard the radio news broadcast announcing the senseless violence wreaked upon a peaceful Amish community in

Nickel Mines, Pennsylvania. Most of us know something about this group of peace-loving people who eschew the avaricious, frenetic ways of our materialistic world so firmly they decline the benefits of electricity. Personally, everything I know about them leads to admiration. I admire their industry, their ingenuity, and how staunchly they live their convictions.

To me, it was unthinkable that anyone could do what was being reported. Could it be true that a man who had lived in their midst had committed such unspeakable violence against these unassuming Amish families? Apparently so. This man who had been living and raising his own family side by side with the Amish, for no explicable reason, invaded an Amish school, tied up 10 young school girls, shot five of them to death, and critically wounded the other five. After this heart-wrenching massacre, he turned the gun on himself and took his own life.

Sitting in my car, hundreds of miles away from the scene, I was shocked, saddened, sickened, and appalled. My heart went out to the families of those girls and the entire Amish community that had been so unjustly violated. I also need to admit I did not entertain, even for a second, one glimmer of concern or compassion for the gunman, his wife, children, or extended family. It never entered my mind. Such was not the case for the Amish families involved.

As the shock waves crashed over them, the Amish were understandably catapulted into paroxysms of grief and suffering. Can anyone possibly fathom the pain and anguish that must have torn through the hearts of those parents and families as the horrors of those monstrous murders went through their minds? All of them would have every right to burst out in justifiable fury, hatred, and outrage at the gunman and anyone remotely associated with him.

Although they were wounded beyond measure, and at the height of their overflowing grief and pain, these heroic families exercised their ability to expand their attention far enough to realize they were not the only victims of this crime and not the only ones suffering. Virtually on the spot, and without hesitation, they reached out in sincere gestures of compassion and sympathy to those who were possibly even more shocked, and certainly more mortified, than they—the gunman's family. Collectively, and as individuals, the Amish rose above the understandable "natural reactions." Immediately and genuinely, they forgave.

A delegation of Amish leaders promptly visited the gunman's family and extended condolences and forgiveness. Individuals and families did the same. Nearly half of the people paying respects at the gunman's funeral were from the Amish community. As money poured in from around the country to defray burial costs, the Amish families shared that money with the gunman's widow and children. Through their example, I saw something I now esteem even more than "grace under pressure," and that is "grace under pain."

Newspaper reporters covering the tragedy were at first skeptical and then dumbfounded. They heard no strident, vengeful voices making demands, pronouncing epithets, or hurling threats, as might be expected. No tones of hatred or animosity of any kind were expressed, not even from families of the murdered schoolgirls. The Amish mourned, but they did not have to couple it with vengeance, and that hastened the healing on both sides. A community that could have been permanently riven was, instead, brought closer together.

A public statement issued by the gunman's family says it all:

> To our Amish friends, neighbors, and local community: Our family wants each of you to know that we are overwhelmed by the forgiveness, grace, and mercy that you've extended to us. Your love for our family has helped to provide the healing we so desperately need. The prayers, flowers, cards, and gifts you've given have touched our hearts in a way no words can describe. Your compassion has reached beyond our family, beyond our community, and is changing our world, and for this we sincerely thank you.
>
> Please know that our hearts have been broken by all that has happened. We are filled with sorrow for all of our Amish neighbors whom we have loved and continue to love. We know that there are many hard days ahead for all the families who lost loved ones, and so we will continue to put our hope and trust in the God of all comfort, as we seek to rebuild our lives.

Accustomed as we are in this cynical society to witness vindictiveness and retaliation, it is hard for us to believe such a scenario actually could be genuine. "That just doesn't happen" would be the expected response. Nevertheless, it did.

Norms and tendencies are not mandatory behaviors. The examples cited in this chapter illustrate again that humans are thinking beings, wielding independently the power to choose responses. Courageous responses to outrageous acts may not happen every day. Nevertheless, they could.

Chapter 27

Jorge Hernandez

"Picture yourself sitting down to a poker game where you are dealt five cards," says Jorge Hernandez. "You look at your hand, and you don't like it at all, and you say to the dealer, 'I don't like this hand.' The dealer says, 'Well, if you don't want to play that hand, you can fold.' So, you say, 'Okay, I'll fold,' and you're dealt another hand and you try again. Life is not like that. In life, you have to play the hand you are dealt, and that's all there is to it."

A biomedical engineer by love and by profession, Jorge Hernandez has been dealt a difficult hand, and he has played it admirably. He works for a great company that makes medical devices that save lives and relieve pain. Saving lives and helping people live pain-free means a lot to him because Jorge himself has lived with a lot of pain and dealt with many challenges.

Jorge's challenges began almost the moment he came into the world. Born in stark poverty in a small city in Mexico to two loving, but hopelessly indigent, parents, Jorge came to know deprivation's disadvantages up close and personally. Daily survival, in the most literal sense, was frank reality for the seven Hernandez children. It wasn't that his parents were lazy. Far from it. His father worked long hours in a factory, barely earning minimum wage. Try as he might, Jorge's father was never able to raise his family above baseline destitution.

"My mother was a hard worker too. She learned to provide for herself as a young woman. Her father was a priest who could never own or acknowledge his children due to church rules. After her mother died, my mother, being the first born, had to assume responsibility for supporting herself and her siblings." Conditions did not change much after she married Jorge's father and began having children. Year in and year out, the family struggled to survive.

In Jorge's small city, amenities for the children were sparse, but they made the most of what they had—like the frequent arrival of the train from Mexico City. As it approached the city, it would slow down into a curve, shift into reverse, and back into the train station. Many times, some of the children, including Jorge, would wait excitedly for the train at the curve in the tracks. As the train slowed down, they would run alongside, grab the catwalk of a cargo car, and get a short free ride. "When I was a boy, I had many fun rides on that train," he says.

One day, at age 10, Jorge made his usual attempt to jump aboard the train, but that time, something went drastically wrong. He fell under the train; his left arm was severed and his left leg was severely crushed. Nearby medical aid was sufficient to save his life, but due to the onset of gangrene the leg had to be amputated. At the time, one of the doctors involved made the inconsiderate comment, "This boy will not amount to more than a beggar."

Jorge suffered intense pain for days following the amputations. Three months later, he returned to school, worked hard, and caught up quickly, finishing the year second in his class.

A few months after the accident, Jorge was fitted with two crude prosthetic limbs (World War I vintage) made out of aluminum. They were rough and ill-fitting, nothing like today's prosthetic technology. "Oh, the blisters, gouges, and cuts those things would make on my poor tender stumps," he winces. Despite the shortcomings of his new limbs, Jorge didn't spend any time feeling sorry for himself; he made use of what he had. "Since those aluminum members were the best I could get at the time, I worked with them, developed some calluses, and moved forward," Jorge explains.

"I thank my family for never treating me in any special way or granting me any privileges because of my condition," Jorge recalls. "I was just one of the children, and that furthered my attitude of self-reliance essential to my success." Encouraged by his mother, Jorge made a firm promise to her and to himself to get a good education, rise above the poverty that had shackled his family, and make something of his life. After graduating from high school, Jorge left home at age 17 to go to college in Mexico City. "In my mind, there was never any question about my going to college," he recalls.

In those days, there were no jobs for struggling students, but Jorge's superior grades earned him scholarships from the Mexican government. The money was meager, but once again, Jorge made it work somehow. Pinching every peso, he found a place to live, and he paid for his food, transportation, and occasionally some of the books he needed. While attending college, Jorge was able to obtain a new prosthetic leg. Unlike his first one, this limb was state-of-the-art technology, at least for Mexico at the time. "It took me awhile, but I did it. My new leg worked and fit so much better. I felt like a new person. A functional prosthetic arm was never really a necessity, so I just used a cosmetic one."

Jorge studied hard and made the most of his academic opportunity, appreciating it for what it was: the doorway to the better life of his dreams. Honing his mental skills, he earned a bachelor's degree in electronic engineering, a master's degree in electrical engineering, and became a professor of electrical engineering in Monterrey, Mexico, at one of Mexico's most prestigious universities.

Although it was not easy, as far as academics went, things fell into place for Jorge. Other parts of his life were not as straightforward. A cruel reality of life is that often those who deserve some compassionate consideration are instead subjected to ridicule and derision. Jorge was no exception. He endured a difficult adolescence, and the challenges continued on into his teen years. Socially, Jorge was often rejected by girls simply because of his condition. Taking Ownership of his self-esteem, he refused to let Victim thinking take precedence. He resolutely pressed forward with optimism and courage, found the right woman, married her, and started his family. He also moved from academia to applying his intelligence and engineering skills in the electronics industry.

By the time Jorge and his wife had added two children to their family, they had moved to Tijuana where Jorge worked for a subsidiary of a large American electronics company. When that operation was closed, his future was once again uncertain and tenuous. The responsibilities of providing for his family weighed heavily as he asked himself, "Where do I go from here? How do I provide for my family now?"

"I had a friend that worked for another American company, and I contacted him to see if there might be a career opportunity at that plant in Agua Prieta, a border town in Sonora, Mexico." It turned out that a position was available. Jorge was hired and sent to Chandler, Arizona, for training. "At that time I could not speak English—only a little bit. I could understand somewhat and I could read English, but I could not speak well at all," Jorge explains.

One night, alone in the company apartment in Tempe, Jorge was troubled. He was happy for the job and relieved he could provide for his wife and children, but he was anything but thrilled about moving them and living in Agua Prieta. "I was hired to work in Agua Prieta, which to me at the time was not a place where I wanted to raise my children. I really did not want to move my family there. So, I injected my faith in God and hoped for something better to work out.

"I asked God for help, 'I don't want to go work in Agua Prieta,' I said. 'I want to be here in the United States. If you want me to be here, please do what is necessary for me to move here with my family.'

"My prayer was answered. It turned out that the company needed an engineer that could speak both English and Spanish. Again, my English was not very good at all, but I applied for the position and my prayer was answered. The company sponsored me to get a working visa, and I worked in Arizona while my family stayed in Mexico for about nine months. Then I was able to bring my family to the United States to live, and we have been here ever since."

At first, Jorge was in a little over his head in terms of his language skills, but he applied himself diligently to gaining fluency in English as quickly as he possibly could. "I remember attending meetings at a facility in the Phoenix area. There were six people around the table and I was trying to translate what was being said. Before long, the conversation was already two or three guys ahead of me, so I got lost.

"Little by little, by listening and reading a lot, and *just practicing,* I got better and better with the English language. I never took any formal courses; I just did a lot of reading. In time, I developed a good command of the language—spelling and everything."

Jorge Hernandez has learned that the familiar Ownership adage, "where there's a will, there's a way" holds true as long as it truly is a will, not just a whim. Jorge began in poverty, suffered a horribly debilitating injury, worked while he studied very hard in order to get an advanced education, persisted through periods of discouragement, taught himself English, worked his way up through the ranks of business, and became a naturalized citizen the United States can be genuinely proud of.

Today, Jorge Hernandez enjoys a successful career as an electronics engineer. He has been awarded 29 patents in the United States and worldwide. He lives the good life—a life resulting from his courage, self-reliance, and hard work. Jorge enjoys a great income, a beautiful home, nice cars, and a family. Most importantly, Jorge has a high level of self-respect and personal satisfaction. He's had to overcome a lot of obstacles, but that has made his eventual victory all the more sweet.

"I have a family and a wonderful wife who has supported me throughout our married life. I am not rich by a lot of people's standards," Jorge says, "but I have financial independence and a life beyond anything I could have dreamed of as a boy."

Jorge continues, "What I can say is this: If one can only stop and think 'All right, what happened to me—however and for whatever reason—it happened. So, this is it. This is the hand I have to play. Now what do I do?' And, that's the key!—to say, 'What do I do?' Rather than 'What can my family do? What can my bosses do? What can other people do for me? What can the government do for me?' All it takes is a little trying. Small successes will come at first. Then just keep trying and trying a little more. Then one day you will look around and say, 'Oh my, look where I am.'"

Jorge didn't let the *lack* of resources stop him. Having no money, two missing limbs, no job, and no language skills did not intimidate him. He just forged ahead believing he could make things work out somehow. "I knew it was up to me. Nobody could do it for me. I was not about to turn around or quit. For me, there was only one thing to do: go forward. One way or another, I had to make it work.

"I had dreams of becoming an engineer and, yes, there were many, many obstacles to my dream. That's okay. It's really a matter of deciding that it is mostly up to the individual—what one wants to do and what one wants out of life. Ask yourself, 'What do I want? If I have to make sacrifices, if I have to give up entertainment, if I have to give up time spent on this or that, so what? I will invest my time on bettering myself.' When you say, 'I will invest in more education and more skills,' there is always a pay back. I am proof of that. I just kept studying and working. Little by little, I made it. Now I have financial freedom. I am still working, but I have everything I want."

Jorge expresses his faith and optimism this way: "The same omnipotent Love and Providence that brought me to this point will see me through the rest of my life. If you respond to life's challenges with enthusiasm, with faith, and with optimism, you can make it. You can do it," he says.

"One more thing," he adds. "Don't allow that voice that says, 'Poor me, poor me' to be too loud. You can do *anything* you want. Anything worth doing takes effort, but *if I can do it, anybody can do it.*"

Chapter 28

Randy Finley

The maxim, "You will never be given more than you can handle," evokes diverse responses depending on the thinking mode we are in at the moment. When we are in an Owner mode, we can leverage this thought to urge ourselves forward. When we are in Victim mode, we may resort to muttering sardonic expletives under our breath. Whenever this thought passes through my mind, I think of Randy and Jill Finley, and I step back in awe and admiration. During the course of my life, I have not met any two people who have faced more trial and done it with more gentle grace, patience and fortitude than they.

The Finleys had been living in California for a few years. Randy was president and COO of a manufacturing firm and had built the business up, markedly increasing its revenues and profitability during his tenure. In addition to fulfilling all of the daily responsibilities of running the company—streamlining systems, reducing costs, and improving the processes—Randy also had taken on another significant responsibility: He had been charged with preparing the company for sale.

The CEO and principal stockholder was getting to an age where retirement beckoned. This man, known for his hard-fisted (most would say *ruthless*) business practices, was actively pushing to market and sell the business, intending to reap a handsome return on his capital and leadership investment. At times, when people learned he worked for this man, Randy was asked, "How can you work for him? He's a barracuda." Trusting and loyal, Randy's answer was always, "We have established a good working relationship, the company is prospering, and I love my work."

For two intense years, Randy worked long hours to make the company look and be as attractive as possible so it could be sold to some investment banking groups. Under Randy's leadership, everything came together and qualified buyers showed up. For his services, Randy received a good salary and an ample compensation package that included health and life insurance for as long as he worked for the company, along with a 401k plan. The compensation for his additional efforts in preparing the company for sale and the due diligence associated with each potential buyer was to be a substantial amount of stock in the new company—something amounting to millions of dollars. Recognizing Randy's value to the company, each of the investment banking companies made Randy's portion of the deal a mandatory part of the negotiation. Although the CEO was basically echoing what the investors were requesting, on more than one occasion, he assured Randy he would share in the growth of the company and the proceeds of any sale. Nothing was ever put in writing. Randy simply went forward, trusting and toiling.

Several legitimate investment groups stepped up and made sizeable offers. Each offer led to hours of additional meetings, negotiation, due diligence, and the extra rigors the company had to perform for these negotiations (all under Randy's leadership). In the end, no offer was ever good enough for the CEO. Solid, reasonable—in some cases, more than reasonable—offers couldn't satisfy the greed and arrogance of this man, a 21st-century blend of Gordon Gekko and Ebenezer Scrooge. No deal was ever consummated. Since Randy's promise of stock was based on the sale, the CEO had no legal obligation to honor any promises, and he didn't.

During this demanding time period, Randy and Jill were also dealing with additional challenges on the personal side. Their oldest daughter, a young married mother of one, had been diagnosed with non-Hodgkin's lymphoma. With the complications that scenario portended, Randy and Jill decided to move out of California to be nearby to lend help, support, baby-sitting, and whatever else might be required to assist their daughter and son-in-law battle the cancer.

The move added to everybody's load in the Finley family. On Randy's part, he now commuted to Southern California on Mondays, returning home on the weekends to be with the family. The travel and associated stresses did not seem like an onerous added burden for Randy, but he did notice a decline in his energy and resilience. This he simply shrugged off as expected consequences of the increased travel and demands of his work.

Coughing Up Blood

At the height of all of this, Randy was preparing to return home from California at the end of another week. Randy recalls, "As I was leaving work on that Friday night, I felt like I was getting the flu. I just felt terrible. I thought, 'I've got to get up tomorrow morning and catch this flight.' I took some over-the-counter medicine, got up that Saturday morning, managed to get dressed, and took a cab down to the airport. By that time, I was just feeling miserable. Then I started getting a deep cough in my chest. Again, I thought it was just some sort of flu I was coming down with.

"I just got sicker and sicker on the plane. By the time we touched down, I was about as sick as I had ever felt in my life. I could hardly walk from the plane to baggage claim. I had to stand on the moving sidewalk and the escalator. I couldn't even walk down the stairs. I was gasping for breath, and that is when I realized something was seriously wrong.

"I got to the curb and Jill was waiting for me there. I got into the car and I said, 'Honey, I am just feeling really sick.' As we left the airport, I started coughing a little harder. Then I started coughing up blood. Bright orange blood.

"At that point, we both knew I was in trouble. We sped to the nearest hospital and got to the emergency room. They were so good to me; they got me right in. I continued to cough up this bright orange blood and there was a lot of it. Handfuls of this blood. I was so scared; I didn't know what to think.

"The first thing that went through my mind was, 'I'm a dead man. I'm going to go right now. I haven't had a chance to talk to my family. I haven't seen my kids for a week.'

"They got me into the ICU, put in a drip and started pumping me full of drugs, and managed to get me stabilized. The first day I was pretty out of it. I wasn't really unconscious, but I was not really with it either. I remember being aware of what the doctors were saying, but they didn't know that I was overhearing. After looking at my chart and x-rays, one doctor said to another, 'And he's still alive?' Again, I thought, 'This is it. I'm going to die.'"

The next day, Randy was transferred to a renowned university hospital and more tests were run. A few days later, the team of doctors arrived at a diagnosis: Wegener's granulomatosis, a rare vascular disease that attacks the blood vessels serving the kidneys and lungs. The inflammation causes the body to produce an unhealthy, tumor-like tissue called granuloma. The granulomas proceed to destroy and supplant normal tissue. Early diagnosis and treatment often leads to full recovery. If not, Wegener's granulomatosis is fatal.

This revelation assembled some puzzle pieces Randy had not recognized for what they were. He had had a deep and persistent cough, off and on, for several years. When it would appear, it would linger for several weeks. He had always brushed it aside as just a bad cold or bronchitis. Over the same period of time "blood blisters" had appeared on his fingertips from time to time and then would go away. Being so focused on all his other concerns and responsibilities, none of these symptoms sounded any alarms. He just dismissed them and went on with life. With the pieces now coming together and making sense, Randy realized he had had the disease for at least five years, and he knew what that meant. He was certainly not in the early stages of his disease, where a hope for a cure was possible. His prognosis was guarded at best, and the best he could hope for was a period of remission.

What about the Family?

Immediately, Randy's thoughts turned to his family. His concerns need little elaboration, "What is going to happen with my livelihood? What if I'm not able to work? If I am ever able to go back to work, how long will that last? How long do I have?" Jill and Randy were right in the throes of rearing their family. They had had eight children and had been challenged by more than the sheer numbers alone. Their first-born child, a boy, was stillborn. He had been a very active fetus right up until the last few days before the due date. At that point, Jill noticed the ominous absence of activity within her uterus. She was immediately checked out by her physician (her father), and the heartbreaking realization the baby had died was a tragic and bitter moment for all.

"There was nothing Daddy could have done," Jill says. "It wasn't anybody's fault, but he took it hard—harder than Randy and I."

The vacancy left by the death of their first child was filled as Jill and Randy gratefully and happily welcomed seven more children into their family. At the time of Randy's diagnosis, only Sarah, the oldest, was married and out on her own. The next two children, both sons, were in college and expenses associated with that rested firmly on Randy's shoulders, and there were the four other children still at home to care and provide for as well.

If you are beginning to sense how daunting these hours were for Randy and his stalwart wife—the kind of gut-wrenching pressures they both were under—there is one more rather significant part of the picture you need to know and empathize with before we continue. The fourth of the seven living children, Jordan, is a special needs individual. Severely disabled from birth, Jordan is non-verbal and functions on the level of a two-year-old. Due to his low level of functioning (he finally became potty trained at age 15), and because he was 21 at the time of this writing and not many programs exist for adults with special needs, there are not many options for Jordan, or for Randy, or Jill. Jordan lives at home and all of his needs and care rest on the family. Doctors say Jordan is likely to have a fairly normal lifespan. He may well outlive his parents. In all probability, Randy and Jill will care for Jordan emotionally, physically, and financially for the rest of their lives. They will do this in the same manner they have from the day he was born, with love and patience and joy.

It is this next part that sets Randy and Jill apart from most of the rest of us. Not one of their family, closest friends, neighbors, or associates have ever—not even once—heard a complaint or even detected a heavy sigh from these two amazing people. Regardless of their challenges, they accept each new wallop with grace, unpretentious fortitude, and good humor. There seems to be no end to their love and patience. They have demonstrated the quiet calmness that comes from taking Ownership, rather than railing at the world. Those virtues seem to grow with each rock in the landslide of adversities that crashes over them.

I know people who have children with varying degrees of disability. One of those people describes his partially disabled child as "a heavy child." Describing the relief that comes over him when that child goes to bed, the father remarks, "It's like a great weight is lifted off my back when he falls asleep, and the heaviness of life eases." This statement is not made in rancor or with any tone of resentment, just in unguarded honesty. Yet, to put the Finleys' situation into perspective, I would offer this: If the weight that father feels is a pound, the weight Jill and Randy feel must be a ton.

Jordan

Jordan may be non-verbal, but he is not very "non" anything else. He is strong physically, extremely mobile, tirelessly active, and gifted with some savant-like qualities that make him unique and the epitomizing definition of the tongue-in-cheek adjective "a handful." One of his quirks, one that endears him all the more to all who know and associate with him, has earned him the name "The Destroying Angel." Jordan has not only the uncanny ability, but also the zealous desire, to methodically, systematically take things apart. (Unfortunately, for others, especially his family, the converse talent of reassembling them is not part of his repertoire.) Randy explains, "He has a very unique way of thinking of things in reverse. If you give him any kind of a tool and any kind of a contraption, anything that is mechanical, he will figure out how to take it apart. It's *only* taking it apart, and he does it in a very methodical way."

Jordan does not do his dismantling to be a prankster. Nor does he do it to be mean or malicious. That is the furthest thing from his character. It appears he actually thinks he is doing a service and is being useful. Nevertheless, seldom does a day go by in the Finley household when some family member does not walk into a room and find something that has been "fixed" by Jordan, especially if it involves removing screws. That is his specialty. Jill relates the example of walking into her living room, which an hour or so prior was in perfect order, and finding all the living room curtains on the floor. Jordan had removed all the screws from the brackets and rods.

The neighbors are well aware of Jordan's "gift" as well. One neighbor still thinks one of the funniest lines he has ever heard was Randy's quip, "The scariest sight I've ever seen is Jordan coming out of the basement with a screwdriver in his hand." One time, Jill and a group of friends were intending on watching a movie in their family room. Everything seemed to be in perfect order. All of the cords were in place, but she could not get the DVD player to turn on. As she investigated more closely, Jill found the player was just a shell. Jordan had taken the screws out of the back of the unit and carefully removed all the inner workings and stashed them in another part of the house.

Randy says, "Here's the test: Can you ever get mad at Jordan for the things he does that cause destruction? You cannot; because you know what kind of a person he really is—a kind, gentle, loving soul, who only wants people to be happy. I have gone through five lawnmowers in the past 10 years. Jordan thought he was helping me out by pouring what he thought was gasoline into the tank. He takes Clorox bottles out of Jill's laundry room and pours the bleach into the gas tanks of the mowers, one of which was a very expensive Honda I had saved money for a long time to get. What happens when you put Clorox into an aluminum engine? You get a chemical reaction where the engine turns into powder. He has done this five times. Those are the kinds of things from his 'destructive angel' side that we face almost daily. And, you know, we get used to it."

Randy and Jill emphasize in utmost sincerity that despite all the extra effort and patience required to rear and care for Jordan, the joy and love he has brought to the family—and brought out in the family—are beyond calculation. His life has had a great refining and sweet, mellowing influence on every member of the family.

Meanwhile, Back at the Hospital

With a more complete picture in your mind, you can now appreciate even more the poignancy in the "what will become of my family" question on Randy's mind as he lay in the hospital. Coming to grips with the precarious and indefinite state of his health was just the tip of the iceberg. The massive matter underlying that question was the larger impact of it all on his family's security and future.

Could things possibly get worse? Unfortunately, yes. Randy's crisis and the diagnosis occurred in November. By January, Randy was able to summon enough strength to travel to work again and try to resume his role as president of the company. He had virtually no stamina. Just the travel drained a large portion of his reserves. Somehow, Randy was able to function well enough to keep the company thriving, but he knew he could not keep up the pace for long.

Jill and Randy decided to move back to California and buy a house near the company headquarters to ease Randy's travel demands. In April, Jill flew with Randy to California with the objective of buying a house. It became unnecessary. The CEO had brought in a replacement—his son—to take over the company. For all intents and purposes, Randy was forced to step aside "for the good of the company" and resign.

Unbelievably, on top of everything else, Randy and Jill were now facing their oh-so-very-fragile-and-precarious future without the crucial assets of health insurance or life insurance, both of which evaporated instantly the moment Randy was no longer a salaried employee of the company. Randy was offered a consulting contract with the company for six months, take it or leave it, and that was that.

No Rancor, No Malice, No Hatred

How would you feel? What would you do? Most people would lay awake at night fomenting plots of revenge and retaliation in their minds. A lot of us would let our swimming pool fill up with bitter animosity. Some of us might be inclined to look up our Italian ancestry and importune for a contract. As our festering loathing billowed, we might even resort to hiring a Voodoo witch doctor to cast the most vile and excruciatingly painful spell on the CEO. Any person so heartless and callous as to leave a loyal employee, a man who had given his all to serve and enrich him, in such a precarious position deserves nothing less than the most hideous medieval torture.

Those of us who did not take that route, might well instead spend those sleepless hours beating ourselves up with "How could I be so stupid," and "What a naive idiot I was to allow myself to be taken advantage of so blatantly."

None of that Victim wailing for Jill and Randy. With patience in affliction that would make Job remove his hat, these two amazing people simply looked forward and refused to hate or to wallow in regret. They just focused on doing the best they could with what they had available. Randy worked on his resume, while Jill listed the house for sale, simply observing, "We just can't afford this house any more. Something smaller will suit us better."

As for Randy, he asks, "What good would it do to hate or wish things were different? Hey, I am just so grateful to be alive. I could be dead right now, but I'm not. I'm alive, I have a wonderful wife and family, and we appreciate everything we have so much more. We have wonderful relationships with our children. We love them and they love us and each other. Jordan has brought so much unifying love into all of our lives. No one will understand how much having him has blessed our lives. We have so much to be grateful for. I can work and support my family, and we will make it through somehow."

No Quick Fixes

Over the ensuing months, Randy's medication seemed to accomplish its intended effect. The symptoms abated somewhat and he was able to find some consulting jobs for a while. Eventually, he secured a full-time job with a good company—one founded and functioning on high moral and ethical principles. Randy likes his job and has been able to perform his work at a high level. Some days he feels quite good. Other days are not so good. On those days, every movement of his body seems like a chore, requiring extra effort.

Randy and Jill Finley are Owners. Randy says, "Things always seem to work out for Jill and me, as long as we just stick together and deal uprightly with each thing as it comes along."

Randy generates enough income that the family could live a fairly normal life, were it not for the mortgage on their home. The Finleys have had their home up for sale for months. The housing market is down right now and lenders are in a pinch. It is very hard to qualify for the jumbo loans needed for the purchase of this particular home and others like it. So, the prospects do not look good on that front. As of this writing, the house is in foreclosure. If their home does not sell within the next three months, the foreclosure will be finalized.

Chapter 29

Aimee Henderson

Aimee Henderson is not built like Barbie. It seems as though most of the rest of humanity wishes she were.

One Size Does Not Fit All

Some people spend years looking for their passion. They yearn to identify a pursuit that defines who they are and unifies their latent talents, along with the inner beckonings to express those talents to their fullest degree. Aimee is not one of those people. Aimee has known from her earliest recollection exactly what she wants to do and be. She loves to sing, dance, act, and entertain. Calling musical theatre her passion does not go deep enough. For her, it even goes deeper than the marrow of her bones and the DNA of her physical make-up. Her love for singing and dancing emanates from the innermost core of her soul, virtually indistinguishable and inseparable from her life force itself.

What if you *know* your role, yet you don't seem to have been given the right assets to make your dream come true? What do you do if pursuing your dream amounts to the primary source of disappointment, rejection, and heartless ridicule? That is the dichotomy Aimee Henderson has faced throughout her life.

Looking like Barbie would have made life so much easier for Aimee. It doesn't take Stephan Hawking to figure out that if you dream of being the leading lady in a play, it would be very helpful if you somewhat fit the petite, delicate, blue-eyed-blonde stereotype.

Aimee does not fit that image. She is a 5'7", large-boned, brunette—she's fit, but you would not call her slender. Though she is far from unattractive, Aimee's larger frame simply clashes with the ultra-slender, super model image overly touted in the media today. Beyond her physical qualities, Aimee is a warm, witty, out-going free spirit, who loves to laugh and engage with people. She also has a tender heart, one that has suffered more than its share of insults and hurt on the path to her dreams.

Early Lessons

"By the time I was five years old, I was already interested in music and theatre," she says. "I loved dancing. My best friend and I would put on Gloria Estefan CDs and dance for hours. We were pretty obsessed with her music; I don't know why. At this age, I was in my first musical, *Charlotte's Web*. I played a little baby chick and just waddled around on stage."

As would be the pattern for her future, it did not take long for Aimee to face some disappointment. Her mother, Cheryl, recounts one of Aimee's first experiences and how she dealt with it: "In third grade, she had her first real rejection. She still talks about it. There was to be a big school-wide play but it had only four main parts. All the third graders were trying out, and Aimee just knew she should be one of the main parts, but she didn't get it. Even harder for Aimee, a girl in the neighborhood got the part she had wanted.

"Aimee has grown a lot over the years in how she has learned to deal with things," Cheryl observes. "At this age, her first reaction was to be upset with the neighbor girl, constantly talking about how she wasn't any good, that she herself should have gotten that part. Aimee sat in that performance with her arms crossed, just angry. At home she got sad and teary eyed, and she was so jealous. But, from that first experience with disappointment, she learned."

In the fourth grade, while living with her family in England, Aimee added a positive experience to her theatrical resume. She was given a role in a Mother's Day presentation that allowed her to feature her zest for theatrics. Because she was a little larger than most of the other girls in the grade, Aimee was asked to play the part of a Victorian-age mother. Cheryl recounts, "Aimee has always struggled with her size from the day she was born, so she's always had that challenge. From day one, she's always wanted to be up in front of a crowd. She's always had this music—this theatrical flair—she's wanted to express and has always been very dramatic. When we lived in England, she played the Swooning English Mother where she had to faint, and she was quite the hit. The audience thought she was wonderful."

Aimee remembers: "My big line was to swoon or faint, and I did this way over-the-top faint. It was cheesy but everyone loved it. I remember feeling proud of myself because I got a little paper award that I still have in a box. That was my first theatrical accolade, the first time anyone other than my parents gave me any recognition for a performance on stage."

An Owner's Response to Disappointment

Near the end of fourth grade, another big production was planned, and everyone was excited about it, especially Aimee, of course. Again, she gamely tried out for one of the main roles. "I thought I had done a really great job in the audition," she confesses, "and that I really deserved this part." However, when the casting list was posted the next day, Aimee had not gotten the part. In fact, her name did not appear on the cast list at all, not even for one of the minor roles. "As a nine-year-old, that was devastating," Aimee admits. "My first thoughts were not, 'Well, maybe this other person was better.' My first thoughts were, 'The teacher must hate me. I must be horrible, and it's so unfair and so wrong.' I was taking this the way most nine-year-olds would take it. I was just crushed, and when you're nine that's your whole world, and you don't have a broader perspective to draw from. You don't know that things pass and wounds heal. So, I went home and I was so angry at the world. I wouldn't even play with my friends for days because this meant so much to me. I kept thinking everyone at that school must hate me because I didn't even get to be in the musical at all. After two days, that got me nowhere; I was lonely, sad, and angry. At that point, I already had some kind of connection to what I was inside. I don't know how to explain it other than saying I just had a sense that, 'Next time will be different. I know that I can do this, and I know that, whatever comes next, I'll be able to accomplish it. This stinks right now, but I'll make it happen yet.'

"So, I stopped being angry and went and talked to my teacher instead," Aimee explains. "Like every little nine-year-old, I was scared to death. In my mind, my music teacher was the epitome of wonderfulness. She was gorgeous, and I loved her so much that I was afraid to approach her. Somehow I worked up enough courage to go talk with her, and I told her how disappointed I was for being left out of the play. The next day, she and my peers decided to make a part for me in the play and I got to be in it after all. It was a tiny little part but it meant a lot to me. I loved being in the play. My parents remember when I was on stage I mouthed everybody else's lines; I had memorized the whole show.

"I learned something right then about handling disappointment. It is not always easy to do, but it is a valuable lesson. I learned that you have to decide what you're going to do about things that stink in your life. There are a lot of situations where it's up to you to find a solution. Nobody else is going to come find you and say, 'I'm sorry this is hard for you. I'm sorry you didn't get what you wanted and you're so sad.' Let's face it, nobody's going to do that. You have to be the initiator and make something happen. That's what happened in fourth grade; I made something happen."

Challenges of a Competitive Environment

After Aimee's fourth grade year, the family moved back to the United States. Like most adolescents and teenagers, Aimee struggled to find herself. "When I moved back to the U.S., that was a hard transition for me. I hadn't yet figured out who I was or where to put my focus. During that time, I got introduced to singing through a choir class. That was really good for me because I had a teacher who really supported me and thought I had a voice somewhere inside there. I wasn't the best singer naturally—I had the pitch, but that was about it. I'd just sing as loud as I possibly could. I wasn't very good, but I just loved doing it, and I finally had a teacher who was kind of like me. She was kind of eccentric, happy, and loud, and we meshed well. She believed in me and thought I had a good voice, and she gave me a small solo in a choir concert. After that, my parents decided that I could start taking voice lessons."

The decision to enroll Aimee in voice and dance lessons turned out to be pivotal, although it may not have seemed that large at the time. Michele Baer, Aimee's first voice teacher, talks about her admiration for the way Aimee's parents approached this decision. "I observed Aimee going through a difficult time with weight as a pre-pubescent teenager. It was a really tough time for her, and her parents knew that. Cheryl shared with me the issues they pondered. They really debated whether they should talk 'sense' and help Aimee see 'reality' about her weight. Should they put her in a diet class or an exercise class, instead of voice and dance classes?"

After Aimee's parents thought about it, and even made it a matter of prayer, they decided to put the emphasis on building her inner strengths, her self-esteem and self-confidence, rather than her physical attributes. They invested in her strong points rather than her weak points.

"Aimee was almost 13 years old when she came to me," Michele explains. "I cannot say that I saw her on Broadway at that time, but I did think she had great potential. She had a beautiful natural voice, and she was a hard worker. I still have my notes on the pieces I gave her and how fast she progressed. I think dance class, which is obviously a big part of musical theatre, was even more of a stretch because of her physique. I think I could see people saying, 'You really want to dance?' Aimee had more of a natural talent for singing, but dance, that was a different story, and, of course, you have to have both if you are going to excel in musical theatre."

Cheryl comments on this crucial phase of Aimee's progress: "When Aimee started wanting to dance, that was really a struggle for her. Where we lived, there were a lot of girls that danced—a lot of pageant things and a lot of very talented families that really supported their children in their endeavors. It was a little competitive, and there really wasn't a place that wanted Aimee, until we found one little dance studio that had a different outlook on things. They were much more inclusive. Their goal wasn't to turn everyone into professional dancers; they simply wanted to help young people experience the pure joy of dancing. They welcomed Aimee and really encouraged her, and she just blossomed. Aimee *loved* to dance, even though she didn't look like a dancer."

After learning all she could from her first studio, Aimee needed to move on and develop her talents in the more competitive environment. From that point on, the rejection and ridicule she endured was virtually incessant. Although she was accepted into one of the more select studios, Aimee was never placed in any of the top companies, primarily because she "looked so out of place." Snide remarks and snickering were commonplace.

Aimee's father, Steve, says, "There was real emotion with every insult and rejection. It wasn't just, 'Oh well, that's okay.' Every one of those remarks stung. There was real hurt and real disappointment, but with Aimee it was never the final state. She just refused to stay in the misery; she just kept figuring out a way to keep going."

Even when someone would try to say something complimentary, the underlying dismay oozed through. Cheryl recalls, "During this period Aimee always felt like the fat girl, the ugly girl, but she just loved to dance. I remember her performing a dance duet in a church talent show, paired with a girl who looked more like a dancer. Someone said to me, 'Wow, that's really brave of her.' Interpreting that, it was 'Wow, I can't believe she's on the stage when she's so heavy.' They didn't mean it to be like that, but that's really what they were saying. Aimee was up there just dancing her heart out. Afterwards, I had three different women come up and say 'That's so inspiring. She loves it, and she's up there doing it, and it just doesn't matter what other people think of what's she's doing.' I shared that with Aimee and she appreciated that."

"I started doing summer musicals," Aimee recalls. "That's when I figured out it wasn't just about the music or the dancing, it was also about the acting. There was something magical for me when I put all three of those together. That was my mode of communicating who I was and that sparked something inside, and I suddenly became really passionate about musical theatre." The inner sense that she had talent that could be developed if she would stay at it and work hard sustained her. Cruel remarks hurt, but they did not stop her, she just pushed forward through the withering barrage of rejection. When she tried out for the high school cheerleading and pom teams, she was chided for even "thinking that she had a chance." At the tryouts, none of the thin, gorgeous girls she was competing against offered the slightest degree of compassion. Aimee was openly mocked and made fun of. "For a while, I think I may have joined them in looking down on myself," Aimee says. "That type of criticism does affect you, and it's very hard to overcome these feelings of inadequacy at times. For some reason, I could see what I could be, and I refused to let anybody take that away from me.

"For me, those experiences where you feel crushed and like you are 'nothing' are the building blocks of who I have become. In retrospect, I look back and am grateful for them, as painful as they were. That's when I started learning to be less judgmental of other people, and that has helped me shake off any judgments put on me by my peers. I am able to see people for what they are worth. Because of that characteristic, I've been able to connect with people, and that is so important when you are performing on stage."

College Years

Upon graduating from high school, Aimee was eager to throw herself into her dream. She expected to be accepted into at least one of the respected programs she admired. She auditioned for some of the leading theatrical arts programs at the top colleges in the country, and she was summarily turned down in every case.

"I went to several different schools and auditioned at conservatories, and I thought I did really well. I would get the letters back and take them up to my room because I hated being disappointed in front of other people. Every single one that I opened was a 'no.' Hearing that 'no' just gives you that sick feeling in your stomach and you feel like a failure. It was pretty hard to accept that none of the schools wanted me."

Aimee tried college for a year, considering different pursuits, trying different things. Nothing clicked. After her freshman year, she left school and went home for the summer feeling empty and directionless.

That summer, two significant things happened. First, she met and married her husband Russ, whose support rekindled her hopes. Second, through some quirky coincidences, Aimee was able to connect with an outstanding voice teacher, Carolyn McKenna—the right person at the right time for Aimee.

"It's funny how you're led to the things that are meant to be. If you keep pursuing and keep trying, you'll end up being where you need to be. I studied with Carolyn McKenna who really, really believed in me. Her belief in me was not because I was a good person or because I wanted it so badly. She believed in me because she could hear something inside of me that I knew was there, but I couldn't hear myself. I remember several times during my lessons breaking down and crying because it felt so good to have somebody who was so professional actually believe in the talent that I had."

A Big Breakthrough

Carolyn knew how to mold Aimee's talent and prepare her for professional auditions. When she thought Aimee was ready, she encouraged her to audition with the North Carolina Theatre, where they use equity performers from Broadway and do Broadway-level performances.

"I walked into my first audition," Aimee states, "and belted out this song that I had been working on with Carolyn. She taught me how to perform it, sing it, and really communicate it. I was only two bars into the song when a man put his hand up for me to stop singing. I thought, 'Uh oh, I've totally bombed it. They don't even want to hear another note.' This man walked up to me. My hair was really curly and he started messing with my hair. I guess he liked the way it looked for one of the characters, and he handed me a script and told me to come back the next day! Instant call backs are just unheard of!

"So, I came back the next day. At first, my heart dropped a little," Aimee confides. "Here again, I was back in the same old uncomfortable situation that I'd been in so many times before. All the girls I was competing against looked like Broadway stars. Everywhere I turned there was Barbie, Barbie, Barbie. Then, down there at the end of the row was Aimee. They were all incredible dancers, all size two, beautiful teeth, and beautiful hair, and not like me. Memories of the cheerleader tryouts came back into my head. For a moment, I freaked out. Before we started auditioning, I found a quiet corner and I started talking to myself. I went over in my head how far I had come this last year, how hard I had worked, and all the disappointments I had overcome. As I started warming up vocally, I stayed inside myself, thinking and focusing on the price I had paid. As I did that, I realized I *did* have the confidence inside me to do this. If I really wanted this part, it would be mine, and nobody would be able to take it from me.

"I walked back into that room and I delivered my lines. They dismissed everybody else, and right there they walked up and gave me the part! That is so uncommon; they usually debate and have you come back again and again. This time they handed me my script and told me I was going to start in two weeks. At that moment, I realized how much it matters to stay focused and believe in yourself. Whether you're on stage, or anywhere else in life, if you have confidence, not cockiness but confidence, in who you are and what you can do, people will be drawn towards you. It's amazing that the human spirit and human intuition can interact that way. That's something I have really learned."

Aimee's experience with that first professional production led to another production where she was given a more prominent role. Both were great opportunities for her to interact with and learn from Broadway luminaries as she intently observed them practice their art.

Acceptance

Aimee's vitalized confidence was founded on substantial footing. What had happened was not just luck. She had taken the steps and paid the price that enabled her to seize an opportunity, and she knew she could replicate that formula. From that position of strength, she was ready to take Ownership of the next big challenge—getting into one of the elite collegiate musical theatre programs.

One university in particular had always been Aimee's dream, but the openings were few in number and the competition ferocious. As she thought about applying, the old deep-seated misgivings tried to surface once again. "Somewhere in the back of my mind I could hear the voice, 'I'm not good enough, I'm not going to make it, I don't want to be crushed again, I'm tired of being hurt and disappointed,'" Aimee admitted.

When Cheryl talks about Aimee's ability to rebound from rejection and overcome negative thoughts, she says, "Aimee will live with the hurt for a day or two. She will be down, and sometimes she cries a lot. Then she will say, 'Okay, that's enough of that,' and she picks herself up and goes on." Essentially, that's what Aimee did one more time. She listened to the fears for a day or two and then said, "Okay, that's enough of that. I'm going to go for it and I got my 'Aimee attitude' back. I just decided that it was time."

Aimee and Russ rented a truck, packed their belongings, and drove across the country, ready to give Aimee's dream one more try. "My acting audition went great. That's what I do best. The vocal audition was okay, not nearly as good as most of the girls, and the dance audition was the hardest thing I have ever done in my life. I thought I had bombed it."

Typically it takes a month for the admission letters to go out, and some of the applicants Aimee knew did get their letters. Some were accepted and some were not. Aimee's letter didn't come. "I didn't get a 'yes' or a 'no.' Everyone kept asking me if I was in the program or not, and I just had to say 'I don't know.'"

With the pressure mounting, Aimee returned to one of the big lessons she had learned in the past—"There are a lot of situations where it's up to you to find a solution. Nobody else is going to come find you and say 'I'm sorry this is hard for you.' You have to be the initiator and make something happen." Putting that thought into action, Aimee made an appointment with the director of the program and went to his office. "I was really nervous and shaking," Aimee confides. "He explained that over 650 people had auditioned this year to get into the musical theatre program, and only 10 boys and 10 girls are accepted. He also said they had already accepted 10 boys and 10 girls, and my letter was still sitting on his desk. He hadn't put an answer on it yet, and my heart just broke because, obviously, the slots were filled. Then, he told me they couldn't decide what to do with me. I needed tons of work on my voice and dance, but for some reason the committee just couldn't say 'no' to me. They kept going back to my video and watching it and saying there was something there."

At that moment, Aimee's Ownership Spirit took over and made something happen. She poured all her energy into explaining who she was, her background and experience, and how much she loved musical theatre—that the department would never find anyone who'd work harder or be more dedicated than she. She admitted the other girls were talented and deserving, but Aimee did not back down on her petition and made her case that she be accepted too because of the unique qualities she could bring to the program.

"The next evening, the director called me from the committee meeting," Aimee relates. "Thirty faculty members, including the deans of the school of music and the school of dance, had met. He told me they had decided to waive the 10-girl limit, that they were going to take on one more, and they really wanted me to be a part of the program.

"I can't put words to how wonderful that news was; I was overjoyed! At that moment, I felt, I hate to use the word 'vindicated,' but I felt that I had really proven something. A large group of talented people, with expert eyes, had seen that certain 'something' inside of me. They could see that I was different—that I may not fit the ideal stereotype for a singer or dancer—but my 'something,' whatever it is that I bring, had value. Who knows—somewhere, somehow, someday—that different 'something' might just make a big difference in some unique way.

"I guess it was a testament to me that people can judge me anyway they choose, but I think I'll always surprise people and not be what they think. I might be a shape on the outside, but in my heart, where my passion is, I have something of value to offer the world."

At this writing, Aimee Henderson is thriving in this elite program—the program of her dreams. As you would expect, she is totally immersed, making the most of every minute, learning and progressing in her craft.

Don't be surprised if this is not the last time you hear her name.

Section 5

Perspectives:
Power to Change

---

*"People with intelligence must use their intelligence,
people with eyes must use their eyes,
people with the capacity to love have the impulse to love
and the need to love in order to feel healthy.
Capacities clamor to be used,
and cease in their clamor
only when they are used sufficiently.
That is to say,
capacities are needs,
and therefore are intrinsic values as well."*

—Abraham H. Maslow

Chapter 30

The Power to Change Everything

My efforts to offer a spectrum of examples of Ownership in Action has had several purposes: (1) to accentuate that the principles, postures, and tools of Ownership really work and that they apply in real situations that are as varied as life itself; (2) to underscore that none of us is exempt—that change, challenge, and adversity are a part of everyone's curriculum in the University of Life and that there are specific ways we can prepare ourselves to earn "A's" on our "exams"; (3) to emphasize that circumstances are not greater than people; and (4) to demonstrate the power in using The One Grand Key—Ownership. With that key, we, as thinkers of thoughts, can shift from postures of weakness to postures of such strength we can stand strong and courageous in the face of anything and everything that comes our way.

Let me highlight a few summary examples from the Portraits (and add a few extra) to support my points as I conclude my case.

Becoming Undaunted by Difficulty

One of the significant lessons Steve Bodhaine has learned in his leadership experience is the literal truth conveyed in the Chinese signs for "crisis": Great opportunities that lead to great rewards often come concealed in a garb of distasteful, even dangerous and daunting, circumstances.

Too often we see only the surface features of the situation and view our possibilities and outcomes based on that surface impression.

If the "opportunity" looks hard or intimidating in any way, we tend to look for a way to sidestep or evade the situation, but we don't *have* to quail and flee. As Rich Hamill says, "The only person who can tell you you can't is yourself, and you don't have to listen." We can train ourselves to stand our ground and take on those tough situations by taking control of our thoughts and intentionally calming our qualms.

Like Steve Bodhaine and others, I have proven this through my own experience. To help myself stay calm and put forth more courage in moments when I am tempted to look for an excuse or an "out," I redirect my thoughts with one particular phrase: "When it looks like death, it's probably life; run to it!" For me, it kills fear as effectively as the new wonder-drug antibiotics kill bacteria.

Case in Point

Not long ago, I was invited to meet with a high ranking corporate leader, for whom I have done a fair amount of work over the past several years. This man is a strong results-oriented leader and understands the value of sound processes. He upholds them vigorously. He also knows that processes do not run themselves, that there is an inescapable human element involved, and that human beings are diverse, complex, and unpredictable.

This leader had two purposes for our meeting: (1) to describe a difficult situation that had eventuated between two teams that played extremely crucial roles in the company's production process, and (2) to enlist my help in resolving the difficulty.

The two teams involved—each composed of smart, strong-willed people—needed to cooperate and work together in a mutually collaborative effort on a high stakes project. In fact, for the product's end user, the outcome was literally a matter of life and death. Unfortunately, the working relationship between the two teams was in a shambles. Contention had risen to the point of caustic name-calling and emotionally charged accusations and threats.

As I began to grasp the dynamics of the situation, knowing how much was at stake, I began to seriously question in my mind whether anyone could be successful in resolving the issues and contentions within this group in the needed time frame. Getting these two teams to put genuine effort into building a trusting, cooperative relationship seemed as likely as getting Red Sox fans to cheer for the Yankees.

Frankly, for a moment in the conversation, my doubts started gaining the upper hand. My mind started conjuring scenes of me walking into a meeting with these people and promptly being "chewed up and spit out" within the first 10 minutes. At first, the only thing I could see them agreeing upon would be that they didn't need any of this "warm, fuzzy, soft-skills crap," especially with so many tasks and deadlines bearing down upon them. Then, I thought of my mantra, "When it looks like death, it's probably life; run to it!"

When that thought ran through my circuitry, a couple of quick flashbacks came to mind wherein I'd faced daunting situations and critical audiences before. Some of the best things that had ever happened to my company came out of them. That was all I needed, and I was able to squelch the doubts and unfounded fears. True to the previous pattern, this experience turned out to be "life," not "death." Not only did the initial presentation go over so well that an immediate reversal in attitudes and behaviors ensued, but a sizeable chunk of future business came along with it, adding a meaningful boost to my company's reputation.

Looking back, I would rate this experience in the top three most gratifying experiences of my career. I shudder to think how close I came to side-stepping the opportunity by allowing myself to be daunted by difficulty.

Dividing in Order to Conquer

In the Portraits section, every one of the impressive mountains that were climbed was scaled using the "divide in order to conquer" strategy. Rather than viewing the mountain as a mountain, these Tough-Minded Owners viewed their mountains as a series of steps. Jorge Hernandez lifted himself out of poverty in Mexico and attained financial independence in the United States by using this approach: "I just kept studying and working. Little by little, I made it." Combining this method with a healthy new mindset, Joan Gustafson created a wonderful life for herself and her children that included an enviable ascent to the upper levels of corporate leadership, getting there one stage at a time.

In some cases, Tough-Minded Owners have to break their pace down into even smaller increments—taking things not just a *day* at a time, but sometimes almost a *thought* at a time. Tom Sullivan describes using that approach when the addict inside tries to take over and return him to taking drugs: "When I have that thought, I get scared to death. I get scared that I even entertained that thought. It's then that I know I have to play it out and go to work on myself right then and there."

Playing it Out

The practice of "playing it out" has proven to be a particularly effective way of conquering bad habits and fighting addictive behaviors. Let me share some testimonials to that effect from some of my interviews. One recovering addict describes the harsh reality he deals with like this: "I know I am only one thought away from falling back into my old ways. I know myself well enough that, within a day, I could be right back into my ugly life—my past life of drugs and alcohol. Just by acting out on one stupid thought."

In those moments when recovering addicts are struck with the urge to give everything up for that one fleeting momentary "high," they learn to "Play it Out." In other words, they do not just play the movie up to the "moment of pleasure" and then stop, pretending the high is the end of the story. They continue on to consider the aftermath, consequences, and fallout that inevitably result once the high is gone.

We've all seen the beer commercials that only show the fun moments in the bar when the guy meets the good-looking girl. What they don't show is the scene 40 minutes later, when the guy turns into a sluggish bore with slurred speech, the vomiting, the morning-after hangover, and conversion of the guy's virile physique into the always-attractive beer belly accompanied by the eventual cirrhosis of the liver.

Recovering addicts know that they can fall into the trap of the "short pleasure-trip story," and they learn to counter that trap by playing their movies out to their full end. "When I am tempted to relapse," says one man, "I have to stop and think, 'Okay, this might feel good for an hour or so, but what's going to happen after? The fear and paranoia will come back. I'm going to feel guilty and like I let everybody down, including myself. Then I am going to have to talk to my wife and admit it, and that's going to be painful. If I don't do that, then I'll be hiding out and being a liar again.' When I look at all I will have to go through after I binge, it scares me, and I can see that it's not worth it."

Then, in another classic example of redirection, he adds, "On the other hand, when I picture how great I will feel about myself when I have resisted the temptation, and I can look my wife in the eye without any guilt or deception because I refused to give into the short-term high, it gives me the strength I need to stay clean."

Another View of Divide in Order to Conquer

One of the great things about correct principles is that they have multiple valid applications. We can use the divide-and-conquer principle of Tough-Minded Ownership to battle our internal demons and change things on the inside. We can also employ these principles to change the external world and improve the circumstances we encounter "on the outside."

Becky Douglas is an inspiring example of that application. Having voluntarily undertaken the enormous humanitarian goal of helping the leprosy-affected families of India, she has encountered no shortage of obstacles and frustratingly unjust setbacks. There have been days when she has been sorely tempted to just throw in the towel and give up. However, in those moments of overwhelming frustration, she has been able to keep going by focusing only on the next step on the mountain—finding an answer to the most proximate issue. Once that obstacle is dealt with, she moves to the next most pressing issue and deals with it. And so on.

Will there ever be an end to the obstacles the Douglases and Rising Star Outreach face? Probably not. Ravines, ice flows, crevasses, and cliffs are all parts of the mountain. When you and I choose a mountain to climb, we also choose the terrain and treacherous features that make up the mountain. Don't let that stop you. The highest, most formidable mountains on earth have all been conquered, and they were conquered one step at a time.

Heightening Their Creative Efforts

The Douglases' story also stands out as a remarkable example of what can be accomplished once one begins to unleash the creative potential of thoughts empowered by a worthy cause or higher purpose. Likewise, every time Jorge Hernandez seemed blocked by lack of resources or opportunity, he created something "out of nothing" and willed himself forward. Aimee Henderson's pathway to her goal is one long saga of using creative effort and hard work to make something happen that would not otherwise have occurred.

Buying a Business with No Money

A good friend of mine, Sam, had been working as the general manager for a privately held company for about two years when a choice opportunity presented itself. The president and principal owner needed to step out of the business, and Sam saw it coming. He knew he would have to find another position or else make an offer to purchase the company. The problem with the second option was he didn't have the money to buy a multi-million dollar enterprise. Sam was not daunted. He knew opportunities like this did not come along every day—he knew this company inside and out and saw that it had tremendous upside potential.

After careful consideration, Sam approached his boss with the idea of buying the company. After in-depth negotiations, the two men agreed upon a purchase price. Sam now faced a fairly large task—where to get the money. Fired by his dream, he set his creative efforts to work.

"Initially, I went to traditional sources knowing I would need an equity partner and some owner financing to supplement a bank loan and line of credit. My goal, of course, was to do that in such a way that I could have a good share of equity in the company for putting the deal together. My first approach was to reach out to our largest customer to buy part of the business. We spent a lot of time negotiating a deal that would allow me to run the company and have a good piece of the ownership. I continued to negotiate with this potential partner exclusively as my deadline to secure financing approached. Unfortunately, the deal they finally offered me fell far short in several ways. They were not willing to put up all of the money—they required additional partners. They were also not willing to grant me the equity I needed; worst of all, they wanted complete control. On the eve of my deadline, after having spent months in negotiations with them, I had to walk away from their proposal and go back to the owner and tell him I didn't have the money."

The force of Sam's conviction persuaded the owner to extend the deadline, and it also drove his creativity. Sam began to think about how he might restructure the entire equity position of the deal to include a select cadre of customers—people and organizations that already had an appreciation for the company's mission and values. "I got inspired to think about developing a partnership that would include a core group of our customers," Sam said. "I also knew I would have many of them in town during our annual convention, our largest and most significant event of the year. So, in the midst of the intense and demanding schedule of the convention, I assembled a group of candidates and did an investment presentation one evening at my home," Sam recounts. "It was a crazy, overwhelmingly busy few days, but it worked. I was able to reach an agreement with the most influential core group, and in an amazingly short time, it all worked out. I was able to assemble a full group of investors so I could pay the owner the asking price and end up with the equity portion that I needed."

The Banking Piece

Building a consortium of investors was a major step, but that was only part of the feat. There still remained one other essential component—a strong banking relationship that would lend the rest of the money needed to close the deal and provide a credit line for sustaining operations. The banking piece turned out to be even more of a "miracle" than the partnership, especially the timing of it.

"I needed to find a bank that would loan the rest of the money, including an operating line of credit," Sam says. "I had gone to several banks and had been turned down by most of them. Only by the fluke of one casual interaction in one small bank's lobby was I able to ultimately fund the deal. I was actually depositing the earnest money for the deal into my attorney's trust account at a bank I had never been to. While there, I bumped into one of the bank officers, who asked about my deposit. When I explained what I was trying to do, she casually asked, 'Have you talked to us?' This bank was a small local bank that had never even been on my radar screen. At the time, I had two larger banks that had already told me, 'Yes, we think we are going to do this for you.' So, I was working both of those deals and feeling pretty confident about getting my financing. Out of courtesy to this bank officer, I said, 'Well, sure, I'll get you some information,' which I did.

"As the weeks went by, one of the banks that had given me early indications that they were going to do the deal backed out of it. I was now down to one bank, but this last bank had given me even stronger indications that they were going to do the deal. In the meantime, I got a call from this smaller bank, asking me more questions. I answered the questions but was still sure that the bigger bank was going to come through.

"As the deadline drew near, the pressure was mounting. There would be no chance for another extension this time—I had to have the money by the deadline hour or the deal would be off. Even at that late hour, I was still not very invested in the relationship with the smaller bank, but just as a backup plan, I called one of the top officers and he said, 'I think we can do this.'

"On the very day of the deadline, a mere two hours before my meeting to finalize the sale, the first bank notified me that they were *not* going to fund the deal. I was shocked, thinking that all this effort was going to be for naught, but one hour later, just 60 minutes before I had to show evidence of my financing, I got a fax confirmation from the smaller bank with a loan commitment for the full amount I needed. I was able to walk into my meeting with the owner and the lawyers and sign the papers.

"I'll never forget standing by the fax machine watching that loan confirmation come through. Without that chance meeting in the lobby of that one small bank, I would never have been able to complete the deal."

Observation

If you were to talk to a few dozen entrepreneurs, asking them to recount the ups, downs, and narrow passages they had to squeeze through in order to start and grow their businesses, the plot line in this part of Sam's story would come to sound familiar. Almost every one of them will point to a fortuitous coincidence that ended up saving their venture at the last moment. Sam says, "I am a believer that you get lucky once in a while, but it's usually a result of you being out there and doing something. It will often come from where you least expect it, but it was the fact that you were out there swinging that made it happen. The door would have never opened because you wouldn't have been in the room. I believe that luck is far more likely to come to those who tenaciously persist in reaching their goal and creatively respond to the circumstances that are presented to them along the way."

Redirecting Negative Trains of Thought

When the pressures of our trials grow intense, our minds almost automatically run through numerous escape scenarios. Some of them are not constructive. For example, the hopeless-helpless circuits in our heads are often activated by the Victim-toned questions of, "Why?" "Why me?" and "What if?" Lingering on those unproductive, irrelevant questions leads to inaction and dissipation of will and energy.

Carrie Nielsen wrestled with the "fairness" of having two special needs children when she had kept her moral standards high throughout her life, while others had not. She was able to drive away her useless cares by noting that, despite her occasional feelings of inadequacy, she was able to provide a wonderful life for her special children.

This "why *not* me" response also came out plainly in the example of Scott and Teri Fitch. The Fitches found it helpful to step out of their own world of care and look around a little bit. They recognized they were not the lone sufferers on the planet—other people carried heavy bags too and each person's trials seemed appropriately suited to that particular person.

Jeff and Katy Johnson learned that burdening oneself with second-guessing and sadness is another one of those unproductive options. Over time, they came to realize they were the ones who could turn the one grand key that would change their state. Amid circumstances that hadn't changed at all, they simply chose to set aside their sullen feelings and cheer up. "[After] about 18 months, we decided that was long enough, and we made the conscious choice that we were going to be happy again."

Edie Eger went beyond redirecting to actually *revolutionizing* her view and emotional relationship to the soul-wrenching experiences of the Holocaust. "The healing journey is not going to ever truly take place without the choice to open up inside," she reminds us.

Altering Circumstances by the Force of Commitment

Ownership does not let the status quo prevail simply because "that's the way things are around here." Ownership is being willing to channel energy and intellect into assessing and upgrading what's there by actively dealing with what's there. Aimee Henderson refused to let other people's stereotypes squelch her dreams. She did not simply let things "just work themselves out." She made things happen that would not otherwise have happened and reshaped the circumstances by the force of her commitment.

Terry Sutter led a business unit through a complete "quality makeover" within one year, saving a vital account and winning a prestigious Quality Supplier Award, by the force of his commitment. Randy Finley provides for the extensive needs of his family, notwithstanding the physical pain and weakness imposed upon him by an incurable, degenerative disease. Most of the time his body does not even remotely feel like working, yet by the sheer force of his commitment, he continues to improve his circumstances.

In this book, you have read about businesses that have been built, and businesses that have been accelerated, by the force of commitment manifested in the form of *Ownership Spirit.* You have read about diseases, deaths, and disasters; betrayals, birth defects and bad luck; injustices, injuries and insults—adversities of all sorts and kinds—none of which ultimately succeeded in diminishing the lives of the people who chose to overcome them. The over-arching truth is that every one of these lives became greater and more noble *because of* their choice to apply Tough-Minded Ownership when they could much more easily have chosen the Victim role.

Each customized lesson offered by The University of Life holds infinite worth for our personal development and for the expanded good we can do with our increased strength. May we all stay awake to the fact that *Ownership Spirit* has the power to convert adversity into ascendancy and let us courageously *Own* our individual challenges.

None of the people in this book is a superhero. None of us is. When it gets down to the bottom line, we all share a common reality. Each of us is a thinker of thoughts with the capacity to learn how to think better thoughts. If we will Own that one truth and keep perfecting our use of that One Grand Key, there is nothing in our lives that we cannot change.

Options for bringing *The Ownership Spirit*® to your organization

Dr. Deaton and Quma Learning deliver the training:

+ Keynote Speeches
+ Conference Workshop and Breakout Sessions
+ Half-day, One-day, and Two-Day Seminars
+ Customized Organizational Programs and Consulting

Or Dr. Deaton and Quma Learning can help your organization deliver the training:

+ Train-the-Trainer Certification
+ DVD-Assisted Training (includes Facilitator's Guidebook)
+ *The Ownership Spirit*® Interactive CD-ROM (Computer-based training)
+ Leading the Ownership Spirit Exercise and Activity Binder

Options for individual learning and reinforcement

+ *The Ownership Spirit*® *Handbook* by Dennis R Deaton
+ *The Ownership Spirit*® Audio CD (Live seminar recording— 3-disk set)
+ *The Ownership Spirit*® Interactive CD-ROM
+ *The Book on Mind Management* by Dennis R Deaton
+ *Own It!* (Teen accountability and empowerment course) www.OwnItU.com

Contact Information

Quma Learning Systems, Inc.
480-545-8311; 800-622-6463
Email: info@quma.net
    www.Quma.net
    www.QumaLearning.com
    www.GrandKeyEd.com
    www.OwnItU.com

Index

About the Author

Dennis R Deaton is the co-founder and CEO of Quma Learning Systems, and chief designer of Quma's most sought-after seminars, including *Creating Connections, Destination Thinking for Leaders®,* and *The Ownership Spirit®.*

Among the clients for whom Dennis has done extensive classroom training are: Boeing, CenturyLink, Charles Schwab, Dupont, Honeywell, Medtronic, Motorola, ON Semiconductor, Scottsdale Insurance, Texas Instruments, University of Phoenix, and Universal Technical Institute.

Dennis is a popular speaker at conferences, meetings, and conventions. He is the author of *The Book on Mind Management, Money: An Owner's Manual,* and *The Ownership Spirit Handbook.*

Dr. Deaton also is co-founder of Grand Key Education, the company that developed Own It!, the first teen empowerment and accountability course ever offered to schools and the public. Own It! is a highly engaging, video saturated, cutting-edge way for young people to acquire the life skills taught in The Ownership Spirit.

He received his bachelor's degree from the University of Utah and his doctorate, cum laude, from Washington University in St. Louis.

Dennis has been described as

"A man with something to say,
and the gift to say it."